# Dr. Earl Mindell's
# CBD
## AND HEALTH FOR
# DOGS

Earl Mindell, R.Ph., Ph.D.

TURNER
PUBLISHING COMPANY

Turner Publishing Company
Nashville, Tennessee
www.turnerpublishing.com

Cover design: Maddie Cothren
Book design: Mallory Collins

Library of Congress Cataloging-in-Publication Data
Mindell, Earl.
[Nutrition and health for dogs] 1st Edition
Earl Mindell's nutrition and health for dogs / Earl Mindell with Elizabeth Renaghan.— 2nd ed.
p. cm.
Rev. ed. of: Earl Mindell's nutrition & health for dogs / Earl Mindell and Elizabeth Renaghan. 1998.
Includes bibliographical references and index.
ISBN 978-1-59120-203-5
1. Dogs—Nutrition. 2. Dogs—Health. 3. Dogs—Food. I. Renaghan, Elizabeth. II. Mindell, Earl. Earl Mindell's nutrition & health for dogs. III.Title. IV.Title: Nutrition and health for dogs.
SF427.4.M56 2007
636.7'0852--dc22

9781684422999    Paperback
9781684423002    Hardcover
9781684423019    eBook

Printed in the United States of America
17 18 19 20 10 9 8 7 6 5 4 3 2 1

# Contents

Acknowledgments v

Introduction vii

**Part One—Creating Optimum Nutrition for Your Dog**

1. Feeding Your Dog for Naturally Great Health 3
2. Vitamins for Your Dog 25
3. Minerals for Your Dog 41
4. Nutritional Needs for Special Circumstances 53

**Part Two—Natural Methods for Your Dog's Optimum Health**

5. The Importance of a Strong Immune System 71
6. Natural Flea Control for Your Dog 95
7. Understanding Homeopathy 105
8. Natural Prevention and Treatment of Common Dog Diseases 113
9. Natural Remedies for Common Ailments 133

**Part Three—The Dog Hit Parade**

10. Breed-Specific Health Problems 153
11. CBD: The Miracle Remedy For Your Dog 277

Resources 285

References 289

References 298

Index 301

About the Authors 312

# Acknowledgments

First and foremost, we would like to thank Virginia Hopkins for putting this project together and for her inspiration and editing through the years.

I am deeply grateful to Dr. Beverly Cappel-King, who shared her time and considerable expertise as a holistic veterinarian. A heartfelt thanks to our friends and family for their support and for believing in this book for so many years, with a special thanks to the four-legged members of our families: Dudley, for his unconditional love and patience.

# Introduction

During more than forty years of writing about health and nutrition, hundreds, and maybe even thousands, of people have thanked me for giving them the information they need to lead a healthy, energetic life. I have found that once a person learns how the food he or she is eating affects every aspect of life, and then experiences the difference when positive lifestyle changes are made, there's no going back. There is nothing like optimal health to convince a person that diet, exercise, clean water, and taking some supplements works wonders.

As I learn more about the nutritional needs of dogs, I find confusion and misconceptions abound. Few people, including veterinarians, realize that a dog's body functions much the same as a human body and has similar nutritional needs. You could probably go into your refrigerator right now and make a nutritious, balanced meal for your dog.

The commercial dog food industry is a multimillion dollar business that primarily depends on hiding the truth about what is good nutrition. For example, many in the dog food industry have perpetuated the myth that your dog is healthiest and happiest when she or he gets the same food every day. That's no more true than it would be for you. Your dog thrives on a variety of fresh foods, including fruits and vegetables. If you compare your dog's nutritional needs to the ingredients in the majority of commercial dog foods, you will understand why dogs are dying younger than they should and are plagued by chronic illnesses.

The foundation for your dog's good health is the same as it is for you—good nutrition, exercise, clean water, and love. For optimal health, you can build on that foundation with specific food and supplements. I'll tell you about the specific nutritional needs your dog has that are different from yours, and how to keep his or her immune system strong.

It is also important to support your dog nutritionally against those illnesses that she/he might be predisposed to genetically. Just as with people—one family may have a high incidence of cancer and another a high incidence of heart disease—different breeds of dogs are genetically predisposed to certain illnesses. In this book you will learn which illnesses your breed is prone to and how to avoid or delay the onset of the more common illnesses.

The focus of this book is on how your dog's body functions nutritionally, what your dog's nutritional needs are, and easy, flexible, affordable ways to keep your dog in optimal health through all phases of his/her life.

The nutritional information I'll give you is a guideline for formulating a diet and supplement plan for your dog. Every dog is different and has varying nutritional needs. I'll explain to you why each nutrient is needed, so you can create a diet for your dog's specific needs. The recommended amounts to feed are also meant to give you a general sense of what's appropriate for that size of dog. What your dog actually eats needs to be balanced for her or his unique combination of age, level of exercise, and individual metabolism. In the same way, your dog's multivitamin-mineral supplement doesn't have to exactly fit the recommended dosages (we are very grateful to Dr. Beverly Cappel-King for providing these) as long as they are close and contain the proper balance of vitamins and minerals.

You will find that as you pay closer attention to your dog's health, your bond with your best friend will become stronger, and that having a dog in your life will become an even greater privilege and joy than it is now.

## PART ONE

# CREATING OPTIMUM NUTRITION FOR YOUR DOG

# 1

## Feeding Your Dog for Naturally Great Health

You are what you eat. It's a common saying that few people take seriously, and yet good nutrition is the foundation for good health. If your dog doesn't have a soft, shiny, and clean coat,; eyes that are bright, clear, and alert; clean teeth; pink gums; and a lean, muscular body, then she is not in good health. The good news is that you can restore and maintain your dog's health through proper nutrition.

Most commercial dog food is low in nutrients and high in additives and preservatives. Dog food companies are not required to make human-grade dog food, meaning it is not fit for human consumption; and yet, with a few exceptions, your dog's body functions similarly to yours and has similar nutritional requirements for optimal health.

A dog isn't conditioned to complain about her aches and pains as we are, and she will instinctively hide physical problems, because in any pack of animals the predators look for the weakest members. That is why it is important to do a quick, head-to-tail health check of your dog each month. Start with the head and look for clean teeth and ears, dark pink gums, and bright clear eyes. Work your way back, looking for any signs of weight gain or loss, a soft, shiny, clean, mat-free coat and a clean underbelly free of fleas and flea dirt. As you're going over your dog's coat, take note of how it smells. Unless she has recently rolled in something potent, it should not have any odor. That doggy smell is a sure sign of ill health. Last, and the least desirable, check your dog's rear end to be sure it is clean, with no sign of worms.

If your dog doesn't pass the health check, a simple change in diet could bring her back to optimal health. If your dog shows any signs of ill health, including subtle changes such as a dull, dirty coat, it is a good idea to first bring her to your veterinarian for a thorough health check. In this chapter, you will learn what to look for in a commercial dog food and what to avoid. I will take the mystery and labor out of home-cooked meals and help you integrate fresh foods into your dog's diet. In later chapters, I will also give you feeding guidelines for special needs, such as obesity, recovering from illness, and pregnant and nursing dogs.

If you are not feeding your dog all-natural, human-grade dog food and are going to change to all-natural food or home-cooked meals, make the change slowly. Time after time, I have had people tell me they tried home-cooked meals or that all-natural stuff and it made their dogs terribly sick with diarrhea and mucus stools. What made the dogs sick was their body's attempt to detoxify from the toxin-filled food they had been eating. The dogs' bodies were struggling to come back to a natural state by getting rid of all the chemicals and preservatives that had been accumulating. A gradual change to a natural diet will detoxify your dog gradually, creating less of a shock to her system and fewer side effects, such as diarrhea.

Each dog is a unique individual with specific nutritional needs. Although Golden Retrievers look alike and generally have similar personalities and health problems, each Golden Retriever has different dietary needs depending on how her body processes foods, activity level, age, genetic makeup, environment, and a whole host of other internal and external factors. In this chapter, I will give you nutritional guidelines to use as a starting point in tailoring a diet to specifically meet your dog's needs. As you gradually introduce new foods to your dog, watch her carefully for any negative or positive reactions. Keep an eye out for things like changes in her coat, eye clarity, energy level, and weight gain or loss.

## WHAT TO LOOK FOR WHEN CHOOSING A COMMERCIAL DOG FOOD

Although there are over 300 pet food manufacturers in the United States with over $11 billion dollars in annual sales, your choice of truly high-quality foods is extremely limited. Most commercial dog foods are canned, semi-moist, or dry. Semi-moist can be eliminated from your list of choices because it is very high in sugar and other flavor additives that are addictive and and have no nutritional value. Canned and dry dog foods are your remaining choices, with dry foods being the most popular because they are less expensive and easier to use. Here are your three most important criteria in choosing a dry dog food:

The first thing to look for is meat that is human grade or United States Department of Agriculture (USDA) inspected. USDA inspected meat is, by definition, fit for human consumption. Optimally, buy a dog food made of organic, human grade, or USDA meat. Organic meat comes from animals raised without the use of antibiotics, growth hormones, such as estrogen or steroids. If the meat is not USDA or human grade, it is most likely coming from diseased, drugged, and decaying animals, including dogs and cats. There are many reports of rendering plants throughout the United States that receive dead dogs and cats, process them into meat meal, and sell them to dog food manufacturers. These animals are most likely riddled with diseases, such as cancer, heart disease, and kidney and liver disease. Sodium pentobarbital, which is used to euthanize dogs and cats, survives the rendering process and will be in the meat meal that is sold to the dog food manufacturers. A rendering plant in Baltimore has been known to process over 1,800 animals a month, including dogs, and sells their products to Alpo, Ralston Purina, and Heinz pet food companies. This meat can be listed on the dog food label as meat meal or meat and bone meal.

The second criteria in choosing dog food is to look for natural preservatives. Check the label for the antioxidants vitamin E and vitamin C. Stay away from chemical antioxidants such as ethoxyquin, butylated hydroxyanisole (BHA), and butylated hydroxytoluene (BHT). Ethoxyquin is a chemical that is manufactured for use in making rubber and preserving animal feed. It must be labeled as a poison by the manufacturer, is listed as a pesticide by the USDA, and has been banned from use in human food. The Occupational Safety and Health Administration (OSHA) lists BHA and BHT as chemical hazards in the laboratory. They have been linked to various forms of cancer, most commonly bladder, kidney, and liver cancer.

Natural antioxidants, such as vitamins C and E, are the best preservatives because they are natural to your dog's body and she can use what she needs and easily excrete any she doesn't need.

The third criteria for dry dog food is freshness. Look for a brand with a maximum shelf life of six months. Just as you look for the expiration date when you buy milk, yogurt, or cottage cheese, start looking for the date on the bag of dry food. Look for a bag that is under three months old and please don't buy a forty-pound bag of food for your Chihuahua. By the time a Toy breed eats forty pounds of dog food, it will be stale and rancid. Rancid fats and oils cause oxidation, a process within your dog's body in which unstable oxygen molecules, known as free radicals, attack healthy cells in an attempt to stabilize themselves. The healthy cell becomes unstable from the attack and is now a free radical looking for a healthy cell to stabilize it. Free radical damage contributes to allergies, arthritis, cancer, as well as eye, heart, and kidney disease. The smell of rancid oil in dog food is often not detectable, which makes the date on the bag your only indicator of freshness. Some dog food companies put the date the food is made on the bag and some put the expiration date.

The person you buy the food from should know which system the company uses. Buy enough food for a maximum of one month and either keep it in a dark, dry area in a tightly closed container or close the bag tightly. Canned dog food won't have an expiration date on it, but the other two criteria are the same: human grade meat and natural preservatives. Ideally, your dog should be eating fresh, naturally preserved food made with meat that you would put on your dinner table. See Resources in back for a list of dog food companies that fit these criteria. I have indicated the companies that use organic meat and would highly recommend that you feed your dog organic meat if it is available in your area.

## HOW TO READ HOW TO READ HOW TO READ

Dog Food labels are just as confusing as people-food labels so you aren't going to try to read and understand each ingredient. You can scan the label and look for red flags.

The ingredients are listed in descending order by weight. The ingredient that weighs the most is first but is not necessarily the primary ingredient. If you add a cup of beef and a cup of oats, the oats will weigh significantly less than the beef.

Meat should be the first ingredient. If the label doesn't specify the type of meat, such as beef, chicken, or lamb, cross that food off your list. If the meat is simply listed as meat, it could be dog, cat, or a decaying raccoon someone found on the side of the road on the way to work.

Steer clear of by-products. They can be any part of the animal except for the meat, hair, horn, teeth, and hoofs, which means it could be feathers, feet, and heads. Minced feathers and feet won't directly hurt your dog, but their nutritional value is highly questionable.

Meal and digest are fine. Meat meal is chopped or ground meat, bone, and organs. Poultry meal is chopped or ground meat, bone, and skin. Digest is meat that is pre-digested through a chemical or enzymatic process. You wouldn't want your only source of meat to be digest, so be sure there are additional sources, such as meal. You also want meat that is naturally digested with enzymes—not chemicals. If the shelf life of the food is six months or less, you can feel confident that the meat is naturally digested and doesn't contain chemicals.

The next ingredients listed are usually the grains and fats. Look for whole grains, such as ground brown rice. Avoid terms like hulls, mill run, or by-products. These are the waste that's left after the grains are processed for human consumption. Ironically, what is considered waste is the most nutritious part of the grain, but it still doesn't give you the complete balance of nutrients that whole grains do.

Fats should be specifically identified. It should say *beef fat* or *poultry fat*, not simply animal fat, and it should be naturally preserved, usually with vitamin E.

The rest of the ingredients can range from a simple list of vitamins and minerals, which you will recognize after reading this book, to various plants, such as vegetables, herbs, and kelp.

*Stay away from beet pulp.* If you see beet pulp on the label, cross that food off your list. Beet pulp is another common ingredient in dog food that would be thrown in the garbage by the sugar-beet processor if the dog food manufacturers didn't buy it. Many dog food manufacturers add beet pulp to their dog food in an attempt to satisfy the myth that the harder a dog's stool is the better. Your dog's stool should not be rock hard; it should be soft and slightly formed. As beet pulp passes through the intestine and the colon, it absorbs water and swells up to ten times its dry state, which causes it to pass very slowly and produces hard stools.

Diarrhea for more than a day or two is one of the few early indicators you have that your dog has an intestinal disorder. An artificial stool hardener, such as beet pulp, will put you days behind in identifying and treating an illness. Beet pulp also has a high sugar content. Dogs get just as addicted to sugar as we do, and it also makes them fat, hyperactive, and diabetic.

Gastric torsion is one of the leading causes of death in large and giant barrel-chested dogs, such as the Basset Hound, Bernese Mountain Dog, Bloodhound (leading cause of death), Boxer, Briard, Bullmastiff, Chinese Shar-Pei, Chow Chow, Doberman Pinscher, English Setter, German Shepherd, Gordon Setter, Greyhound, Irish Setter, Labrador Retriever, Russian Wolfhound, Saint Bernard, Scottish Deerhound, Standard Poodle, and Weirmaraner. The exact cause of gastric bloat and torsion has not been determined, probably because there is not one exact cause, but many breeders believe that feeding dry food without adding water is one cause. Dry food fed without water absorbs water from the stomach and swells. Adding beet pulp will cause additional swelling and additional risk. (*See* Chapter 9 for more on gastric torsion.)

You have probably studied the guaranteed analysis on pet food labels, scratched your head, and wondered what it should mean to you. Because there are no regulations on the quality of ingredients in dog food, unless you know the ingredients are high quality, it is useless information. The guaranteed analysis lists minimum or maximum percentages of ingredients, such as crude protein, fat, and fiber. The catch is, they don't have to tell you exactly what sources the protein, fat, and fiber come from. Lots of foods contain protein, but your dog's ability to absorb and use protein varies. Eggs are a great protein source because your dog's body will absorb and use all the protein in an egg. An old leather shoe is a poor source of protein because your dog's body can't absorb the protein in an old leather shoe, and yet it could be legally listed on the ingredient label as meat by-products and could be included as a source of protein. If the food contains high-quality ingredients, then you can use the guaranteed analysis to narrow down your choices of dog food by finding a brand with optimal amounts of protein, fat, and fiber.

If you are going to feed your dog dry or canned food, be sure all the ingredients have nutritional value. Also, add a variety of fresh, live foods every day. Contrary to what the dog food manufacturers would like you to believe, a variety of nutrient-rich foods is the best way to give your dog a balanced diet.

## HOME-COOKED MEALS

Many people shy away from home-cooked meals for their dogs. They don't know where to start, they think it will be too time-consuming or they are worried that their pets won't get proper nutrition. Preparing homemade food does take more time than throwing a cup of dry food in a dish, but not much more, and it is really very simple.

Your dog is an omnivore, meaning she eats both animal and plant foods. In the case of a dog, the need for animal food is predominant. The approximate nutritional proportions for a dog's healthy meal are 25 percent organ meat (liver, kidney, heart), 25 percent muscle meat, 25 percent grains, and 25 percent vegetables. For example, for a fifty-pound dog, one meal might consist of one-half cup liver, one-half cup ground beef, one-half cup minced or grated carrots and broccoli, and one-half cup brown rice and oats, sprinkled with a multi-vitamin supplement.

Ground meat is an economical and easy source of muscle meat. Buy the ground meat that is packaged by the store because meat that is packaged in the store usually means it was ground in the store. This reduces the risk of contamination that occurs in large meat-processing plants or in transporting the meat. As much as possible, try to vary the type of meat you feed. This will give your dog a variety of nutrients and help reduce the chances of developing an allergy to one type of meat. If you can find bones with lots of meat on them, that is a healthy, fun way to feed muscle meat to your dog. To avoid splintering, always feed bones raw. I don't recommend poultry bones. Although it is unusual, Dr. Beverly Cappel-King has treated several dogs that have punctured their intestines eating poultry bones.

If your dog is lazy and inactive, you might want to avoid turkey, and if she is hyperactive you might want to try adding turkey to her diet. Have you ever wondered why, after a turkey dinner, you never want to do the dishes or play a game of touch football, you just want to take a nap? Turkey contains the amino acid tryptophan, which acts as a mild sedative.

If possible, try to find an affordable source of organic organ meats. The liver and kidney are the organs that filter waste from the body and toxins can accumulate there. If you have a grocery store nearby that sells organic meat, the butcher may be able to lower the price if you buy in bulk. If you don't have a big freezer your friends may be interested in organic organ meat for themselves and/or their dog(s). Your local health food store may also know of a source. If you can't find an organic source, it is best to skip the organ meats.

If you feed your dog raw meat, which is the healthiest way to do it, freeze the meat in meal-size packages and take out enough each morning for the next day and put it in your refrigerator.

For the carbohydrate portion of the meal, buy whole grains, such as amaranth, barley grits, brown rice, buckwheat, millet, oats, whole-wheat couscous, or quinoa, which is a whole grain that's high in protein. Your dog's saliva doesn't contain the starch-digesting enzymes that humans have, so she can't digest large pieces or quantities of starchy food. Add some extra water, and cook the grains a littler longer than you would for yourself. If you can see grains in your dog's stool, that means she isn't digesting them and they need to be cooked longer. Cooking breaks down the starches in the grains, making them easier to digest. You can cook enough for a week at one time.

Most vegetables are good for your dog. Dark green leafy vegetables and orange, red, and yellow vegetables are the most nutritious. Onions should be avoided because they contain a substance called n-propyl disulfide, which alters and eventually destroys the red blood cells of dogs, causing hemolytic anemia and sometimes death. If your dog has arthritis, try avoiding vegetables from the nightshade family (eggplant, peppers, potato, tomato), as these vegetables can sometimes aggravate arthritis.

Either slightly cook the vegetables or, to preserve the enzymes, chop or grate them finely and serve them raw. I often just give my dog a little bit of what the rest of the family is getting for dinner and leave some in the fridge for the next morning. After all, dogs aren't the only ones who should eat their peas and broccoli.

You don't have to be strict about the food proportions you give. Older dogs who have never eaten vegetables may not have a taste for them unless they're well disguised in a little butter or olive oil. Dogs fed vegetables early in life will be more inclined to eat them plain and raw. Every dog's needs are different and will vary throughout her life. Those quantities are a guideline. If she tends to leave grains in her dish, cut back a little on the grains. Meat, grains, and vegetables are the basics. After those, any whole nutritious foods can be added, such as beans, cottage cheese, eggs, fruits, unsalted nuts, and yogurt.

How much food to feed each day will also vary with each dog. Just as every person's body uses food differently, so does a dog's. You will be giving your dog more food with home-cooked meals than with a dry dog food, because since dry dog food doesn't have water in it, it is concentrated. As a starting point, use the following guidelines for total amounts to feed each day:

- 1–2 cups for small dogs, up to 20 pounds;
- 2–7 cups for medium dogs, 20–50 pounds,
- 7–10 cups for large dogs, 50–100 pounds;
- 10–14 cups for giant dogs, over 100 pounds.

Many dog owners find that once their dog gets used to her home-cooked meals, she will eat what she needs and leave the rest, becoming trim, fit, and full of energy. Unless they have experienced trauma around food, such as not getting enough to eat as a newborn, dogs will eat to meet their energy and nutritional needs. Most overweight dogs get that way because their food contains addictive sugars or is high in calories with little nutritional value.

Mix together the meat, grains, and vegetables, add supplements (which you will learn about later in this section), mix thoroughly, and serve with a smile, knowing you are putting your dog on the road to a long, healthy life.

## FRESH FOODS

Fresh foods have been forgotten in most canine diets. There are hundreds of human studies testifying to the fact that a diet high in fresh, raw fruits and vegetables is key to a long, healthy life. Where are the studies on dogs that would prove the same thing? The majority of studies done on dog nutrition are funded by dog food manufacturers who could not call their foods *complete and balanced* if they did a nutritional study that included fresh foods. Fortunately, a few studies are being done that are independent of the dog food manufacturers. One impressive study of 900 cats found those who were fed a diet that included raw meat and raw milk led long healthy lives, while the cats fed pasteurized milk and cooked meat suffered from many ailments, including gum, heart, kidney, and thyroid disease.

The difference between raw meat and milk, and pasteurized milk and cooked meat is that the raw food contains enzymes. An enzyme is a protein molecule produced by living organisms. There are at least 1,300 different enzymes in the dog's body, each with a different function, such as digesting food or processing waste materials in the blood. Enzymes are essential to all life on earth.

**Fresh Foods = Long Long Life for Taffy**

Taffy, a border collie who once held the *Guinness Book of Records* title for Canine Longevity in Britain, is another impressive testimony to the benefits of fresh foods. Taffy ate fresh foods and lived to be twenty-seven years old.

According to Humbart Santillo, author of *Food Enzymes, The Missing Link to Radiant Health*, "There is a connection between the strength of our immune system and our enzyme level. The greater the amount of enzyme reserves, the stronger our immune system, the healthier and stronger we will be." Enzymes are only found in raw food because they are destroyed in food that is heated over 105 degrees Fahrenheit. Any food that is baked, fried, heat-processed, or roasted does not contain enzymes.

Not surprisingly, there is a high incidence of digestive-enzyme deficiencies in dogs. Although many enzymes are made by the body, it's also important to get them from raw foods. Most dogs get no fresh food their entire lives unless they can get away with sneaking in a few mouthfuls of grass when they go outside.

Digestive enzymes help break down your dog's food, enabling the nutrients to be absorbed. Normally, living creatures begin life with plenty of digestive enzymes, which can be depleted if they are never given any fresh, raw food. The enzymes in raw food do not replenish your dog's reserves as much as they digest a portion of that food, so your dog's body does not use as many.

German Shepherds are prone to a digestive-enzyme deficiency, which causes many intestinal problems including poor digestion and the inability to absorb the nutrients from foods. Nutrient deficiencies cause a long list of chronic problems, including allergies, diarrhea, skin problems, and vomiting. A diet of fresh raw foods is all these German Shepherds would need to properly digest and absorb their food. For severe cases, there are digestive-enzyme supplements for dogs.

Try to give your dog as much fresh, raw meat, vegetables, and fruits as you can. If you feed your dog raw vegetables from the time she is a puppy, she'll usually always like them. If your older dog won't chew on a carrot, then grate, mince, or blend it and add it to her food. If you are in the kitchen preparing fresh whole foods and your dog shows an interest in them, give her some. Sometimes dogs will be more willing to try something new if they think it is people food. And yes, raw beef, lamb, and poultry is very good for your dog. Not only will the enzymes help digest the meat, they will also help clean your dog's teeth.

## WATER

Oxygen is the only nutrient that is more important to sustaining life than water. Your dog could live for weeks without food, but would only last a few days without water. Approximately 60 percent of your dog's total weight is water. That means, if she weighs fifty pounds, then thirty pounds of that weight is water. The entire body is highly dependent on water, including the blood, brain, and muscles, which are each over 70 percent water. The most important nutrient you give your dog is water, so it is vital to provide access to pure, clean water at all times.

Although 70 percent of the earth is covered by water, it 's hard to find clean drinking water. The Environmental Protection Agency (EPA) data shows that the tap water of approximately 30 million people in the United States fails to meet at least one of their health standards each year. And these are shamefully inadequate standards to begin with—they allow about 100 contaminants that should not be found in tap water. Throughout the United States, more than 2,000 contaminants have been found in drinking water supplies, and your tap water can contain such contaminants as aluminum, bacteria, cancer-causing industrial compounds, chemical salts, chlorine, fecal material (e-coli), fluoride, gasoline, lead, nitrates, parasites, pesticides, radioactive gases, sulphates, and viruses.

According to the U.S. Centers for Disease Control, 1,000 to 1,200 people die each year from contaminated drinking water and another 400,000 to 7 million people become sick. These numbers probably reflect only a small portion of the actual deaths and illnesses from contaminated water because there is no official reporting system for water-related health problems. Gathering statistics on these problems is difficult because many doctors don't consider water when diagnosing an illness, but the toxins in water cause gradual deterioration of the body over many years. Human healthcare professionals who consider the role of polluted water in illness are rare, and it is unheard of among health-care professionals who take care of dogs. When was the last time you called your vet because your dog had diarrhea or vomiting and he or she asked about your dog's drinking water?

The average dog weighs about sixty pounds, while the average person weighs more than twice that. The smaller the dog, the higher the metabolic rate and the more susceptible they are to pollutants because their bodies process everything more quickly, including toxins. What might take months to make a human sick might take only days to make a small dog sick. The same drinking water that is making 27 million people sick each year is undoubtedly making a significantly higher number of dogs seriously ill and shortening the lifespan of many Toy breeds.

## GET THE LEAD OUT

Among the hundreds of contaminants in our drinking water, lead is probably the most common and the most dangerous. Over 98 percent of homes in the United States have pipes that contain lead or lead solder, leaving over 30 million people drinking water with high levels of lead. High concentrations of lead can permanently damage the brain, central nervous system, and kidneys, and cause anemia, digestive problems, headaches, heart disease, hyperactivity, muscle and joint pain, reproductive problems, mental challenges, slowed growth, and even death.

In 1986 Congress amended the 1974 Safe Drinking Water Act and banned all future use of lead pipe and lead solder in public drinking water systems. This, however, does not include your faucets which, to this day, may contain up to 8 percent lead. A study of water that sat in twenty-five new faucets for a few hours contained from 30 to 1,300 parts per billion of lead, which is 2–100 times the daily amount that can cause serious symptoms in people. Again, whatever the danger to people, the danger to your dog is magnified. If you must use tap water for yourself and your dog, run the water for a minute first to clear out any accumulated toxins. If you believe your dog has been exposed to lead, give her an extra mineral supplement for a few days. Magnesium and zinc are instrumental in helping rid your dog's body of lead.

Hundreds of the contaminants that enter the water through the air, ground, and pipes are eliminated from municipal water supplies by the addition of chlorine, which is yet another contaminate. Some communities are also poisoning their water supply with fluoride.

## THE GREAT FLUORIDE SCANDAL

The decision to add fluoride to the drinking water can be attributed to one of the most successful and deceptive marketing campaigns in contemporary history. Before fluoride was added to drinking water, it was considered an extremely toxic environmental pollutant that destroyed crops and animals. The handbook, *Clinical Toxicology of Commercial Products*, considers fluoride to be more poisonous than lead. Because it was considered an environmental pollutant, industries whose waste products contained large amounts of fluoride (mostly aluminum and fertilizer manufacturers) were incurring huge expenses to dispose of their waste. The need to inexpensively dispose of fluoride waste products was brought to the government's attention by the *right* people, which prompted the mysterious transformation of fluoride from an environmental pollutant to a supposedly harmless substance that would be trickled into the nation's water supply to prevent tooth decay.

The studies used to support the proposal to put fluoride in drinking water to prevent tooth decay are in direct opposition to studies that were done independently of the companies that needed to get rid of their fluoride. It reminds me of the two men who went for job interviews at a company's research facility. The first man went to his interview and was given a research project and asked how he would conduct the study. The man went through a lengthy discussion on how he would conduct his study and left feeling very confident he would get the job. The second man went in for his interview and was given the same research project and was asked how he would conduct the study. The second man got the job simply by asking one question: What results do you want?

Studies done by researchers who did not have a financial interest in fluoride found it to be linked to arthritis, cancer, discolored teeth, headaches, immune disorders, skin problems, stomach pain, and weak bones. Fluoride has *not* been linked to a reduction in tooth decay or stronger bones in any independent study. One of these independent studies involved over 39,000 children throughout the United States, ages five to seven. The children using fluoridated water did not show any reduction in tooth decay when compared to those children using non-fluoridated water.

The United States is one of the few countries left in the world that puts fluoride in its water. The same decline in tooth decay that we have seen in America has also been seen in countries that do *not* use fluoride in their water. And, in fact, this decline in tooth decay is attributed to better dental hygiene and better nutrition, not fluoride.

Another fluoride myth is that it will build strong bones and repair weak, brittle bones. Using fluoride will make bones *look* denser on X-rays for a few years, but in truth the bone is actually weak and brittle, and after four to six years the fracture rate of people taking fluoride increases dramatically. Isn't it fascinating how the studies promoting the use of fluoride-like drugs, such as Fosamax for osteoporosis, all end at four to six years?

Avoiding fluoride is not easy, so if you're in a community that doesn't add it to their water supply, consider yourself lucky. Boiling water concentrates fluoride, and the only filtration system that removes fluoride is a reverse osmosis system. If fluoride is in your tap water, use bottled water that guarantees it does not contain fluoride, distilled water, or water from a reverse osmosis system.

## THE BIGGEST WATER-BORNE CARCINOGEN

Chlorine is added to municipal water systems to destroy microorganisms that carry disease. Unfortunately, this disinfectant can also make you and your dog sick. Chlorine in water creates cancer-causing by-products called trihalomethanes that are formed during the chlorination process.

The Natural Resources Defense Council estimates that trihalomethanes cause more than 10,000 cases of rectal and bladder cancer in humans a year. According to the National Cancer Institute, drinking chlorinated water doubles your risk for bladder cancer. Fortunately, most water filters remove chlorine.

If you use well water, you have probably been congratulating yourself on having clean, untreated water, but the only contaminants you are avoiding are chlorine and fluoride. The same nearby farms, fields, golf courses, landfills, military bases, orchards, pesticide-spraying neighbors, and underground gasoline storage tanks that pollute municipal water supplies are also poisoning your well water.

In your dog, short-term bouts of diarrhea or vomiting, hyperactivity or more serious long-term effects, such as arthritis, cancer, kidney and liver disease, could all be caused by polluted drinking water.

There are a few easy solutions to clearing up the contaminants in your tap water. First you can have your water tested to find out what contaminants you need to eliminate. To do this, call the Environmental Protection Agency's safe drinking water hotline at 1-800-426-4791. If you live in Washington D.C., call 703-412-3330. They will give you a list of certified testing labs in your area. You can also go online at www.epa.gov/safewater.

Once you find out which contaminants you need to eliminate, look in the yellow pages of your phone book under *water* and *water purification systems*. Depending on the level of contaminants and your budget, you can buy a filter for your faucet, a reverse osmosis system, or a water distiller. (*See* Resources in back for information on where to buy filters.)

New technology for water filtration is coming out every year, so do some research before buying. If you don't want to bother having your water tested or changing filters, you can have bottled water delivered to your house. Alternatively, if you have the time and inclination, there may be a nearby place where you can bring your own container and get bottled water for around 25 cents a gallon. Whatever your source, be sure there is a written evaluation of what's in the water.

If you and your dog travel a lot or go camping, you can buy purification filters at most sport or department stores. Read the label carefully. Some types of portable filters only purify water from freshwater rivers, lakes, or streams, and not tap water. Look for one that filters chlorine and parasites, such as giardia.

## THE WATER BOWL

Your dog's water bowl can also be a source of contaminants. Use a glass, stainless steel, or American-made ceramic bowl (many foreign-made ceramics contain high levels of lead that will leach into the water). Plastic and aluminum will also leach and contaminate the water you worked so hard to keep clean and fresh.

Place the water away from any possible contamination by pesticides, cleaning sprays, or other animals. Wild animals, such as rodents, carry many diseases that could be lethal to your dog. Rodent urine has recently been found to carry a deadly strain of leptospirosis that is different from the vaccine your dog gets.

Clean your dog's water bowl at least once a day and if you are not home during the day, be sure it's large enough to last through the day.

## TREATS

Many people serve their dogs only the highest quality foods at mealtime and then fall short when it comes to treats. Even a few low-quality treats a day can compromise your dog's health. The same cautions I gave you in choosing a dog food hold true for treats, and the best treats are fresh raw foods. I once knew a Golden Retriever named Tyler who thought the best treat in the world was an ice cube. His owner was on a tight budget so she used ice cubes for rewards.

You can use carrot sticks, dried meat, or home-cooked cookies. If you like to cook, you can try making homemade treats and store them in the freezer. For a refreshing treat on a hot day, give them to your dog right from the freezer. (*See also* Resources in back for dog food manufacturers that make high-quality treats.)

The following are two of Dr. Beverly Cappel-King's favorite recipes for dog treats.

### Dr. Bev's Delectable Dog Cookies

1 1/2 cups whole wheat flour

1/8 cup chopped unsalted seeds and nuts

1 tablespoon vegetable oil

1 egg

1 tablespoon molasses

Add any or all of the following, to taste: fresh garlic or garlic powder, grated cheese, or nutritional yeast.

Combine all ingredients into a firm ball, adding milk if more moisture is needed.

Roll the dough out and cut it into your dog's favorite cookie shapes. My dog prefers cats, rabbits, and squirrels. Place them on a greased cookie sheet and bake at 300 degrees Fahrenheit for 30–40 minutes, or until the cookies are crispy.

### The King of Dog Cookies

1 1/2 cups cooked rice, oatmeal, or other wholegrain cereal

1/4 cup whole or skim milk powder

1/4 cup vegetable oil

1/4 cup wheat bran

1/4 cup whole wheat flour, rye flour, or corn meal

Add any or all of the following to taste: fennel seed, fresh garlic or garlic powder, grated cheese, nutritional yeast, oregano.

Make a firm ball, adding milk if more moisture is needed.

Roll the dough out and cut it into your dog's favorite cookie shapes. Place them on a greased cookie sheet and bake at 300 degrees Fahrenheit for 30–40 minutes or until the cookies are crispy.

Feel free to take great liberties with these recipes. Try different flours, wholegrain cereals, cheeses, nuts, seeds, and spices. If you want to make a big batch and keep them in the refrigerator or travel with them, squeeze a vitamin-E capsule into the dough, as a preservative.

## Animal-Origin Chew Toys

Dogs need to chew. Chewing is not only good for your dog's emotional well-being, it is good for his health. Chewing prevents boredom and keeps teeth clean, gums healthy, and jaws strong. If your dog lived in the wild, he would spend hours chewing on his prey. Your puppy should always have something to chew on or, as many dog owners have found, he will find something to chew and won't discriminate between the antiques and the old furniture, although many dog owners would argue that their dogs will only eat antiques.

Among the huge variety of chew Toys available are animal-origin chew Toys which range from the familiar rawhide chews to the ever-increasing variety of animal parts, such as ears, feet, hooves, and horns. It seems that every time I go into a pet store there is a new animal part on the shelf being marketed as an all-natural chew Toy for my dog. These are animal parts that would otherwise be thrown away because humans won't eat them. Remember, *all natural* doesn't always mean nutritious. Sticking to food with nutritional value is one of the keys to creating optimal health.

Lack of nutrition isn't the only reason I don't recommend rawhide or animal-part chew Toys. They can also endanger your dog's life. Foods with very little nutritional value are harder to digest, which means they sit in the stomach and intestine longer than highly digestible foods. Large chunks of indigestible foods, such as rawhide or pig's ears, have caused a wide range of illnesses—from mild intestinal problems to complete intestinal blockage and death.

A Golden Retriever named Sunny is one of many dogs Dr. Beverly Cappel-King has treated for intestinal problems associated with animal-origin chew Toys. Sunny was brought to Dr King with symptoms of vomiting and constipation. When Dr. King palpated her stomach, she could feel something unusual, so she took X-rays. They showed nothing, and neither did an ultrasound or endoscopy, so, as a last resort, Dr. King did exploratory surgery and found a piece of rawhide the size of a lime embedded inside Sunny's intestine.

There have also been many instances of dogs choking on animal-origin chew Toys. As the dog chews, these products become soft and sticky, and get easily caught in the throat. Many rawhide chew Toys also contain the chemical preservative propylene glycol, a component of antifreeze that has a sweet taste the dogs begin to crave after a few rawhides. The chew Toys may also contain dangerous chemicals, such as arsenic, bleach, cyanide, formaldehyde, lead, and mercury. The short-term consequences of ingesting these chemicals can include itching, sore throat and pancreatitis. Long-term they can cause an overall deterioration of the body, resulting in such diseases as cancer, kidney failure, and liver disease.

You also need to be careful of chew Toys like hooves that can splinter and puncture your dog's intestinal wall. I don't see any reason to take these types of risks when there are safe alternatives that will satisfy your dog's need to chew.

As with humans, variety is the spice of life for dogs, so I keep a wide assortment of safe, non-food chew Toys of all shapes, sizes, and textures around the house—fuzzy shapes that squeak, ropes, and rubber balls, to name a few. Tennis balls act like Brillo on your dog's teeth, wearing them down quickly, so reserve them for games of fetch. And avoid brightly colored Toys that contain harmful dyes, plastic Toys that will leach the plastic, and synthetic fabrics.

A raw bone from your butcher is great for safe, long-term chewing that will provide good nutrition, clean your dog's teeth, and keep his jaws strong and his gums healthy. They are inexpensive and will satisfy your dog's chewing needs for days. It is important to serve them raw because cooking bones makes them splinter. A frozen bone is another great treat for your dog on a hot day. If you don't have an outside area where you can leave your dog to chew on his bone, an old sheet or blanket will protect your carpet and other fabrics from being stained by the fat.

# 2

# Vitamins for Your Dog

Just like humans, dogs need vitamins for the growth and maintenance of a healthy body. It would be ideal if your dog could get vitamins from her food, but even the highest quality non-organic dog food (home-cooked or bought), will not provide enough vitamins to maintain optimal health. You need to use supplements, and here's why. Most produce is grown in soil depleted of nutrients and sprayed with pesticides. And meat, unless it's organic, comes from animals given estrogen-like hormones to fatten them up, and antibiotics to prevent the diseases caused by overcrowding and stress. Excess estrogen can cause cancer, and overexposure to antibiotics can create resistant bacteria that no antibiotic can stop. Whether you live in the country or the city, your dog experiences a daily bombardment of physical stressors from pollutants and toxins, such as car exhaust and pesticides. And when your dog is further stressed by environmental or emotional factors, her need for vitamins is that much higher.

Unless you are treating your dog for a specific health problem or a stressful environment, the best way to provide daily vitamins is with a multivitamin supplement. Give half the daily dose with the morning meal and half with the evening meal.

For each vitamin your dog needs on a daily basis, I will give you dosage recommendations for adult small, medium, large, and giant dogs so you

---

### Dog Sizes

Small dogs weigh up to 20 pounds.

Medium dogs weigh from 20–50 pounds.

Large dogs weigh from 50–100 pounds.

Giant dogs weigh over 100 pounds.

---

can choose the appropriate multivitamin.

There are many sources of quality dog multivitamins. (*See* Resources in back for mail order sources of vitamins if you can't find a vitamin that contains the correct dosages.)

## WHAT ARE VITAMINS?

Vitamins are organic substances found naturally in eggs, fish, fowl, meat, and plants. With the exception of vitamin C, your dog can't produce her own vitamins and needs you to provide them through food and supplemental sources.

Vitamin A, C, D, E, K, and the B-complex vitamins are referred to as essential vitamins for dogs because they are important to sustain life. These vitamins are divided into water-soluble vitamins, which include the B-complex vitamins and vitamin C, and fat-soluble vitamins, which include A, D, E, and K. The water-soluble and fat-soluble vitamins are processed differently in the body. The water-soluble vitamins (B-complex and C) are absorbed in the small intestine, used as needed, and any excess is excreted in the urine. The fat-soluble vitamins (A, D, E, K) are stored primarily in the liver and any excess is excreted in the feces. The important difference between these vitamins is that the fat-soluble vitamins (A, D, E, K) are stored in the body, creating a greater risk for toxicity, but a lower risk of deficiencies, while the water-soluble vitamins (B-complex, C) are not stored, increasing their potential for deficiencies, while decreasing the chances of toxicity. See Table 3.1 below for a quick reference on the essential vitamins, their functions within the body, their nutritional sources, and any health problems related to excesses and deficiencies of each vitamin.

## TABLE 3.1. ESSENTIAL VITAMINS

| FUNCTION | SOURCE | DEFICIENCY | EXCESS |
|---|---|---|---|
| **A** | | | |
| Skeletal growth, skin, epithelial tissue, vision, reproduction, immune system | Yellow, orange, and dark green vegetables and fruits, fish liver oils, liver, egg yolk, milk | Skeletal abnormalities, skin disorders, loss of tissue integrity, night blindness, reproductive failure | Skeletal abnormalities, oversensitivity to sensory stimuli, cleft palate in puppies |
| **B-Complex B$_1$ (thiamin)** | | | |
| Digestion of carbohydrate and protein. | Whole grains, liver, pork, legumes, nuts, yeast | Stool eating, lack of appetite, impaired central nervous system, convulsions, muscle weakness | Non-toxic |
| **B$_2$ (riboflavin)** | | | |
| Digestion of carbohydrates and fat, cell growth | Eggs, yogurt, milk, organ meats, cheese, green vegetables | Stool eating, skin disorders, impaired central nervous system | Non-toxic |
| **B$_3$ (niacin)** | | | |
| Processes amino acids, carbohydrates and glucose, utilization of fatty acids | Liver, meat, yeast, milk, egg yolk, whole grains, legumes | Skin disease, diarrhea, madness | Non-toxic |

| FUNCTION | SOURCE | DEFICIENCY | EXCESS |
|---|---|---|---|
| | **$B_5$ (pantothenic acid)** | | |
| Occurs in all forms of living tissue, synthesis of fatty acids, cholesterol, and steroids, production of cortisone and hormones, utilization of fat and carbohydrates | Liver, kidney, egg yolk, dairy products, yeast, legumes, wheat germ, peanuts | Lowered antibody response, premature graying, low blood sugar, Addison's disease, deterioration of adrenal glands, digestive disorders | Non-toxic |
| | **$B_6$ (pyridoxine)** | | |
| Processes amino acids, proteins, hydrochloric acid and magnesium; helps produce antibodies and red blood cells | Liver, meat, yeast, milk, whole grains, egg yolk | Anemia, dental decay, heart disease, liver disease | Neurological damage |
| | **$B_{12}$ (cobalamin)** | | |
| Processes amino acids, fatty acids carbohydrates, and fat, absorption of protein, production of red blood cells | Liver, kidney, meat, fish, poultry, eggs | Anemia, brain damage, fatigue, low red-blood-cell count, senility | Non-toxic |

| FUNCTION | SOURCE | DEFICIENCY | EXCESS |
|---|---|---|---|
| **Biotin** | | | |
| Processes fat, protein, and vitamin C | Liver, kidney, egg yolk, yeast, milk, legumes | Anemia, skin disorders, hair loss, heart disease, weak muscles | Non-toxic |
| **Folic Acid** | | | |
| Production of red blood cells, processes protein, builds antibodies, growth and division of cells | Liver, yeast, green vegetables | Anemia, vaccine reactions, watery eyes, lack of appetite | Non-toxic |
| **Choline** | | | |
| Utilization of fat and cholesterol, cell and nervous tissue structure and function | Organ meats, fish, egg yolk, yeast, wheat germ, dairy products, legumes, whole grains | Impaired central nervous system, liver, and thymus gland, heart disease | Diarrhea |
| **C (ascorbic acid)** | | | |
| Collagen production, absorption of vitamins, growth and maintenance of tissue cells, gums, blood vessels, bones and teeth, antioxidants | Citrus fruit, green vegetables, potatoes, berries | Weak immune system, bladder stones, urinary tract and skin infections, skeletal abnormalities | Non-toxic, diarrhea, low sulfur |

| FUNCTION | SOURCE | DEFICIENCY | EXCESS |
|---|---|---|---|
| **D** | | | |
| Absorption of calcium and phosphorus | Fish liver oils, yeast, egg yolk | Defective bone growth, softening of bones | Calcium deposits, bone resorption, kidney damage |
| **E (tocopherols)** | | | |
| Antioxidant, enhances immune system, utilization of sex hormones, vitamin D, and cholesterol | Nuts, brown rice, wheat germ, eggs, whole grains, soybean and sunflower oil, seeds, green leafy vegetables | Reproductive failure, low red blood cell count, heart disease, muscle degeneration, anemia, kidney disease | Non-toxic, increased need for vitamins A and D |
| **K** | | | |
| Blood clotting, production of protein | Liver, green vegetables, | Hemorrhage, internal bleeding | Anemia |

## Water-Soluble Vitamins

The B-complex vitamins are grouped together because they work well as a team. The team is made up of thiamin ($B_1$), riboflavin ($B_2$), niacin ($B_3$), pantothenic acid ($B_5$), pyridoxine ($B_6$), cobalamin ($B_{12}$), biotin, folic acid, and choline. The effectiveness of one B vitamin is, to a large extent, dependent upon adequate amounts of the other B vitamins. For example, pyridoxine ($B_6$) is necessary for the absorption of cobalamin ($B_{12}$). Natural food sources rich in B vitamins never contain only one B vitamin. It's best to supplement the B vitamins together unless you're treating a specific illness with one B vitamin.

The B-complex vitamins help ward off stress, alleviate neurological problems, are essential for cell maintenance and growth, the production of antibodies and red blood cells, and the absorption of protein, fat, and carbohydrates. Alfred J. Plechner, DVM and Martin Zucker, authors of *Pet Allergies, Remedies For An Epidemic*, have found that hyperactivity and aggressiveness in dogs can sometimes be remedied by a B-complex supplement.

You can give your dog some extra B-complex when you know she is going to be stressed, or when her immune system is compromised. Vaccinations, surgery, and a serious injury or shock to the body are the most extreme cases for which your dog's body needs a lot of extra support from the B vitamins. The B-complex vitamins will also reduce the toxic effects of antibiotics and radiation from X-rays or radiation therapy.

Other indications for giving your dog a B-complex vitamin are highly stressful situations, such as traveling, separation anxiety, the show ring, nausea during pregnancy, or being a stressed mother. Neurological disorders, such as degenerative myelopathy in German Shepherds, can be helped with the B-complex vitamins. Any breed, such as the Boxer and German Shepherd that are susceptible to digestive disorders, can benefit from some extra B-complex vitamins. Toy and short-nosed breeds, such as the Bulldog, Pekingese, Pomeranian, and Pug, are prone to tooth and gum diseases and can benefit from some extra vitamin B-complex.

Cortisone, drugs for high blood pressure, hormone therapy, and sulfa drugs rob your dog's body of B-complex vitamins, so be sure to give your dog a supplement if she is on any of these drugs. Sulfa drugs are given for bacterial diseases and are sometimes referred to as antibiotics, though technically they are not. If your veterinarian has prescribed a drug that begins with sulfa, such as sulfanilamide, it is a sulfa drug; or you may see a brand name, such as Albon, Bactrovet, Primor, or Tribrissen. If in doubt, always ask questions.

Nutritional sources of the B-complex vitamins are blackstrap molasses, brewer's yeast, dark green vegetables, eggs, kelp, kidney, liver, milk, and peanuts. The high heat used to process some brewer's yeast depletes it of B vitamins so be sure you are buying *unprocessed* brewer's yeast if you use it as a nutritional supplement. Unprocessed brewer's yeast is inexpensive and readily available at health food stores. When you give your dog and yourself eggs, buy eggs that are from organically fed free-range chickens. Free-range chickens get the majority of their nutrients from the pasture and are free of antibiotics and hormones. And yes, raw eggs are good for your dog. The myth that raw eggs are not good for dogs came from the fact that raw egg whites can prevent the absorption of biotin (one of the B-complex vitamins). This is true, but the egg yolk supplies your dog with plenty of biotin to counteract the effects of the egg whites. Feeding the egg raw keeps the food alive and enables your dog to absorb the nutrients more efficiently. Eggs are a great source of protein, B vitamins, vitamin A, vitamin D, vitamin E, amino acids, magnesium, selenium, and zinc. I give my dog an egg for breakfast every Sunday morning, the same day I splurge on a big breakfast.

Vitamin B-complex comes as a tablet, a powder in a capsule, or you can buy the unprocessed brewer's yeast.

Daily dosages for adult dogs are as follows:

| | Small Dog | Medium Dog | Large Dog | Giant Dog |
|---|---|---|---|---|
| Thiamin ($B_1$) | 1 mg | 2 mg | 3 mg | 4 mg |
| Riboflavin ($B_2$) | 1 mg | 2 mg | 3 mg | 4 mg |
| Niacin ($B_3$) | 1 mg | 2 mg | 3 mg | 4 mg |
| Pantothenic Acid ($B_5$) | 1 mg | 2 mg | 3 mg | 4 mg |
| Pyridoxine ($B_6$) | 1 mg | 2 mg | 3 mg | 4 mg |
| Cobalamin ($B_{12}$) | 1 mcg | 2 mcg | 3 mcg | 4 mcg |
| Biotin | 1 mcg | 2 mcg | 3 mcg | 4 mcg |
| Folic Acid | 1 mcg | 2 mcg | 3 mcg | 4 mcg |

## Vitamin C (Ascorbic Acid)

Unlike humans, who must get their vitamin C through diet or supplements, most animals produce their own vitamin C. Dogs produce vitamin C in the liver from the blood sugar glucose. Each day, adult dogs produce approximately 40 milligrams of vitamin C per 2.2 pounds of body weight. That's about 1,800 milligrams for a 100-pound dog, 900 milligrams for a 50-pound dog and 450 milligrams for a 25-pound dog.

There is an assumption among conventional veterinarians that because dogs manufacture their own vitamin C, there is no need to supplement it. However, holistic veterinarians have found that vitamin C in a dog's diet can clear up a variety of health problems. In his book, *How To Have A Healthier Dog*, Dr. Wendell Belfield points out, "Fifteen years of clinical experience, involving over two thousand cases, has told me that dogs definitely benefit from extra vitamin C. When given supplements, they are much less likely to develop hip dysplasia, spinal myelopathy, ruptured discs, viral diseases, and skin problems. They live healthier and longer."

Vitamin C is a powerful antioxidant that can boost the immune system, reduce cancer risk and the risk of cataracts, and stimulate wound repair. Vitamin C is important for proper bone formation and maintenance, and plays a role in preventing heart disease. Also, when a dog is stressed, she needs additional vitamins for her body to function properly and to protect it from disease.

A report published in the *British Journal of Biomedical Sciences* states that, in humans, a low intake of vitamins A, $B_6$, C, E, beta-carotene, and folic acid have been associated with abnormally low immune-system response and greater risk of cancer.

Cataracts, the filming over of the eye's lens in older dogs, is a common problem in all dogs. Cataracts are caused, at least in part, by oxidative stress to the lens of the eye. Testimony to the power of vitamin C in protecting the eye was shown in a human study that also applies to pets. The *American Journal of Clinical Nutrition* reported that people with cataracts tend to have lower levels of vitamin C in their blood. In a study of 175 people with cataract and 175 cataract-free people, those who were cataract-free used significantly larger amounts of vitamin C than those who had cataracts.

The body requires vitamin C to form collagen, a substance that functions as the glue holding together the skin and the connective tissues, such as ligaments and tendons. Many holistic veterinarians have used vitamin C to prevent and treat hip dysplasia, an abnormal hip development that is very common in all breeds of giant and large dogs. Dr. Wendell Belfield has been preventing hip dysplasia for years by supplementing dogs with vitamin C when they become pregnant, and continuing the vitamin with the puppies after they are born. He has had many cases in which mothers with hip dysplasia have produced litter after litter that are totally free of hip dysplasia. In their practices, veterinarians R. Geoffrey Broderick and Jack Long have also used vitamin C successfully to prevent hip dysplasia. Both report that hip dysplasia has basically disappeared in dogs given vitamin C as puppies.

An article in the *Journal of the American Podiatric Medical Association* reports that vitamin C levels are higher in healing tissue and return to normal after the healing is complete. Vitamin C, in combination with pantothenic acid ($B_5$), has been shown to increase skin strength and the fibroblastic

### How Vitamin C Saved Seymour

A Poodle puppy named Seymour is alive today because of the healing qualities of vitamin C. Seymour was brought to Dr. Beverly Cappel-King with vomiting, dehydration, and severe intestinal bleeding. A test for the parvo virus, which is usually deadly for puppies, came back positive. Dr. King immediately put Seymour on intravenous therapy, which included megadoses of vitamin C to stop the bleeding, potassium for the dehydration, and antibiotics to battle infection. The internal bleeding stopped in about six hours and Seymour is now a healthy, happy adult.

content of scar tissue. A deficiency of these supplements causes prolonged wound healing.

Most fresh, uncooked fruits and vegetables are great sources of vitamin C. Some that your dog might like include asparagus, broccoli, cantaloupe, cauliflower, honeydew melon, kiwifruit, red pepper, snow peas, and strawberries. Whenever you're preparing these fruits and vegetables for yourself, which I hope is often, you can put some aside for your dog. I recommend you give these to your dog raw, to optimize the nutrients and enzymes.

When supplementing vitamin C, use sodium ascorbate, or some other form of buffered vitamin C because plain ascorbic acid may cause an upset stomach. You can buy it in powder form and add it to your dog's food, or get it in a multivitamin. The recommended daily dosage for an adult dog is:

- 500–1,000 mg for small dogs;
- 1,000–2,000 mg for medium and large dogs;
- 2,000–4,000 mg for giant dogs.

For puppies that have not yet been weaned, buy vitamin-C pediatric drops or tablets for humans at your health food store. Put the tablet on the puppy's tongue or under the lip and it will dissolve almost instantly.

Use the following daily dosages:

- Small and medium breeds—50 mg for the first ten days; from the age of ten days to weaning, 100 mg;
- Large and giant breeds—75 mg for the first ten days; from the age of ten days to weaning, 150 mg.

When the puppy is weaned, gradually switch to powder and slowly increase the dosage until you get to adult dosage. For the first six months, slowly increase the dosage to:

- 250 mg for small dogs;
- 500 mg for medium breeds;

- 1,000 mg for large breeds;
- 2,000 mg for giant breeds.

At six months, slowly increase to the adult dosage. For adult dogs, start at the lowest dose and gradually increase the dosage until you see loose stools. Loose stools, or diarrhea, are a sign of too much vitamin C so back off to the last dose.

## Fat-Soluble Vitamins

Vitamin A comes in two forms: preformed and provitamin. Preformed vitamin A is also called retinol and can be found in foods of animal origin, such as egg yolks, liver, and milk. Provitamin A is derived from carotene, a pigment found in dark green, yellow, and orange fruits and vegetables that is converted to vitamin A in the liver. Unlike humans who store their excess vitamin A in the liver, only 30 percent of a dog's excess vitamin A accumulates in the liver until they need it. The remaining 70 percent circulates in the blood, and any excess is excreted through the kidneys and then the urine. The way a dog's body processes vitamin A allows it to tolerate a much higher dose than humans before it becomes toxic to the animal. The maximum daily dose for both dogs and humans is 50,000 IU per day. (Humans should not take that much for more than a week or two.)

Toxic levels of vitamin A in adult dogs inhibit the development of collagen in bone. In growing puppies, toxic levels of vitamin A inhibit cartilage production. However, as you can see from the extremely high amounts of vitamin A it would take to be toxic for a dog, that's not something you need to be concerned about, unless you're giving your dog very high doses of this vitamin to treat a specific health problem. If you are planning to breed your dog and are treating her for a specific health problem with high doses of vitamin A, discontinue its use three months before breeding and do not start the supplements again until after the puppies are born. Vitamin A plays an important role in bone growth and maintenance, healthy skin, protection from respiratory ailments, a strong immune system, vision, wound repair, and the production of sperm in males and normal reproductive cycles in females.

Progressive retinal atrophy (PRA) is a genetic retinal eye disease common to all breeds, including mixed breeds, that causes blindness, but may be prevented and halted by the addition of vitamin A to the diet. Vitamin A combines with protein and produces rhodopsin, or visual purple, which enables your dog to see at night. One of the first symptoms of PRA is poor night vision, which leads to day blindness, and can also lead to cataracts. If your dog is under eight-years-old and seems disoriented or uncomfortable going out at night or into a dark room, have a veterinary ophthalmologist test her for PRA.

Breeds that are susceptible to skin disorders, such as the cairn Terrier, Cocker Spaniel, Golden Retriever, and Labrador Retriever, can benefit from some additional vitamin A in their diet. Vitamin A deficiency can cause bacterial and fungal infections of the skin, hair loss, and scaling. In susceptible breeds, such as those listed above, even slightly inadequate levels of this vitamin can precipitate skin problems. Many people with dogs susceptible to skin problems, who have gone through round after round of treatments, such as medicated shampoos, antibiotics, or steroid hormones, with no success, *have* had success with vitamin A.

Start with 5,000 international units (IU) per day for dogs under 20 pounds and 10,000 IU per day for all dogs over 20 pounds and be patient. You should see an improvement within four to six weeks. If you do not see any improvement in that time period, increase the dose, but do not exceed 50,000 IU per day.

Improvement from the vitamin A supplementation indicates that your dog needs more vitamin A than the average dog to maintain healthy skin, and should remain on the supplements for life. You have not *cured* the disease, you have given your dog's body the ability to prevent it.

Nutritional sources for vitamin A are dairy products, dark green, orange, and yellow fruits and vegetables, eggs, and liver.

Vitamin A comes in liquid and capsule form. As a recommended daily dose, small dogs should be getting 1,500 IU, medium dogs 3,750 IU, and 5,000 IU for large and giant dogs.

## Vitamin D

Vitamin D has many functions in the body, but perhaps its most important role is in building and maintaining bone. It is the agent that enables calcium and phosphorous—the main ingredients of your dog's skeleton—to build and maintain your dog's skeleton.

With plenty of calcium and phosphorous in the diet, your dog has a very low requirement for vitamin D, which would be met by a high-quality dog food or the nutritional sources named below. As little as ten times the daily requirement of vitamin D can be toxic to your dog, so I do not recommend supplementing with vitamin D unless you are sure it is not in your dog's diet, or your veterinarian recommends it.

Nutritional sources of vitamin D are anchovies, egg yolk, fish oils—from bass, cod, mackerel, sardines, or tuna—and yeast.

The recommended daily doses for Vitamin D are: 100 IU for small dogs, 200 IU for medium dogs, and 400 IU for large and giant dogs.

## Vitamin E (Tocopherol)

Vitamin E plays an essential role in the healthy function of all cells in the body. It is widely recognized as a powerful antioxidant, protecting cells from damage. In humans, a diet rich in vitamin E has been proven to reduce the risk of heart disease, some types of cancer, strokes, and viral infections. Vitamin E also plays an important part in the development and function of the immune system. According to a study published in the *Cornell Veterinarian*, vitamin E has an important influence on the dog's immune system, and dogs supplemented with vitamin E produce antibodies against vaccinations significantly faster than dogs on a vitamin E deficient diet.

Clearly, vitamin E has a strong influence on the immune system. Although I recommend daily supplementation of vitamin E, it is especially important to give your dog extra in times of stress or illness. It should always be given when your dog has surgery, vaccination(s), or has experienced serious injury or shock. Dogs susceptible to a blood disease called immune-mediated hemolytic anemia (IMHA), such as the Akita, Alaskan Malamute, American Cocker Spaniel, Basenji, Basset Hound, Beagle, Doberman Pinscher, English Springer Spaniel, Giant Schnauzer, Golden Retriever, Irish Setter, Miniature and Old English Sheepdog, Miniature Dachshund, Newfoundland, Pekinese, Poodle, Rottweiler, Saluki, Shih Tzu, and West Highland White Terrier can benefit from additional vitamin E in the diet. Larger breeds are more susceptible to heart disease and should be given a vitamin E supplement as they approach old age.

Nutritional sources of vitamin E are asparagus, avocados, green leafy vegetables, nuts, seeds, soybean oil, sunflower oil, and wheat germ.

Vitamin E is available in liquid or powder form. The recommended daily dose is 100 IU for small dogs, 200 IU for medium and large dogs, and 400 IU for giant dogs.

## Vitamin K

Vitamin K is necessary for normal blood clotting. Without vitamin K, the liver can't produce the substances that allow the blood to clot. Vitamin K comes in two forms, vitamin $K_1$, found in green plants, and vitamin $K_2$, which is synthesized by bacteria in the large intestine.

Under normal circumstances, there is little need for additional vitamin K because it is, in part, produced in the large intestine. However, there are circumstances in which the bacteria in the large intestine are killed, in effect cutting off production of vitamin K. In this instance, the most common culprit is antibiotics. Give your dog plenty of vitamin K enriched liver and dark green leafy vegetables when she has been given antibiotics, but even more important is a probiotic supplement to restore the bacteria that have been killed. Probiotics are organisms that maintain the health of your dog's intestinal tract. (*See* Chapter 5 for more detailed information on probiotics.)

The most common blood-clotting disorder in dogs is called Von Willebrand's disease. Blood has ten different clotting factors, identified in Roman numerals, such as I, II, III, IV, and V. Von Willebrand's disease involves clotting factor VIII and it would not be helped by vitamin K. There are other less-known blood-clotting defects found in dogs. If your dog is diagnosed with one, ask your veterinarian what the clotting factor is. If clotting factors II, VII, IX, or X are involved, your dog may need vitamin K supplements. Factor-II deficiency is most common in Boxers and English Cocker Spaniels, factor-VII deficiency is most common in Alaskan Malamutes, Beagles, and English Bulldogs, factor-IX deficiency is found in Beagles, Chesapeake Bay Retrievers, Doberman Pinschers, German Shepherds, Golden Retrievers, Manchester Terriers, Miniature Schnauzers, Pembroke Welsh Corgis, and Scottish Terriers, and factor-X deficiency is found in American Cocker Spaniels.

Nutritional sources for vitamin K are dark green leafy vegetables and liver.

# 3

## Minerals for Your Dog

Minerals are inorganic elements that are essential for the growth and maintenance of a healthy body. Amazingly, these elements that are vital to life comprise only four percent of your dog's total body weight. Minerals are found in food, soil, and water. Plants absorb minerals through their roots from the soil and water, and animals get their minerals from eating plants and other animals, as well as drinking water, just as your dog will. The best nutritional sources of minerals are fresh organic fruits and vegetables, free-range organic meat and fresh spring water. If organic free-range food is not available, or not affordable, you will need to supplement your dog's diet with minerals.

With the exception of organic farming, food is depleted of minerals, or even worse, it contains the wrong balance of minerals. Dirt in its purest form is loaded with minerals, but today's soil is so overused and loaded with toxins that it has been depleted of most of its nutrients. Since most farmers plant crop after crop in the same soil without replenishing the minerals, any plants grown in this mineral-deficient soil will be unhealthy, in turn causing the farmers to use chemical fertilizers and pesticides that *further* deplete the soil of any nutrients. If, instead, farmers were to till in lots of organic compost and let it sit for a year, they would have a rich soil packed with minerals.

Minerals are dependent on each other and many other nutrients for proper absorption and functioning in your dog's body. A mineral deficiency may not always be caused by a lack of the mineral in your dog's diet, it may be caused by your dog's inability to properly *absorb* the mineral. Absorption problems can be genetic, or they can be caused by an imbalance of another vitamin or mineral. For example, an imbalance of calcium, copper, or iron will interfere with the absorption of zinc.

Minerals are separated into two categories. Macrominerals account for most of the body's mineral content, and microminerals or trace minerals, are found in the body in very small amounts. The macrominerals include calcium, magnesium, phosphorous, potassium, sodium, and sulfur, and the microminerals (trace minerals) include boron, chromium, cobalt, copper, fluoride, iodine, iron, manganese, molybdenum, selenium, silicon, and zinc.

Trace minerals can be toxic *even at low doses* and are highly dependent on each other for proper absorption. Your best bet is to give them to your dog in a multivitamin-mineral supplement. The recommended daily doses in this chapter can be used as a guideline for finding a good supplement. You will notice that some of the microminerals do not have recommended daily doses. This is because they haven't been studied in dogs, as they are not considered essential to life, but they are all-important in a healthy diet.

You also won't necessarily find all the minerals listed here in a supplement for dogs. I have noted which minerals a healthy dog will get plenty of from home-cooked meals or a high-quality commercial diet. (*See* Resources in back for a mail-order source if you can't find a multivitamin-mineral supplement that includes the approximate recommended dosages.)

## Macrominerals

Close to 99 percent of the calcium in your dog's body is found in his skeleton. Most of the remainder is in the blood. Calcium keeps bones and teeth strong, and the fluids balanced. It helps regulate the heartbeat and is necessary for normal blood clotting. Without calcium your dog wouldn't be able to utilize magnesium and phosphorous and, to make things even more complicated, the ratio of calcium to phosphorous to magnesium is very important. Excess calcium causes decreased phosphorous absorption and excess phosphorous causes decreased calcium absorption. Calcium without magnesium makes the calcium useless because it needs magnesium to be absorbed by the body. Your dog's body can easily regulate the balance of these minerals when it gets adequate amounts of them all in the diet.

Nutritional sources of calcium are beans, blackstrap molasses, leafy green vegetables, nuts, salmon, soy, and sardines. No, I didn't leave milk out by mistake. Contrary to popular belief, milk is not a good source of calcium because there is not enough magnesium in milk for the calcium to be used efficiently.

Calcium is so well known for *building strong bodies* that many people, especially large and giant dog owners, make the mistake of over-supplementing calcium, which can be as detrimental as a deficiency. As with the other minerals, stick to a multivitamin-mineral supplement using the following recommended daily dosage: small and medium dogs, 100 mg, large and giant dogs, 200 mg.

## Phosphorous

Phosphorous is found in every cell of your dog's body, with the highest concentration in combination with calcium in the bones and teeth. Phosphorous is necessary for your dog to utilize calcium and therefore, like calcium, is critical for proper growth and maintenance of the skeleton.

Nutritional sources of phosphorous are beans, fish, meats, organ meats, and poultry.

A healthy dog will get plenty of phosphorous from a high-quality diet. Daily doses are: small and medium dogs, 50 mg, large and giant dogs, 100 mg.

## Magnesium

Approximately 60–70 percent of the magnesium in your dog's body is in the skeleton. Magnesium is the third member of the calcium, phosphorous team that builds and maintains strong bones and teeth, and enables your dog's body to use sodium and potassium. Magnesium is important for proper muscle and nerve function and helps the body absorb calcium, vitamin C, vitamin E, and the B-complex vitamins. Magnesium is active in producing enzymes that prevent blood clots, and it helps prevent lead toxicity by drawing lead out of bone and other tissue sites. Convulsive seizures (epilepsy) have been seen in dogs with a magnesium deficiency. The American Cocker Spaniel, Australian Cattle Dog, Basset Hound, Beagle, Belgian Malinois, Belgian Sheepdog, Belgian Tervuren, Bichon Frise, Border Collie, Collie, English Springer Spaniel, German Shepherd, Greyhound, Irish Setter, Italian Greyhound, Keeshond, Labrador Retriever, pointer, Poodle, Pug, Saint Bernard, standard Manchester Terrier, and Vizsla are all prone to convulsive seizures. If your dog has seizures and is getting his recommended daily dose of magnesium, very gradually add more magnesium to his diet. Too much magnesium will result in gas and loose stools.

Magnesium is also a heart-healthy mineral. Studies done in the 1970s found that dogs recovered from heart failure faster when given magnesium intravenously. Giant and large dogs (over 50 pounds) are more prone to heart problems than medium and small dogs, with the Boxer, Doberman Pinscher, German Shepherd, great Dane, Irish Wolfhound, Newfoundland, and Sussex Spaniel showing a stronger history of weak hearts. Be sure they are getting plenty of exercise and their daily dose of magnesium.

Nutritional sources for magnesium are apricots, bananas, beans, leafy green vegetables, meat, milk, wheat bran, and whole grains.

Recommended daily doses are: small and medium dogs, 50 mg; large and giant dogs, 100 mg.

## Sulfur

Sulfur is found everywhere in the body, with the highest concentrations in the hair, nails, and skin. Sulfur's high concentration in the skin makes it a key component in healing wounds. A sulfur deficiency can cause coat discoloration and skin conditions, such as dermatitis and eczema. Those of you with dogs that are more prone to dermatitis or hot spots, such as the Airedale Terrier, Akita, Basset Hound, Bichon Frise, Dalmatian, German Shepherd, Golden Retriever, Great Dane, Great Pyrenees, Irish Setter, Labrador Retriever, Lhaso Apso, Poodle, Pug, Scottish Terrier, Sealyham Terrier, Smooth Fox Terrier, Soft-Coated Wheaten Terrier, and the West Highland White Terrier need to keep an extra eye on their coats for any signs of skin problems and be sure to keep up with their multivitamin-mineral supplement. Sulfur is absorbed in the intestine and is depleted when intestinal bacteria are destroyed by such substances as antibiotics. Don't forget the spoonful of yogurt or probiotic supplement when giving antibiotics.

Dogs that have skin allergies may need some extra sulfur, which I recommend you supplement in the form of methylsulfonylmethane (MSM). (*See* Chapter 10 for more detailed information.)

Nutritional sources for sulfur are dairy products, eggs, fish, meat, and molasses.

A healthy dog will get plenty of sulfur from home-cooked meals or a high-quality commercial food.

## Potassium and Sodium

Potassium and sodium work together to maintain normal fluid balance in the cells of your dog's body. Normal fluid balance in cells is needed for proper nerve and muscle functioning. A sodium deficiency will result in dry skin, exhaustion, fatigue, listlessness, loss of equilibrium, loss of hair, lower water intake, and poor growth. Commercial dog foods have plenty of potassium and sodium chloride (salt). If you are preparing home-cooked meals for your dog, there will be plenty of potassium in the food and you can add a pinch of salt.

A potassium deficiency can result in dehydration, lesions of the heart and kidney, muscular paralysis, poor growth, and restlessness.

Nutritional sources for potassium are bananas, beans, dried apricots, prunes, sweet potato, squash, fish, meats, poultry, wholegrain cereals, and yogurt.

Recommended daily doses for potassium are: 25 mg for small dogs, 50 mg for medium dogs, 75 mg for large dogs, and 100 mg for giant dogs.

Recommended daily doses for sodium are: 100 mg for small dogs, 200 mg for medium dogs, 350 mg for large dogs, and 500 mg for giant dogs.

# Microminerals (Trace Minerals)

### Iron

Iron teams up with cobalamin (vitamin $B_{12}$) copper, and protein to form hemoglobin molecules. Hemoglobin molecules are found in the red blood cells and carry oxygen from the lungs to the rest of the body. If your dog is tired all the time, he may be anemic due to an iron deficiency. Part of your monthly health check includes your dog's gums. Look for bright, dark pink gums; light pink or almost gray gums are a sure sign of anemia. Anemia is very often the result of a more serious problem, such as an infection, so if you suspect your dog is anemic, bring him to your veterinarian for a complete exam.

Nutritional sources for iron are beef, beans, chicken, liver, pork, and turkey.

Current recommended daily doses are: 9 mg for small dogs, 18 mg for medium dogs, 30 mg for large dogs, and 40 mg for giant dogs.

Recent human studies have found that too much iron is a potent risk factor for heart disease and it is not yet known if the same applies to dogs. Heart disease is very common in dogs, so be cautious about giving your dog too much iron. If you are feeding home-cooked meals or a commercial food that has iron listed as an ingredient, buy a supplement that doesn't contain iron.

## Boron

Boron works with calcium and magnesium to build and maintain strong bones.

Nutritional sources for boron are fruits and vegetables.

## Chromium

Chromium helps manufacture insulin and then helps the insulin maintain the proper level of sugar in the blood. Chromium is also active in the digestion of carbohydrates. Semi-moist dog foods became popular because they are easy to keep and serve, and because even the fussiest dogs love them. The secret to their success is lots of sugar which dogs love and become addicted to. Too much sugar will deplete your dog's body of chromium, putting him at risk for diabetes. If you are feeding semi-moist foods, slowly wean your dog off them with home-cooked meals or a commercial dry or canned dog food that fits my guidelines for choosing a commercial dog food.

Nutritional sources for chromium are brewer's yeast, broccoli, ham, turkey, and shellfish.

## Cobalt

Cobalt is found in cobalamin (vitamin $B_{12}$), which is a unique relationship because cobalamin is the only vitamin that contains a trace element. Cobalt is involved in the production of red blood cells and the absorption of iron. A cobalt deficiency could cause an iron deficiency, resulting in anemia. Adequate amounts of cobalamin will give your dog enough cobalt.

Nutritional sources for cobalt are meat and shellfish.

## Copper

Copper is another mineral that is important for proper bone growth and maintenance. Copper is involved in putting color in your dog's skin and hair. It is required to convert iron into hemoglobin and is important in keeping the immune system functioning normally. Copper deficiencies result in anemia, improper bone formation, and loss of hair and skin color. The majority of copper is found in the liver so an excess can cause liver damage.

The Bedlington Terrier, Doberman Pinscher, and West Highland White Terrier are prone to a disease that causes an inability to use and store copper properly, which can result in liver disease and other problems. For these dogs, choose a multivitamin-mineral supplement that doesn't include copper.

Nutritional sources for copper are beans, calf and beef liver, nuts, seeds, shellfish, and whole wheat.

Daily recommended doses are: .5 mg for small dogs, 1 mg for medium dogs, 2 mg for large and giant dogs.

## Fluoride

Dogs require *very* small amounts of fluoride, which they will get through their diet. If your town adds fluoride to your water, please don't give it to your dog. Fluoride toxicity can cause arthritis, bone malformations, cancer, and damage to the adrenal, kidney, and liver glands. You can use a water filter if you are disciplined enough to change the filter frequently. The best and easiest way to give your dog pure water is to buy bottled water or use a reverse osmosis water purification system in your house.

## Iodine

Iodine is essential for production of the thyroid hormone that regulates your dog's metabolism. Since the addition of iodine to salt, the instances of iodine deficiency in dogs have disappeared. Most commercial dog foods have salt added—most have too much salt. If you are preparing home-cooked meals for your dog, the pinch of salt you added for sodium will also give your dog his daily requirement of iodine. If your dog has a thyroid problem, you can add an iodine supplement to his diet, or sprinkle powdered seaweed on his food.

Recommended daily doses are: 0.2 mg for small dogs, 0.4 mg for medium dogs, 0.7 mg for large dogs, and 1 mg for giant dogs.

## Molybdenum

Molybdenum is active in processing carbohydrates and can protect your dog from excess copper.

Nutritional sources for molybdenum are brewer's yeast, cereal grains, and liver.

## Silicon

Silicon is found in your dog's bones, hair, nails, and teeth. It helps heal wounds and protects against skin disorders. If your dog has something foreign in his system, such as a bacterial infection, an infection from an abscess, or worms, silicon will work to eliminate the foreign object from his system. Silicon is a type of sand that is found in dirt and the stems of certain grasses and plants. When your dog eats dirt, grass, or plants, he may be adding silicon to his system to help him eliminate a foreign object. Try to steer him away from grass, though. Dogs don't digest grass, and the sharp edges on the blades of grass irritate the throat and intestine. Be sure he has access to pesticide-free dirt and plants, and if he continues eating these substances for any length of time, bring him to your veterinarian.

## Manganese

Manganese is an antioxidant mineral that is necessary for the utilization of biotin, thiamin (vitamin $B_1$), vitamin C, and vitamin E. It is also needed for bone and cartilage growth, collagen formation, fat metabolism, normal reproduction, pituitary gland function, and the production of fatty acids.

Nutritional sources for manganese are beets, eggs, green leafy vegetables, nuts, peas, and whole grains.

Recommended daily doses are: 0.75 mg for small dogs, 1.5 mg for medium dogs, 2.6 mg for large dogs, and 3.75 mg for giant dogs.

## Selenium

Selenium is a great co-worker. It works with vitamin E as an antioxidant to boost the immune system and prevent cancer and heart disease. It also works with iodine for proper thyroid function. Selenium protects your dog's body from cancer-causing substances, such as the toxic metals cadmium and mercury, by binding with them and flushing them out of the body.

An article in the *Journal of Federation Proceedings* reports that dogs with a selenium and vitamin E-deficiency have a lower antibody response to vaccines than dogs who are not deficient. A few days before and after any vaccinations, be sure to add some extra vitamin E and selenium to your dog's diet.

Nutritional sources for selenium are broccoli, chicken, eggs, fish, garlic, organ meat, red grapes, red meat, and shellfish.

Recommended daily doses are: 25 mcg for small dogs, 50 mcg for medium, large, and giant dogs.

## Zinc

Zinc works alone and with B-complex vitamins, calcium, copper, and vitamin A in a vast number of bodily functions. Zinc is crucial for the production of enzymes. It has some antioxidant and antibacterial properties, helps in protein digestion, improves antibody response to vaccines, regulates white blood cells, and supports the immune system. Zinc is important for a healthy coat, nails, and skin, and protects your dog's liver from excess poisons, such as cadmium, copper, and lead. Zinc teams up with vitamin C in the production of collagen, which makes it another important nutrient when your dog's body is trying to heal a wound.

William H. Miller, V.M.D., has found that zinc, along with vitamins A and E and the essential fatty acids, are the most important nutrients for the skin. Color abnormalities on solid-colored dogs, such as browning out, red tinges, or white tipping, may be caused by a zinc deficiency. Alaskan Malamutes, bull Terriers, and Siberian huskies are prone to a genetic condition that causes a decreased capacity for zinc absorption from the intestines. This condition is often missed because the only symptoms are skin disease and a loss of appetite. The huskies and Malamutes will respond quickly to a zinc supplement and will need to be on the supplement for life. Unfortunately, bull Terriers are prone to a more complicated form of this condition and they do not respond to zinc supplementation. I am certain there is a missing nutritional link, in addition to the zinc, that the bull Terriers need. Doberman Pinschers, German Shepherds, German short-haired pointers, Great Danes, and Labrador Retrievers are also prone to skin problems from a zinc deficiency. The deficiency can be caused by a zinc-deficient diet, parasites, or by over-supplementation of nutrients that interfere with the absorption of zinc, such as calcium, copper, and iron.

Nutritional sources for zinc are beans, brewer's yeast, eggs, lamb, liver, pork, and wheat germ.

Recommended daily doses are: 10 mg for small dogs, 15 mg for medium dogs, 30 mg for large and giant dogs.

# 4

## Nutritional Needs for Special Circumstances

Dogs, like people, have changing nutritional needs in the varying stages of their lives. Younger dogs have a lot of energy and need foods to promote growing; pregnant dogs need proper nutrition to create new life; and older dogs are sedentary and need easily absorbed nutrients. If your dog becomes ill, her body will need the proper nutrients to heal. In this chapter you will learn how to make adjustments to your dog's diet to meet her special nutritional needs.

### PUPPIES

Puppies are irresistible to even the grumpiest of people. They make the sick forget their pain and the elderly feel young. These fun-loving balls of fur need a puppyhood filled with the same pure joy and happiness that they give us. A key to your puppy's happiness, health, and longevity is to build a strong body and a strong immune system with high-quality food and a stress-free environment. (You will learn more about the immune system in Part Two—Keeping Your Dog's Immune System Strong.)

Your puppy's immune system will get its foundation for health from its mother in the first twenty-four hours after birth. As with humans, these critical hours are the only time the mother produces a special milk called colostrum. Colostrum gets the immune system off to a strong start by providing antibodies and other immune-supporting nutrients that will guard against disease as the immune system matures.

Your puppy's first six months of life will be her fastest growth period. She will need the proper nutrition to build a strong, healthy body. Large breeds reach full size at approximately ten to sixteen months and small breeds reach full size anywhere from six to twelve months. That is a lot of growing in a short time when you think that humans take twenty years to reach maturity. Your puppy will eat approximately twice what she will eventually be eating as an adult, and during some growth spurts she may exceed that.

Feed your puppy the same food she was getting from her previous owner until she gets used to her new home. For a digestive system that hasn't matured, the stress of a new home, combined with the stress of new foods on would put her tiny body on overload. Little things like time changes in her routine and new rules can be very confusing and stressful. You want your puppy's body to be concentrating on growing and maturing, not warding off stress and learning to handle new foods.

## Vitamins for Puppies

You can start with a multivitamin-mineral supplement right away. With the exception of vitamins C and E, do not give your puppy more than the recommended dosage on the label of the multivitamin-mineral supplement unless you are under the supervision of a veterinarian. More is not better and could be harmful. Vitamin C is a water-soluble vitamin (it is not stored in the body and will not become toxic) that will aid in proper bone formation, boost the immune system, and is an antioxidant. (*See* Chapter 3 for more on vitamin C.)

If your multivitamin-mineral supplement does not provide the following daily doses, buy a powdered vitamin C to bring her up to these doses. For weaned puppies start with a daily dose of:

- 100 mg for small and medium dogs (up to 50 pounds as adults);
- 150 mg for large and giant dogs (over 50 pounds as adults);

For the first six months, slowly increase the daily dose to:
- 250 mg for small dogs (up to 20 pounds as adults);
- 500 mg for medium dogs (20–50 pounds as adults);
- 1,000 mg for large dogs (50–100 pounds as adults);
- 2,000 mg for giant dogs (over 100 pounds as adults).

At six months slowly increase to the final adult daily dose of:
- 500–1,000 mg for small dogs;
- 1,000–2,000 mg for medium and large dogs;
- 2,000–4,000 mg for giant dogs.

For puppies not weaned, Chapter 3 gives instructions and doses for vitamin C. The dosages I have given you are guidelines. Humans are told to take vitamin C for bowel tolerance. The same goes for dogs. Your dog's body will tell you when the dosage is too high by getting gas or diarrhea. If your puppy develops either problem, you have given her more than her body needs, so back off on the dosage until she grows into a higher dose.

Vitamin E plays an important role in the development and function of the immune system and is a powerful antioxidant.

If your multivitamin-mineral doesn't provide the following daily dosages, you can buy vitamin E in capsule or liquid form at your local health food store.
- 100 IU for puppies under 20 pounds.
- 200 IU for puppies 20–100 pounds.
- 400 IU for puppies over 100 pounds.

For stressful physical or emotional situations, such as vaccinations or dog obedience classes, double the daily dose of vitamin E for a few days before and a few days after your puppy is stressed. (*See* Chapter 3 for more on vitamin E.)

## Feeding and Caring for Your Growing Puppy

When your puppy becomes comfortable with her new home, very gradually change her diet. Add a small amount of new food to her old food, gradually increasing the new food and decreasing the old food. Find out exactly what your new puppy has been eating, including proportions and how the food was prepared. If she has been eating commercial food, ask for the brand name and where you can buy the food.

At six weeks, your puppy's teeth will begin to come in, and at seven to eight weeks she will start chewing. This is the time to hide the antiques and keep all kinds of interesting Toys on the floor and in her cage or her sleeping area. When your puppy starts to chew, very gradually introduce solid foods. Until your puppy is about one year old, her energy and nutrient needs will be double what she will eventually need as an adult.

If you are going to use a commercial dog food, feed her puppy food for one year and then switch to the adult food. Use the feeding amounts on the package as a starting place and adjust the amount for your dog.

If you are preparing home-cooked meals, feed approximate proportions of 30 percent muscle meat, 30 percent organ meat, 20 percent grains, and 20 percent vegetables. Part of the protein requirement can be met with high-protein grains, such as buckwheat and quinoa, and for one meal a day give her additional protein from such sources as cottage cheese, eggs, and naturally cultured yogurt. For dogs that have trouble digesting lots of protein, including Bedlington Terriers, Dalmatians, and West Highland White Terriers, feed the meat raw (I highly recommend this for all dogs), or cut down on the meat a little and give them protein from other sources, such as those mentioned above.

Avoid soy, because a puppy's digestive system can't utilize the amino acids from soy. Puppies will eat approximately twice as much as an adult dog the same weight, which translates to:

- 1–2 cups per day for puppies weighing up to 10 pounds;
- 2–7 cups per day for puppies weighing 10–25 pounds;
- 7–10 cups per day for puppies weighing 25–50 pounds;
- 10–14 cups per day for puppies weighing over 50 pounds.

Feed your puppy four times a day until she refuses a meal, then cut back to three times a day until she is not hungry for three meals, at which point you cut back to two meals a day for life. Two meals a day, rather than one, puts less stress on the digestive system and allows your dog to utilize more of the nutrients from each meal.

Feed enough so your puppy doesn't lick the bowl clean. A little left over means she had her fill. Give her a few minutes to come back to the bowl and then pick it up. Please don't overfeed or over-supplement your puppy. An overfed, over-supplemented puppy will experience overly rapid growth, which will not give you a bigger dog, but a dog plagued by *obesity and skeletal problems*. If a puppy grows too fast, the bones and joints don't get a chance to form properly, causing problems, such as hip dysplasia, hypertropic osteodystrophy, and osteochondrosis. Those are all very painful skeletal abnormalities that involve inflammation and abnormal growth of the bones and joints, and will give your puppy a lifetime of painful chronic skeletal problems. Hip dysplasia is an abnormal growth of the hip found in all sizes of dog—it is the most common skeletal abnormality in large and giant breeds. A fat puppy will also result in a fat adult. A lean puppy is a healthy puppy.

## PREGNANT AND NURSING DOGS

Breeding a dog is a serious undertaking that requires a lot of hard work and money. If you are new to breeding, carefully research the entire process from conception to adoption. If you are considering breeding because you want to be surrounded by adult dogs and puppies, consider foster care for your local animal shelter or breed-rescue organization instead. The shelters and breed-rescue organizations throughout the country are overflowing and desperately need people to care for puppies and adult dogs. Most of the shelters and rescue organizations pay all the dog's expenses, such as food, Toys, and trips to the vet. Your responsibility is to love, train (if you are caring for a puppy), and feed the dogs.

If, after careful consideration, you do decide to breed your dog, it is important for her to be in optimal health before conception. A trip to the veterinarian for a complete exam is a good investment in the future of the mother and her puppies. It is especially important to have the following breeds checked by a veterinarian because they are more prone to complications during birth: Boston Terrier, Bouvier des Flandres, Cardigan Welsh Corgi, English Bulldog, Greyhound, Pembroke Welsh Corgi, or Pug. The health of the mother will be directly reflected in the health of the puppies. An unhealthy mother will produce unhealthy puppies, and after conception it will be too late to play catch-up with her health.

With a clean bill of health from your veterinarian, you are ready to prepare your dog for her pregnancy. Two weeks before your dog comes into season, put her on red raspberry-leaf tea or powder and keep her on it until six weeks after the puppies are born. Red raspberry leaves tone the uterus and help bring fluid to the birth canal. After birth, the red raspberry leaves help tighten the uterine muscles, preventing infection. Make the tea by putting 1½ teaspoons red raspberry leaves in a cup of water and bring it to a boil. Take it off the stove and let it sit overnight. In the morning, strain out the leaves and keep it in the refrigerator. Use the following daily dosages:

- 1 tablespoon for small dogs (up to 20 pounds);
- 2 tablespoons for medium dogs (20–50 pounds);
- 3 tablespoons for large dogs (50–100 pounds);
- 4 tablespoons for giant dogs (over 100 pounds).

(*See* Resources in back for direct-mail sources of supplements if you can't find red raspberry leaves or aren't much of a cook.)

For the first six weeks of your dog's nine-week pregnancy, she can eat her normal diet and probably won't need much more food than usual. At six weeks, her nutritional needs will start to increase, and by the time she has her puppies (whelping), she will be eating approximately 50 percent more than normal. She needs more food and more protein. If you are feeding home-cooked meals, you can follow the guidelines for a puppy. Feed her as much as she will eat without licking the bowl clean, and feed her as many times a day as she is hungry. Her increased need for protein can be satisfied by increasing her meat ration, giving her grains with high protein, such as buckwheat and quinoa, and giving her additional protein-enriched foods, such as cottage cheese, eggs, and naturally cultured yogurt. If you are feeding commercial food, you can switch to puppy food, or add some of the above protein-enriched foods to her usual diet.

If her appetite seems to decrease before delivery, it may be because the puppies are pushing on her abdomen and it is uncomfortable to eat a lot of food at one time, so try giving her smaller meals. A loss of appetite could also be caused by nausea, which can be helped with a cup of ginger tea and honey. If she doesn't like the ginger tea, add some homemade chicken or beef broth (not the commercial brands that are loaded with salt and MSG). Signs of nausea are drooling or repeated swallowing when you offer her food. To make fresh ginger tea, grate a tablespoon of fresh ginger into a cup, add boiling water and let it steep for ten minutes. Strain out the ginger, add honey and serve.

Right after giving birth (whelping), she may also lose her appetite for a short time. Try giving her raw, uncooked honey and yogurt for energy. Also offer her some homemade chicken or beef broth to keep her strength up, and be sure she has lots of fluids. It is very important for her to always have clean, fresh water available. When the puppies become mobile, keep water right outside their pen so she doesn't have to leave her puppies for it.

As the puppy's appetites grow, so will their mother's. The second and third weeks of nursing are the most stressful. By then she will be producing milk equivalent to 4–7 percent of her body weight per day, which means a fifty-pound dog will be producing a whopping two to three-and-a-half pounds of milk per day, or about one to two quarts of milk. That is a tremendous amount of fluid to keep up with. Keep her on the high protein diet and, rather than increasing the amount of food you give her at each meal, increase the number of times per day you feed her. Most mothers can't take in as much food as they need in one or two meals. She may need up to seven meals a day to keep up with milk production for her puppies. If at any time she seems stressed, B-complex vitamins, vitamin E, or a homeopathic remedy can help calm her.

A pregnant and nursing dog will go through many physical and emotional changes in a short amount of time. Women have nine months to slowly adjust to the physical changes of pregnancy, while dogs have a mere nine weeks to produce a litter of puppies. Keep a close eye on her and her needs. She may refuse food in the morning and be ravenous in the afternoon, or your playful, energetic dog may suddenly want to be left alone to sleep in a nice warm quiet place.

## OLDER DOGS

As dogs age, they eventually start to slow down and are happy sitting under the big oak tree watching life go by. All dogs will age, and they will all age at a different rate, depending on their size, breed, and how they are cared for throughout life. A dog that is in optimal health throughout her life will age more slowly than a dog plagued by chronic illnesses. If you have an older dog in poor health, it is not too late to bring her back to health. Many of the symptoms attributed to old age in dogs are merely a lack of good nutrition.

As your dog's activity level slows down, her metabolism will decrease and she will not burn as many calories, resulting in weight gain, one of the biggest problems among older dogs. As your dog ages and slows down, her whole body is aging and slowing down, and her digestive tract, heart, kidney, liver, and brain can't work as efficiently as they used to. Some small adjustments to your dog's diet and exercise program will give her a better chance for a healthy, pain- free old age.

As your dog's body ages and functions less efficiently, she will not be able to digest food as easily or absorb as many of the nutrients from her food. The lack of nutrients may cause an older dog to become lethargic, and can lead to many of the chronic illnesses that so many people, including veterinarians, shrug their shoulders over and attribute to old age. But aging is not an illness, it is a stage of life. To adjust for these changes, your dog needs highly digestible, low-calorie foods, and a multivitamin-mineral supplement that is easily absorbed—a powdered multivitamin-mineral supplement will be more easily absorbed than a pill. If the multivitamin-mineral supplement is not specifically made for the older dog, give her one-third more than what is recommended for an adult dog. A one-year human trial giving vitamin and trace-mineral supplements to older people showed a significantly decreased infection rate and enhanced immune system function. The same applies to your dog. (*See* Resources in back if you can't find a proper supplement at your local pet supply store.)

Use powdered vitamin C, and once a year up the dose a little to bowel tolerance (gas or diarrhea means your dog is getting to much vitamin C), to see if your dog could use some additional vitamin C. Double the vitamin E to daily doses of 200 IU for small dogs, 400 IU for medium and large dogs, and 800 IU for giant dogs.

To compensate for a less efficient digestive tract, well-cooked carbohydrates will be easier for your dog to digest than meat, so cut back a little on her meat and add more carbohydrates. A heaping spoonful of plain yogurt with active cultures at each meal will also aid in digestion by keeping her intestines rich with much-needed bacteria. Digestive enzyme supplements are also available for dogs. Follow the directions on the label for appropriate dosages. Some older dogs lose their sense of thirst, so add extra water to her meals and when you cook the grains.

To avoid weight gain, in addition to cutting back a little on her meat, buy the leaner cuts of meat and add more vegetables if she starts licking the bowl clean or seems to be hungrier than usual. If you are feeding her a commercial dog food, cut back on the food a little and add vegetables if she seems hungry.

To avoid dental problems that can lead to eating problems, give your dog a marrow bone once or twice a week. They are much less expensive than having your dog's teeth cleaned, and chewing a bone is much more fun for your dog than going to the dentist.

Feeding all the right foods is only half the key to keeping your dog healthy in her older years. Exercise will help keep the joints agile and the organs strong and functioning, maintain muscle strength, and prevent arthritis and weight gain. An exercise program for older dogs needs to be fun and of shorter duration. Rather than one long walk, take her for two walks a day. The expression *use it or lose it* goes for your dog too, and just as with people, dogs need some encouragement to exercise as they grow older.

As your dog ages, you may also notice some behavioral changes, including aggression, barking, confusion, shyness, trouble sleeping, and the desire to be in the background observing rather than the center of attention.

Older dogs who suddenly start snapping when bothered by other dogs or people, or who seek solitude, may be in pain. Growling is their only defense if, for example, they can't run because of the pain of arthritis. If you observe your dog being uncharacteristically snappy or grouchy, make an appointment with your veterinarian for a thorough physical exam.

Barking, confusion, and shyness are very often signs that some of your dog's senses aren't as sharp as they were. Your dog depends heavily on her smelling and hearing to identify people, places, and animals. If the hearing is impaired or there is an ear infection, familiar sounds may now be perceived as a new sound, which can cause barking and confusion. Dogs also use their sense of smell to identify animals, people, and their surroundings. If the sense of smell is diminished, your dog will have trouble identifying friend from foe, which can cause shyness, or aggression towards people, animals, or places she has known all her life. A diminished ability to smell may also decrease the appetite. Try cooking the meat just a little bit to heighten the smell and get the juices running.

If your dog has trouble sleeping through the night, be sure her bed is supportive for achy bones and away from cold drafts. Melatonin, a hormone that is released from the pineal gland to induce sleep in response to darkness, can be helpful. Use ½ mg for small and medium dogs and 1 mg for large and giant dogs. Give one hour before bedtime and try to give it at the same time every night.

Starting at age seven for large and giant dogs, and age ten for small and medium dogs, I also recommend a visit to the veterinarian every six months rather than yearly.

## OVERWEIGHT DOGS

If you are at the end of your wits trying to keep your dog thin, you can take comfort in the fact that you are far from alone. An estimated 35–50 percent of pet dogs are overweight. Obesity is one of the most common health disorders in dogs. That would be an astounding fact if the sole cause of weight problems in dogs was their owner's feeding habits.

Your dog eats practically nothing, is always hungry, and yet is still fat—does this sound familiar to you? If it does, you and your dog are probably the victims of the multi-million dollar processed dog food industry that survives on marketing, *not* on the quality of their products. Many of the commercial dog foods are so loaded with non-nutritional calories that your dog will be obese before she will ever be able to meet her nutritional needs through the food. It would be the nutritional equivalent of you trying to stay thin on a diet of potato chips.

A neighbor of mine who had struggled with her dog's weight for years finally switched to a high-quality commercial diet, and was so amazed when her dog became lean and energetic in just a few weeks that she became a distributor of their product. If your dog is overweight and you are feeding a commercial food that doesn't fit into my nutritional guidelines in Chapter 1, a simple change to a high-quality food may solve your dog's weight problems. (*See* Resources in back for affordable sources if your local pet supply store doesn't carry high-quality dog food.)

Before you put your dog on a diet, bring her to your veterinarian to be sure there isn't a medical reason for her weight gain. If your dog gets a clean bill of health, and you are feeding her a high-quality food and she is still overweight, you are either feeding her too much and/or she isn't getting enough exercise.

What seems like an occasional treat or just a few table scraps can add up quickly when a dog is only thirty or forty pounds to begin with. The smaller the dog, the truer this is, and the harder it is to keep her slim. The secret is to cut down on the calories your dog consumes and keep her moving.

Obesity will take years off your dog's life by putting stress on all her organs and her skeleton. A study of the development of obesity in dogs at the University of Mississippi Medical Center found that, as dogs become obese, they develop high blood pressure, and it becomes dramatically worse during exercise. Not surprisingly, the obese dogs in the study were not able to exercise as much as they could when they were lean. Along with heart disease, obesity in dogs causes arthritis, diabetes, and lung disease. And for overweight dogs, there is no such thing as routine surgery. They are at higher risk for complications, including death, during and after surgery. Lean dogs live longer, healthier lives, with significantly fewer trips to the veterinarian.

Your dog's healthier new diet and exercise program should be introduced very slowly, starting with my first rule for nutritional health: Do not feed your dog anything that has no nutritional value for her.

If your dog has mastered the begging technique and you entertain a lot, ask your guests, as they settle in by the hors d'oeuvres, not to feed your dog. If you are used to scraping your dishes into your dog's dish after dinner, skip the fat and limit the leftovers to food that is good for her. If eliminating all non-nutritional consumption doesn't take the weight off, shave some more calories by giving her fewer treats, or substitute low-calorie treats, such as a carrot or an ice cube. If cutting the calories of the in-between meal snacks doesn't work, very slowly reduce the size of her meals. If she seems hungry during any of the adjustments in her diet, add more finely chopped fresh vegetables to her meal.

If you don't exercise your dog at all, start with short walks and very gradually lengthen them as she loses weight. If you already have her on an exercise program, slowly increase her exercise to at least twenty minutes per day. Never force your dog to exercise.

Every time you are tempted to give your dog junk food or one too many treats, give her a hug, a good pat and a lot of praise instead. Sharing love is more gratifying than sharing food.

## DOGS RECOVERING FROM ILLNESS

Have you ever noticed that some dogs are always sick? If your dog becomes ill and doesn't have the nutritional tools to bring her body back into balance, she will become less and less able to ward off disease and the illnesses will mount.

The most potent medication you can give your dog when she is recovering from an illness is a daily dose of good nutrition. Nutrients are what the body uses to restore diseased or damaged tissue.

Whether your dog has a minor ailment or is recovering from major surgery, it is important to provide her body with the nutritional tools it needs to repair itself. Inadequate nutrition causes slow wound healing, decreased immune response, a higher infection rate, and a longer recovery rate. When your dog is healing, she will use nutrients faster, so you need to increase her supplement levels.

Each day your dog's body relies on a certain amount of nutrition to keep her body running smoothly. If she gets diarrhea with daily doses of vitamin C higher than 1,000 mg, that means her body uses approximately 1,000 mg of vitamin C in addition to what her body naturally produces.

If she has surgery and the entire 1,000 mg of vitamin C goes to repair the wound, it leaves the rest of the body depleted of vitamin C. Vitamin C plays a major role in wound healing, so if she has had any surgery increase her vitamin C. Be sure to watch for loose stools, which are an indication that you are giving her more than she needs. A study of nutrition and wound healing found that vitamin C levels are higher in healing tissue and return to normal after the healing is complete. So, if she has had major surgery, don't be surprised if she needs twice her usual daily dose. As the wound heals, her need for extra vitamin C will decrease, so a week after surgery slowly decrease the dosage until you are back to her usual daily dose.

If your dog is scheduled for surgery, start boosting her immune system and strengthening her body a week before the surgery. If emergency surgery is necessary or your dog is fighting a disease, start building her nutritional forces as soon as she is able to keep food down. Don't ever force an ill dog to eat or you will risk causing her to vomit, which will only make things worse and can cause serious problems, such as choking or pneumonia. Drooling or swallowing repeatedly when you offer her food are signs of nausea. Take the food away and try again later.

A week before, and two weeks after surgery, or during an illness, increase the multivitamin-mineral supplement by one-third. Immediately after surgery, or if there is any type of trauma, give the homeopathic remedy arnica, in tablet form, for bruising and swelling. Follow the instructions on the label. Traumeel cream is another homeopathic remedy that you can apply to bruises or closed wounds to help with pain, swelling, redness, and heat.

After surgery, your dog's immune system is busy healing the surgical wound and detoxifying from the anesthesia and other drugs. The body removes anesthetics through the lungs, kidney, and liver. Essiac and milk thistle are helpful to support the kidneys and liver as they flush out these toxins. For Essiac, follow the instructions on the label. Daily dosages for milk thistle are: 80–100 mg for small and medium dogs, 150–175 mg for medium and large dogs, and 175 mg twice daily for giant dogs. Most milk-thistle capsules contain about 175 mg.

If your dog has to stay in the hospital overnight, ask your veterinarian if you can come in and feed her. She may eat more readily with you there, and you will be able to keep her on her usual high-quality diet with the proper supplements.

Stress is another factor that suppresses the immune system. If your dog has to stay in the hospital overnight, she may be in a very stressful situation, with bright lights, people coming and going, and other stressed dogs that can't sleep either. B-complex vitamins, vitamin E, or a homeopathic remedy will be beneficial for these types of stressful times.

The most frequent prescriptions a veterinarian writes are for antibiotics. If your dog is on antibiotics, be sure she is also receiving a daily dose of probiotics, the friendly bacteria that maintain the health of your dog's intestinal tract. Antibiotics destroy the friendly bacteria in the intestines, and this interferes with her ability to digest food and absorb the nutrients she needs to become healthy. A high-quality, preferably organic, yogurt that contains active cultures is a good source of probiotics. You can also buy a probiotic supplement in the refrigerated section of your health food store.

If you have the time to tend to her, and a clean, warm, quiet, safe place where she can recover, the optimal place for your dog is at home. She should be free of drafts or disturbances and have access to fresh air and sunlight.

Once you have your dog settled in to a nice comfortable place, you will probably start wondering, "How will I know if my dog is in pain?" If your dog has had surgery or a traumatic accident, she *is* in pain, but without the anticipation and fear humans create when in pain. If people are hurting, it scares them and they immediately want to relieve the pain, when, in most cases, if they had just stayed still and let their bodies heal, they would be fine with little or no pain medication. Try to detach from *your* fear of pain and calmly observe your dog. If she is so uncomfortable that she is shaking, panting heavily, refusing to get up, or unable to sleep, for example, then I would recommend pain medication. Start her on one buffered aspirin with food every eight hours. For giant dogs, use two buffered aspirin, and for dogs less than twenty pounds use one buffered baby aspirin. Do *not* use ibuprofen or acetaminophen. Ibuprofen will cause an upset stomach and is toxic to the liver, and acetaminophen is poisonous to dogs and can kill them. You can also try kava, which can help relieve stress and pain. For small dogs, use half the recommended dose, and for all others follow directions on the label. The homeopathic remedy *symphytum* is useful for bone pain and the homeopathic remedy *hypericum* (St. John's Wort) is good for nerve pain. If these don't relieve the pain, then talk to your veterinarian about getting a prescription for a stronger painkiller.

If you are caring for her at home and she isn't eating, you may need to stimulate her appetite with something that has a strong odor, is very tasty, and is easy to digest, like chicken broth or homemade turkey. Feed as many small meals as she will eat and don't be afraid to pamper her by hand feeding, warming the food, or puréeing the food so it is easier for her to eat. Every bite counts when a dog is recovering from illness. Give her only highly nutritious, protein-enriched foods and remember the fresh water. Keep water near her at all times, and if she isn't very mobile really spoil her by bringing the water to her—you may have to put a little on her mouth to entice her to drink. And the last, but certainly not the least important ingredient for a speedy recovery is lots of tender loving care.

## PART TWO

# NATURAL METHODS FOR YOUR DOG'S OPTIMUM HEALTH

# 5

## The Importance of a
## Strong Immune System

Support of the immune system is one of the most important roles that proper nutrition plays in your dog's health. The immune system protects your dog from illness and supports the repair of his body when injured. Our environment is always teeming with microscopic organisms that have the potential to infect your dog with any number of minor to life-threatening diseases. How your dog's immune system responds to these organisms determines his health.

Have you noticed that when a cold or flu is going around, some people always get it and others never get sick? Those who stay well have an active, healthy immune system to protect them. Those who get sick from infectious diseases have an immune system that is in less than optimal condition.

The immune system is a complex network within the body that produces millions of cells each day. Each cell's mission is to seek out and destroy foreign invaders called *antigens*. An antigen, which is short for *antibody generating*, is a foreign invader in the body, such as a bacteria, fungus, parasite, pollen, or virus. Elimination of antigens is accomplished primarily by white blood cells that use the lymphatic and blood vessels to move through the body. One drop of blood contains 5,000 to 10,000 white blood cells, and two-thirds of them are part of the immune system.

The major players in the immune system's defense strategy against infection are called natural killer (NK) cells, T-cells, and B-cells. The natural killer cells mount the first and most rapid attack against the antigens. The next line of defense is white blood cells called T-cells, which are produced by the thymus gland, a primary gland of the immune system. If the T-cells need backup, they can call on helper T-cells, which are able to call on the last and most powerful line of defense, the B-cells.

B-cells are white blood cells that produce and secrete proteins called antibodies. The antibodies bind to the antigen, inactivating it so that scavenger cells can digest it. Although the white blood cells are the primary workers in the immune system, and the thymus gland is the primary producer of the white blood cells, the adenoids, bone marrow, spleen, and tonsils also play important roles in the functioning of the immune system.

Your dog will begin his life with the antibody immunity he gets from colostrum, a special milk his mother produces for twenty-four hours after his birth. He will continue to get some antibodies from his mother's milk, but when he is weaned, it is time for his own immune system to take over. As your dog grows in a stress-free environment, with proper nutrition, he builds on the immunity he received from his mother by producing antibodies that will successfully fight off infections introduced through the environment or vaccinations. Keeping your dog's immune system strong requires proper nutrition, as well as an awareness on your part of what will weaken his immune system. Some breeds are more susceptible to immune system stress than others. Akitas, Scottish Terriers, Shar-Peis, and West Highland White Terriers are prone to immune-system disorders, so it is especially important to avoid situations that will weaken their immune systems.

## WHAT WEAKENS THE IMMUNE SYSTEM?

Anything foreign that enters your dog's body, such as an allergen, bacteria, a toxin, a vaccination, or a virus, will trigger his immune system into action. The immune system is designed to masterfully handle millions of invasions a day, but it does have a stress point. It can become weak if it is malnourished, overexposed to toxic substances, or repeatedly suppressed by stress.

There are warning signs to alert you if your dog's immune system is weakened. Allergies, arthritis, chronic diarrhea, fatigue, recurring infections or skin problems, or slow-healing wounds are all signs that the immune system is weak and vulnerable to more serious illnesses. You can keep your dog's immune system strong with good nutrition, careful monitoring of his environment, and by providing additional nutritional support for those times when his immune system will be stressed.

## VACCINATIONS

Most dog owners dutifully bring their dogs to the veterinarian every year for shots, not knowing what the vet is injecting into the dog or why. I can't tell you exactly how this practice of yearly vaccinations began, but I can tell you this schedule is not based on scientific evidence. In fact, the evidence is that dogs and cats are drastically *over*-vaccinated.

According to Dr. Ronald Schultz, a respected expert on clinical immunology and vaccinology from the Department of Pathobiological Sciences at the University of Wisconsin, there is no scientific justification or immunologic requirement for annual revaccinations. There is mounting consensus among veterinarians that annual revaccinations are causing serious side effects in dogs, such as aggression, allergic reactions, anaphylaxis (hypersensitivity to vaccines), impaired immune function, and a long list of chronic diseases.

Veterinarians concerned about this are now doing yearly antibody titer tests before they vaccinate. An antibody titer test is a simple blood test that measures your dog's antibodies to a specific disease, such as the distemper or parvo virus. If the antibody titer remains in the protective range, there is no need to revaccinate your dog.

---

### Antibody Titer Tests Safely Avoid Yearly Revaccinations

Lincoln, a chow mix, is typical of the many dogs having antibody titer tests done rather than revaccinations, who have all have proven that yearly revaccination is unnecessary. His initial vaccination series was done when he was a puppy, and now, at age ten, his titers for distemper are still in the protective range. And he has only needed two boosters for the parvo virus, one when he was two years old, and the next at age nine—he remained protected for seven years.

Distemper can be transmitted through the air and I suspect that Lincoln has been exposed to small amounts from wildlife, such as coyotes, foxes, and raccoons, throughout his life, keeping the distemper titers in the protective range.

---

Vaccines are a very small dose of the disease you are trying to prevent. The injection of the infectious organism into your dog causes the immune system to mount a defense by producing antibodies. Antibodies are the protein substance produced by the immune system to destroy specific foreign invaders. For example, when your dog receives his rabies vaccination, specific rabies antibodies are produced that will kill the rabies virus if it enters the body.

A dog's immune system will only produce so many rabies antibodies. If he receives a rabies vaccination when he already has plenty of rabies antibodies, his immune system will still be able to destroy the rabies virus if he is exposed to it, but he will not produce additional antibodies. Not only was your money wasted on the vaccine, your dog's immune system was put under tremendous stress from battling the rabies virus, weakening it, and leaving your dog vulnerable to other illnesses.

Vaccinations aren't all bad. They are a useful addition to preventive medicine when given with care, and only when needed. Please don't give a stressed or sick dog a vaccination—sick in this case meaning anything but optimal health. If your dog is fighting allergies, fleas, or skin problems, he is not in optimal health. Leave his immune system alone to fight that battle and bring him in for a vaccination when he is strong and healthy.

There are many factors, such as new people and pets in a household, the show ring, or thunderstorms, that can cause your dog emotional stress. If your dog cowered under the bed all night because of a thunderstorm, postpone his vaccination for a day or two.

For longer term stress, such as going to a show or introducing someone new into your dog's life, give him a few days to rest and get used to the new routine. If you adopt a dog, wait until he gets used to his new home before you take him to the vet. Be especially careful if you adopt a puppy, because a puppy's immune system isn't fully developed and the additional stress of a trip to the vet, along with a vaccination, could weaken his immune system for life. Imagine being a mere eight weeks old. You have recently been weaned and taken away from your mother, and some stranger comes and takes you away from your home. You are then thrust into a big noisy car that moves, knocks you to and fro, and makes you feel nauseous. Finally, the car stops and this stranger brings you into a strange house with a big furry cat that is hissing at you and two little people that won't let you go hide, take a nap, and figure this all out. In addition to the stress of a new home, this new puppy will be getting used to new food and water, and the last thing he needs on top of all these new stressors is a vaccination.

Each dog adjusts to new experiences differently. Some dogs are more high strung than others. Keep an eye on him and when he seems comfortable with the surroundings and easily fits into the new routine, make an appointment with the vet for vaccinations.

Puppies should go through an initial vaccination series. The types of vaccines your puppy needs will vary depending on his lifestyle and the part of the country you are in. For example, if he will be staying in a kennel while you are away, you might want to vaccinate for kennel cough, or if there have been incidences of leptospirosis (a potentially deadly bacterial disease) in your area, vaccinate for leptospirosis. Unless your veterinarian works with your local shelter she/he may not know if there have been any recent outbreaks of disease among the wildlife that could affect your puppy. Talk to your local shelter or animal control officer about any recent outbreaks of disease in the wildlife or local pet population.

State law requires that all dogs must have a current rabies vaccination, and many states go so far as to bar veterinarians from treating dogs whose owners refuse to give them a rabies vaccination. Most towns have expensive fines for dogs without a current rabies vaccination. This is because rabies is deadly to animals and people. If nothing else, do have your dog vaccinated for rabies. The state also mandates the frequency of the rabies shots and at what age puppies must be vaccinated. You veterinarian will have information on when to vaccinate a puppy for rabies.

Parvovirus and distemper are common throughout the United States and are potentially deadly in dogs. All puppies should be vaccinated against these two diseases and then, starting at one year old, have yearly antibody titer tests done. If possible, avoid combination vaccines. These are single shots containing more than one vaccine. When you show up for your dog's shots, many veterinarians will automatically give what is commonly known (and seen on your receipt) as a DHLPP. Those initials look harmless until you translate them to distemper, hepatitis, leptospirosis, parainfluenza, and parvo. Those are five different diseases your dog's immune system suddenly has to battle. Have you ever had a flu shot? It only contains one virus and most people spend at least twenty-four uncomfortable hours with a sore arm and minor flu symptoms, so just imagine getting one combination shot for chicken pox, flu, hepatitis, measles, and tetanus.

Space vaccines a minimum of one week apart, and preferably wait four weeks between vaccinations. Puppies should have their vaccinations anywhere from six weeks to twenty weeks old (five months). The reason for waiting twenty weeks would be to give the immune system time to mature, but this must be weighed against the risks of your puppy contracting the disease. If you have your puppy vaccinated earlier than twenty weeks, he will need to receive each vaccine twice because the antibodies a puppy receives from his mother (maternal antibodies) during the first six weeks of life can interfere with the effectiveness of the vaccine.

A typical vaccination schedule for a puppy would be:

- First distemper at ten weeks;
- First parvo at fourteen weeks;
- Second distemper at eighteen weeks;
- Second parvo at twenty-two weeks;
- At one year, start the yearly antibody titer tests.

If your puppy is isolated from contact with other dogs and wildlife, then it is safe to hold off on vaccinations until he is twenty weeks. By twenty weeks, the maternal antibodies will no longer interfere with the effectiveness of the vaccine, so you only have to give each vaccine once. If you adopt an older dog and don't know his vaccination history, have antibody titer tests done. It is very important to ask for a vaccine titer. The lab can educate your veterinarian about protective ranges and whether you need to revaccinate. (*See* Resources in back for a list of labs that do antibody titer tests.)

## EMOTIONAL STRESS AND THE IMMUNE SYSTEM

Emotional stress can affect a dog's immune system, and the owner is often the source of emotional stress because most dogs are very sensitive to their owner's emotions. If you are upset or stressed, chances are good that your dog will become stressed. Have you ever noticed your dog's reaction when there is a high level of stress in the room? He will be highly attentive and worried, or he may hide under something or leave the room. I know several dogs that won't leave their owner's side when the owner is sick. These dogs are emotionally stressed by their owner's illness. If your dog's emotions mirror your own illness, mustering up some strength for a happy reassurance that you will be okay would be very calming for him and probably you as well. What could be more stress-reducing than patting your dog?

### Natural Therapies and TLC Rout Hilda's Stress-Related Bone Cancer

Dr. Beverly Cappel-King is seeing a strong connection between bone cancer in dogs and stress. In nearly every incidence of bone cancer that she treats, the family has recently gone through a highly stressful event, such as divorce, illness or a loved one leaving. A four-year-old Doberman named Hilda is one example out of many. Hilda and her owner are inseparable. Except for the few hours a day when Hilda's owner is at work, they are together. Hilda's owner decided to get a second job and three months later Hilda came in from playing and was limping on her left front leg (a common place for bone cancer in Dobermans). Hilda was diagnosed with bone cancer. Her owner immediately quit her second job and made Hilda the center of her life. She even went so far as to call ahead when she took Hilda with her to visit friends and asked them not to ask why she was limping, but to tell her how beautiful she was. Dr. King gave Hilda antioxidants, herbal remedies, homeopathics, minerals, and vitamins to build up her immune system, and six months later X-rays showed a clean bone. Hilda and her owner have since had three and a half years of cancer-free health and happiness, and Dr. King attributes Hilda's recovery more to her owner's positive, loving energy than the remedies she gave Hilda.

Every breed and every individual dog responds differently to stress. Some dogs are totally relaxed most of the time (Bloodhounds and Golden Retrievers come to mind) and some dogs are in a near-constant state of stress (border collies and some Toy breeds come to mind). Notice what causes stress in your dog and try to minimize those situations when possible.

Stress increases the production of adrenaline which inhibits the production of your immune system's first line of defense, the white blood cells. The thymus gland, which produces much of the immune system's white blood cells, will begin to shrink if it constantly suppressed by stress. A shrunken thymus gland will not produce an adequate number of white blood cells, resulting in suppression of the immune system, and leaving your dog susceptible to illness.

High levels of stress have also been proven to trigger autoimmune diseases, such as arthritis, hemolytic anemia, lupus, and various skin diseases. In an autoimmune disease, the immune system becomes confused and attacks healthy tissues in the body.

Sudden, extreme stress causes the fright-or-flight instinct to kick in, which shuts down the immune system. The immune system was elegantly designed by nature to shift bodily resources to running or attacking in the face of danger, but if it is overused it can be a killer itself. If your dog was facing an attacking bear in the woods, the fright-or-flight stress response could save his life, but just as with people, chronic stress means the immune system is shut down too much of the time.

If your dog is highly stressed by events, such as a ride in the car, a thunderstorm, or an unwanted separation, the fright-flight instinct causes his heart to beat as fast as it can so he can run away from the car, the thunderstorm, or the fear of being alone. The only way his heart can work that hard is by borrowing resources from other parts of his body that aren't needed for running, such as blood from the stomach or thymus gland. The parts of his body that aren't essential for running, such as the the digestive system and the immune system, will be suppressed or put on hold.

Imagine what happens to a dog's health if he is so terrified of riding in the car or being at the vet that his immune system shuts down. Then the vet gives him the DHLPP vaccination (five diseases) and he is put back in the car. Finally home, he jumps out of the car and runs onto a lawn that was recently treated with pesticides. He drinks from a bowl that was downwind of the pesticide spray, and also contains chlorine and benzene. He takes a nap in the grass, and as he sleeps, his immune system comes back to life and finds five diseases, along with a heavy onslaught of pesticides and the usual water contaminants to battle. Even an immune system that was healthy and strong before the visit to the vet couldn't cope with that much stress. You may not notice immediate symptoms from this type of stress reaction, but it *will* take a toll on your dog's body, setting the stage for heart, kidney and liver disease, as well as arthritis and cancer.

If your dog is in a constant state of stress from hyperactivity or oversensitivity, there are natural remedies, including the B-complex vitamins, homeopathic remedies, and magnesium, that have a calming effect. Valerian and kava are other natural remedies that can be used on occasion to treat stress. (*See* Chapters 3 on vitamins, 4 on minerals, and 8 on homeopathy, for more information.)

## ENVIRONMENTAL THREATS TO THE IMMUNE SYSTEM

There are more than 80,000 different chemical compounds in use today, and a year from now thousands more will have been added to the list. Each year approximately 20 billion tons of chemicals, pollutants, and radioactive waste are released into our environment. The majority of these toxins have never been tested for their long-term effects on you and your dog. If you buy into the often-said, "They wouldn't sell it if it weren't safe . . ." think back to asbestos, DDT, Fen-phen, leaded gasoline, PCB's, thalidomide, and Vioxx, to name a few government-approved products that are now banned because they made people seriously ill.

Rachel Carson, the author of *Silent Spring*, summed up the accumulating effects of toxins: "The fact that the suburbanite is not instantly stricken has little meaning, for the toxins may sleep long in the body, to become manifest months or years later in an obscure disorder almost impossible to trace to its origins." In 1979, the United States Surgeon General issued a warning about the serious consequences of our already polluted environment when he said, "There is virtually no major chronic disease to which environmental factors do not contribute, directly or indirectly."

Toxins are not natural to your dog's body and will trigger the immune system into action. But many toxins can't be eliminated from the body, so they sit in fatty tissues for decades, harming cells and creating an environment for cancer. Short of wearing a space suit, you can't possibly avoid all environmental toxins, so you need to give yourself and your dog the extra protection of a healthy lifestyle. Proper daily nutrition and some extra support for the immune system when your dog is unavoidably stressed is good health insurance.

## THE PLAGUE OF PESTICIDES FOR
## THE IMMUNE SYSTEM

Pesticides are used in such abundance, both agriculturally and in residential communities, that they are one of the biggest environmental threats to your dog's immune system. In the United States, a staggering 800 million pounds of pesticides are used each year on crops and foods, and an additional 70 million pounds are used on urban lawns. With approximately 870 million pounds of pesticides used every year, you would think that insects would be extinct by now. On the contrary, according to the Natural Resources Defense Council—since 1940 pesticide use has increased tenfold while crop losses to insects have doubled.

Pesticides are in and around nearly every home in the United States, and they are killing more than pests: they are killing people and their pets. It's comforting to think that the poisons in pesticides are only poisonous to insects and weeds, but that's not true. It just takes a correspondingly higher dose to kill people because they're bigger.

Dogs spend most of their lives sleeping and playing on the ground and carpet and that's where the highest concentrations of pesticides are found. A nine-home study found pesticides in every one of the homes, with the highest concentrations in the carpet dust. So, even if you don't use pesticides on your lawn or in your home, your dog is still at risk. Pesticides move through the air and the ground, so if your neighbors use pesticides, or if you live near a farm, you and your dog are being exposed. Pesticide runoff from lawns pollutes the sidewalks and roads. When your dog goes for his daily walk with you, he picks up pesticides through his nose and the pads of his feet where it will be absorbed directly into the bloodstream.

Studies of human populations have found that people exposed to pesticides have higher incidences of birth defects, cancer, kidney and liver disease, and nervous system disorders, with children having higher incidences of illness from pesticides than adults. There is no reason why those same studies wouldn't also apply to dogs, with the children's rates of illness being more applicable because a dog's size and lifestyle of playing close to the ground would more closely mimic a child than an adult. The *Journal of the National Cancer Institute* reports that the incidence of leukemia in children is six-and-a-half times higher in homes where pesticides are used. That statistic alone should be reason enough for you to ban all pesticides from your home.

Pesticide poisoning can cause immediate symptoms, or the toxins can slowly weaken the immune system, causing your dog to become sick after years of exposure. Symptoms of pesticide poisoning can include all or one of the following: anxiety, behavior problems, cancer, diarrhea, fatigue, fever, headaches, heart, liver, and kidney disease, hyperactivity, immune-system disorders, incontinence, nausea, respiratory illness, seizures, and vomiting.

You can't eliminate your dog's exposure to pesticides, but you can keep it at a minimum. Start in your own backyard with organic gardening. You will be amazed at how easy and inexpensive it is and how much healthier your plants and lawn will be. To ward off pests, I spray a mixture of hot (spicy) oil, dish soap, and water on my fruit trees and they thrive. Throw away all the toxins inside your house as well. From the flea to the mouse, there are effective, inexpensive, natural ways to eliminate them from your house. Your local library or bookstore will have plenty of material on natural pest control. Finally, be aware of where your dog walks and plays. Avoid neighborhoods, playgrounds or golf courses where a lot of pesticides are used. Wildlife habitats are tucked away in many parts of the country and are wonderful for a nice long walk in any season and weather.

## ALLERGENS AND THE IMMUNE SYSTEM

An allergen is anything that causes an allergy. It can literally come from anything in your dog's environment, including the air, animals, bedding, chemicals, detergents, food, furniture, and plants. Allergens can be absorbed through the skin, ingested, or inhaled, and if they cause an allergic reaction, the most common symptom is itchy red skin. Dogs, like people, can also develop sneezing, red, runny eyes and nose, and post-nasal drip. Symptoms of post-nasal drip are wheezing or trouble breathing. Allergies are a useful red flag that your dog's immune system is weakened.

Allergies occur when the immune system overreacts to a foreign substance or allergen, such as pollen. The allergen stimulates the release of a substance called histamine, which triggers irritation, inflammation, and itchiness in the skin.

Early detection of an allergic reaction will make a big difference in treating it. The more advanced an allergic reaction, the longer the battle to bring the immune system back into balance. Many dog owners let allergies go until their dogs have scratched themselves bald and their immune systems are highly oversensitive. At the first sign of an allergic reaction, put on your detective cap, figure out what is causing it, and, if possible, eliminate it from your dog's environment. While you look for the culprit, start building up your dog's immune system and keep notes on when the allergies seem to flare up. Notice if they are better when you are away from home, whether they are seasonal, or if they seem worse when your dog wakes up in the morning or at the end of the day. It may take a year of seasonal changes, with the environment changing both inside and outside your home, to pinpoint the exact cause of the allergies. Be persistent, keep an allergy diary nearby, and look to the light at the end of the tunnel—an allergy-free dog.

Allergies are only one of the many causes of skin problems, so if you have put forth your best effort and still can't clear up the skin problems, they may be caused by something else, including genetics, hypothyroidism, or a nutrient-absorption problem. Your best bet is to find a holistic veterinarian to work with you and your dog to bring the body back into balance and strengthen the immune system. (*See* Chapter 10 for more information on allergies.)

## AIR POLLUTION AND THE IMMUNE SYSTEM

The mention of air pollution usually brings to mind the yellowish haze often seen over Los Angeles and New York. Few people consider that, when they shut all the windows in their house and turn on the heat or air conditioning, they could be breathing air more toxic than downtown Manhattan at rush hour. The Environmental Protection Agency studied levels of air pollu-tion indoors and outdoors for five years and found that indoor air pol-lution is 100–200 times higher than outdoor air pollution. Unless you faithfully clean your ducts, filters, and vents, you and your dog could be breathing asbestos, bacteria, cleaning chemicals, dust mites, mildew, mold, pesticides, pollens, rodent feces, and tobacco smoke.

If you are building a new home, remodeling, or just sprucing up your house, keep a careful eye on labels and choose products that are toxin-free. New carpets, paint, or wood can contain toxins that are lethal to you and your dog's immune system. If you are buying new carpet look for the *green label* stating that the rug has met voluntary emissions' criteria. Have the retailer air out the carpet before installation, and air out your house for a few days after the carpet is installed. The rubber latex contained in carpet backing and the carpet adhesives very often emit toxic fumes that can cause headaches, lethargy, nausea, red, watery eyes, skin irritations, and vomiting. If health problems persist, the best thing you can do for yourself and your dog is to have the carpet removed.

It's become common to hear of business and homeowners who have experienced serious health problems after having carpet installed. Many of these people subsequently had their carpet tested in a laboratory, and there were findings of toxic fumes at extremely high levels. In one instance, a mouse died after only forty minutes of exposure to air blown over the carpet, and another three mice died after twenty-four hours.

If you have ever painted with oil or latex-based paint, you have smelled the fumes from the approximately 300 toxic substances that can come from the paint. The fumes will linger long after the smell is gone, and can cause you and your dog headaches, nausea, runny, watery eyes, and throat and lung irritation. There are good quality paints with lower levels of toxins—look for paints that are labeled as a clean air choice.

Pressed woods, such as fiberboard, particle board, or plywood, can also be a threat to you and your dog's health. A toxin called urea formaldehyde is used in the glue of many pressed woods and it will cause coughing, nausea, red watery eyes, throat, lung, and skin irritation. Choose woods, such as softwood plywood, strand board, or wafer board that contain glue made with the less toxic phenol formaldehyde.

The Environmental Protection Agency estimates that in the United States we spend over one billion dollars on medical costs for cancer and heart disease caused by indoor pollutants. When you consider that these same indoor pollutants are twice as toxic to a dog half the size of an adult, it is staggering to think of the medical costs dog owners must pay out of their pockets due to illness from indoor pollution.

If you see your dog rubbing his eyes or face, with his paws, on the furniture, or on the ground, he is probably feeling a burning in his eyes or throat from any one of these products. Immediately bring him out to fresh air and rinse his eyes with clean, fresh water. If possible, have any moves or renovations timed so you can keep your windows open for a few days to air out the house after you are finished. If you are painting, put your dog outside, or take him to a friend's house during the painting and for a few hours afterwards, and for yourself leave the windows open while you paint.

The air may be cleaner outside, but it is far from pollution-free. Twice as many people die each year from airborne pollution than from auto accidents. In the most polluted cities in the United States, lives are shortened an average of one to two years from airborne pollution. In a report titled, *Acid Rain and Transported Air Pollutants*, the Congressional Office of Technology Assessment concluded that air pollution may cause 50,000 premature deaths in the United States every year. The list of air pollutants is endless, ranging from the obvious pollens and auto exhaust to unsuspecting substances, such as latex antigens. You did read that right: a study of air pollution and latex allergy found latex antigens in abundance in urban air samples. The study concluded that the latex antigens came from automobile tires.

You and your dog must breathe the air, so you both need to be sure you are getting the cleanest air possible. Exercise together at a time of day when the air pollution is at its lowest, and stay away from busy roads. If your dog rides in the back of a truck with an enclosed cab be very careful of poisoning from the exhaust. Always have fresh air available, and if you open a window on the cab cover be sure it is not over the exhaust pipe. If you stop for gas and the window to the cab is over the gas tank, close the window and open the back of the cab so your dog has plenty of fresh air. If you are stuck in traffic, open the window. Studies show that toxins from car exhaust inside the car are two to four times higher inside the car than outdoors. Small concentrations of the chemicals in automobile exhaust can cause lethargy, eye, lung, and skin irritation, and higher concentrations will cause cancer, fatigue, and headaches.

## POISONS AND THE IMMUNE SYSTEM

When you take your dog for a walk, the world looks very innocent. You don't see the hidden dangers that your dog's nose will find in an instant. A dog's habit of eating strange and disgusting things, such as dirt, feces, or grass, is caused by an attempt to satisfy a nutritional void. The likelihood is slim that what he finds is nutritional, and most likely it is poisonous. Dogs may also be harming themselves if the feces came from a sick animal, or if the grass or dirt has been poisoned with antifreeze, oil, or pesticides, or a whole host of other toxic substances that people pour onto the ground.

Propylene glycol, a preservative in rawhide that is also an ingredient in antifreeze, is sweet and highly addictive. If your dog comes upon antifreeze, he will lap it up like candy, when it is, in fact, a poison and will cause serious illness and possibly even death. Not many dogs can resist a dead animal, if only just to play with it and roll in it, but that dead animal could be diseased or may have been killed with a poison. If your dog picks up a piece of wood to chew, be sure it isn't pressure-treated wood, which contains arsenic.

Indoors can be lethal to a puppy that is still chewing. Dog-proof your home just as you would for a child, keeping anything toxic that could be ingested or used as a Toy out of reach. This includes cleaners, medications, paint, and pesticides.

Poisons abound in our environment. Feed your dog a well-balanced diet and keep a careful eye on what he puts in his mouth.

## NUTRITION FOR A STRONG IMMUNE SYSTEM

To maintain a strong immune system, your dog needs high-quality food, clean water, plenty of fresh air and exercise, and a good multivitamin-mineral supplement. Your dog's immune system will need extra nutritional support if he is subjected to anything that could suppress his immune system, such as any of the environmental dangers listed above, stress, or vaccinations.

If you are spending more time at your vet's office than at home, and have to take out a second mortgage to pay for medication for your dog, then his immune system probably needs to be restored back to health. I would recommend you consult a holistic veterinarian who will treat the underlying cause rather than treating only the symptoms. Many holistic veterinarians can diagnose and treat your dog using the results of blood work done by your current veterinarian. Holistic veterinarian Dr. Beverly Cappel-King brought a cat with feline infectious peritonitis back to health without ever meeting the cat or his owner in person. She diagnosed and treated the cat through blood work and keen observations of the cat by the owner during phone consultations.

If your dog has milder symptoms of a weakened immune system, such as lethargy, occasional bouts of diarrhea, or occasional skin problems, you can restore his immune system by following my nutritional guidelines, paying particular attention to the nutrients for a strong immune system, and avoiding anything that will stress and weaken his immune system.

Just as with people, when your dog ages there is a natural decline in the efficiency of the immune system. In a one-year study of thirty-five people between the ages of sixty-one and seventy-nine, some took a placebo and some took a multivitamin-mineral supplement. Those who took the supplement had less decline in their immune function than those who took the placebo. In a similar study, those who took a multivitamin had fewer days of illness due to infectious disease.

Good nutrition will delay and minimize the inevitable decline in immune function that occurs as your dog ages. Be sure that your older dog is getting the nutrients listed below in a form that is easily absorbed, such as a powder or pill that will quickly dissolve in water.

Below I have listed the key nutrients, and their daily dosages, for maintaining a strong immune system. If your dog is older, highly stressed, or has a weakened immune system, increase his multivitamin-mineral supplement by one-third, and follow the guidelines below for nutrients that are not found in a multivitamin-mineral supplement. (*See* Chapters 3 on vitamins and 4 on minerals for more information.)

## PROTEIN

Protein is just as important to your dog as it is to you, and your dog needs an even higher percentage of protein in his diet than you do. A protein-deficient diet will cause a significant weakening of your dog's immune system. As with everything, moderation is the key, however, because too much protein can cause kidney damage.

Buckwheat, eggs, quinoa, and red meat are high in protein and should be included in your dog's diet on a daily basis if the immune system is weakened or stressed. It is ideal to vary your protein sources. Limit eggs to between two and four a week, depending on the size of your dog, and at each meal try to combine different types of protein, such as grains and red meat.

## GARLIC

Garlic strengthens the immune system and has antibiotic, anti-parasitic, and anti-viral properties. Garlic has a long, illustrious career as a healing agent. The Egyptians worshipped it, monks ate it in the Middle Ages to fend off the plague, and during World War I it was used on wounds to prevent infection. Garlic has been found to inactivate cancer-causing substances, and it aids in destroying parasites. One-half to two cloves of garlic per day, depending on the size of your dog, will help to maintain a strong immune system. If your dog is stressed or the immune system is weakened, stick to the daily maintenance dose. Too much garlic can upset the stomach. Because of potential blood-thinning properties, it is not advisable to give your dog garlic before surgery.

## BETA-CAROTENE

Beta-carotene is a powerful antioxidant that protects cells within the immune system from free-radical damage and helps immune-system cells communicate more efficiently. Beta-carotene improves production of natural-killer cells, the first line of defense for the immune system. If your dog's body is deficient in vitamin A, beta-carotene has the unique ability to convert to vitamin A. However, since beta-carotene loses its antioxidant properties when it converts to vitamin A, it's best to give your dog a multivitamin-mineral supplement that contains both beta-carotene and vitamin A, along with plenty of fresh beta-carotene-rich foods, such as dark green leafy vegetables and yellow and orange fruits and vegetables.

## VITAMIN A

Vitamin A is important in the production of the phagocyte cells and T- cells. T-cells are the white blood cells that identify the foreign substances in your dog's body and the phagocyte cells are one of the many types of white blood cells that the T-cells can call on to engulf the foreign substances (antigens). Vitamin A also aids in the fight against bacteria in saliva, sweat, and tears. It is important for healthy mucous membranes, which are found in the mouth, nose, and digestive system, and is a potent weapon in the body's fight against bacterial infections.

Vitamin A comes in liquid and capsule form. Recommended daily doses are: 1,500 IU for small dogs, 3,750 IU for medium dogs, and 5,000 IU for large and giant dogs.

## B-COMPLEX VITAMINS

The B-complex vitamins aid in the production of antibodies and the normal functioning of cells.

## Daily Dosages for Adult Dogs

| | Small Dog | Medium Dog | Large Dog | Giant Dog |
|---|---|---|---|---|
| Thiamin ($B_1$) | 1 mg | 2 mg | 3 mg | 4 mg |
| Riboflavin ($B_2$) | 1 mg | 2 mg | 3 mg | 4 mg |
| Niacin ($B_3$) | 1 mg | 2 mg | 3 mg | 4 mg |
| Pantothenic Acid ($B_5$) | 1 mg | 2 mg | 3 mg | 4 mg |
| Pyridoxine ($B_6$) | 1 mg | 2 mg | 3 mg | 4 mg |
| Cobalamin ($B_{12}$) | 1 mcg | 2 mcg | 3 mcg | 4 mcg |
| Biotin | 1 mcg | 2 mcg | 3 mcg | 4 mcg |
| Folic Acid | 1 mcg | 2 mcg | 3 mcg | 4 mcg |

## VITAMIN C

Vitamin C is an antioxidant that plays a key role in the production of interferon and infection-fighting white blood cells. Interferon, another part of the immune system's defense team, is produced in response to viruses or tumors. The infection-fighting white blood cells, the backbone of the immune system, engulf foreign substances that enter the body. Many holistic veterinarians have had miraculous results giving critically ill dogs megadoses of vitamin C. It helps restore the immune system, thus restoring the body's ability to fight the disease. Vitamin C also inhibits the secretion of histamines, making it a natural antihistamine and a necessary nutrient in the battle against allergens. Physical and emotional stress depletes your dog's body of vitamin C, so keeping up with the daily doses of vitamin C will go a long way in keeping his immune system strong.

The daily dosage for an adult dog is:

- 500–1,000 mg for small dogs;
- 1,000–2,000 mg for medium and large dogs;
- 2,000-4,000 mg for giant dogs.

For a weakened immune system, slowly increase the dose to bowel tolerance.

## VITAMIN E

Vitamin E is an antioxidant that enhances T-cell function and has proven to boost antibody response to vaccinations. Vitamin E is one of the most important antioxidants for protecting and supporting the immune system.

Vitamin E is available in liquid or powder form. The recommended daily dose is 100 IU for small dogs, 200 IU for medium and large dogs, and 400 IU for giant dogs. For stressful situations or a weakened immune system, double the doses.

# Trace Minerals

## Copper

A copper deficiency will dramatically lower your dog's resistance to infection and disease by decreasing the white blood cell and antibody production.

Daily recommended doses are: .5 mg for small dogs, 1 mg for medium dogs, 2 mg for large and giant dogs.

## Iron

An iron deficiency will inhibit your dog's use of oxygen, which in turn inhibits the function of the immune system. The entire immune system is dependent on oxygen to work efficiently. Iron is another nutrient where moderation is the key. Too much iron can generate free radicals that will injure cells on your dog's artery walls, causing heart disease. A blood test will tell you if your dog has an iron deficiency. Your veterinarian will provide you with iron supplements or you can feed your dog plenty of organic foods rich with iron, such as beef, beans, liver, pork, and turkey.

Recommended daily doses are: 9 mg for small dogs, 18 mg for medium dogs, 30 mg for large dogs, 40 mg for giant dogs.

## Manganese

Manganese is an important coworker to many of the vitamins that play key roles in maintaining the strength of the immune system. Manganese is necessary for utilizing the B-complex vitamins, vitamin C, and vitamin E. A manganese deficiency has been found to suppress the production of antibodies.

Recommended daily doses are: 0.75 mg for small dogs, 1.5 mg for medium dogs, 2.6 mg for large dogs, and 3.75 mg for giant dogs.

## Selenium

Selenium is an antioxidant that works with vitamin E to increase the body's antibody production in response to antigens (foreign substances) and enables white blood cells to destroy bacteria and viruses. According to a study on selenium and cellular immunity, selenium deficiency can lead to impaired immune function and reduced T-cell counts. Many M.D.s who use alternative medicine use selenium to fight a wide range of viruses, including AIDS and herpes.

Recommended daily doses are: 25 mcg for small dogs and 50 mcg for medium, large, and giant dogs.

A healthy immune system will give you a healthy dog. To maintain a healthy immune system your dog needs a daily diet of high-quality nutrition and extra nutritional support for those days when he has added stress to his immune system. Just as your dog's body needs more calories if he expends more energy, your dog's immune system needs additional nutrition on the days it has to work harder.

## Zinc

Zinc is important in all phases of immune function. A study published in the *International Journal of Immunopharmacology* on the effect of dietary zinc deficiency on immune function found that dietary zinc deficiency resulted in depressed T-cells, natural killer cell, and antibody functioning. The study also found zinc deficiencies were related to several forms of cancer, including head, neck, and lung cancer.

Recommended daily doses are: 10 mg for small dogs, 15 mg for medium dogs, 30 mg for large and giant dogs.

6

---

# Natural Flea Control
# for Your Dog

Right now, you probably feel less affection for the flea than you do the mosquito. You think of fleas as bloodsucking creatures that were put on this earth to torment you and your dog. A flea is a parasite, so in a way you are right. Parasites are organisms that survive on another organism without contributing anything. I felt tortured and tormented by fleas until one wonderful hot summer came and went without one flea bath, daily vacuuming, or trip to the vet. We had a flea-free summer. Not once did my dog look at me with those sad, please-help-me eyes, after biting and scratching for ten minutes.

My miracle cure was garlic. Knowing the great health benefits of garlic, I had recently started giving my dog garlic with every meal and found that it is a highly effective way to have a healthier, flea-free dog.

Fleas are tiny, brown, wingless insects that thrive on blood and can jump 100 times their height to get to the source of the blood. Pet owners collectively spend millions of dollars every year on an endless quest to rid their furry friends of this minuscule menace. These tiny insects not only cause endless aggravation, they can cause your dog to become seriously ill. Dogs that are allergic to flea saliva experience severe itching and welts from each flea bite. The allergic reaction is triggered by a chemical in the flea's saliva that prevents the dog's blood from clotting until the flea has finished its meal. If left untreated, the dog will chew her skin raw, creating open sores and the possibility of infection. The dog's skin isn't the only thing affected. The immune system becomes weaker and over-sensitized with every bite, leaving the dog vulnerable to additional chronic health problems. On the outside, the dog is biting and scratching, and on the inside the immune system is working overtime to fight the allergic reaction and heal the sores caused by the itching and biting.

To add insult to injury, fleas don't travel alone. They are two parasites in one tiny package because they carry the tapeworm, another parasite, inside them. As your dog is biting and licking, she undoubtedly will ingest a few fleas. The tapeworm inside the flea has a free ride into your dog's small intestine, which is where it lives and prospers. If your dog is infested with fleas, she most probably has tapeworm also. To know for sure, bring a stool sample to your vet and ask him or her to check your dog for worms. You may also see tapeworms around the anus or in the stool. Tapeworms are thin, segmented worms that can reach several feet in length inside a dog, but when you see them outside your dog they usually look like small grains of rice.

Tapeworms attach themselves to the small intestine with hooks and suckers and, like fleas, they live off your dog's blood. The tapeworm has an outer coating that prevents it from being digested in the small intestine. If your dog has a tapeworm, or any other worm, there are natural wormers you can buy from a holistic vet or a health food store. Garlic or capsules of black-walnut hulls are also good for prevention of worms. (*See also* Resources in back.)

Fleas rarely infest a really healthy animal. I find it interesting how the companies that make millions selling dog food that doesn't begin to meet your dog's nutritional needs *also* make millions selling pesticides to kill fleas and further compromise your dog's health. It is a vicious circle that *can* be stopped.

The key to a flea-free household is not to see how many fleas you can kill in a season. You need to make your dog an undesirable food source. If you walk into a restaurant that smells terrible, you will not stay around for a meal, you will find another restaurant. In this section, I will explain how the flea lives and why it wants to live on your dog's body. I will discuss why the chemicals and pesticides you have used for years not only don't work, but are also hazardous to you and your dog, and how you can rid your dog of fleas naturally.

## THE LIFE CYCLE OF THE FLEA

Your dog is exposed to fleas the minute she walks out the door for a walk around the block or a romp in the yard. A flea's ideal environment is warm, dark, and moist, with readily available food, which makes your dog a perfect host. The flea's only nutritional needs are blood. They prefer to live on your dog's belly, back, or near the tail. They may prefer the back end because there is less activity, although really happy dogs with long tails must be a challenge. One female flea can produce 20,000 eggs in three months. The female flea will stay on your dog to lay her eggs, or she will find a warm, dark, and moist environment off your dog to lay them—preferable living quarters off your dog are bedding, carpets, curtains, and furniture. If she decides to lay her eggs on your dog, they will fall off inside and outside your house. In one or two weeks, the eggs hatch into larvae and spin a cocoon where they will stay from one week to a year. They stay in the cocoon if the environment is not warm or moist enough and if there is no food source, such as you or your dog. While in the cocoon, the fleas are protected from insecticides and low temperatures. Normally, fleas take from three to six weeks to go from egg to larvae to adult. If you want to find out whether or not your house is infested with fleas, take your family, including pets, on a vacation. If you have a problem with fleas on your first night home, you will wake up itching and scratching. Sound familiar? I have known people who walked into their homes after being away and could watch the fleas jumping onto their bare legs. They're hungry because their food source has been gone.

The remarkable ability of flea larvae to stay in their protective cocoon for so long is probably the biggest reason that the fight against fleas can be so difficult. You have to be patient and persistent.

## FLEA COLLARS, SHAMPOOS, SPRAYS, POWDERS, AND PILLS

In simplest terms, flea collars, powders, shampoos, sprays, and spot-on drugs are used externally on your dog to kill the adult fleas.

The spot-on drugs, such as Advantage or Frontline, are chemicals that a veterinarian puts on your dog's skin where it is absorbed into the sebaceous glands. The sebaceous glands secrete oil into your dog's coat to keep it healthy and shiny. When the fleas come into contact with the chemicals, their nervous system is destroyed and they die.

Flea-control chemicals that come in pill form, such as Program, are insect-development inhibitors. Insect-development inhibitors prevent the flea eggs from developing into adult fleas by interfering with the synthesis of chitin. Chitin is the primary substance used to form the arthropod exoskeleton. An arthropod is an animal that has no spinal column or backbone, and an exoskeleton is the hard shell that protects the animal's body and holds it together.

What the collars, pills, powders, shampoos, sprays, and spot-on drugs all have in common is that they are all pesticides. According to veterinarian Michael W. Lemmon, "Popular flea collars often contain powerful nerve gases. They can also kill some pets, and can do damage to children and adults handling the pet wearing the poisonous flea collar." These pesticides are toxic to the fleas but are also toxic to you and your dog. Carbaryl (sevin), a pesticide used in many external flea-control products, adversely affects human sperm, the nervous system, motor function (the ability to move) and the production of melatonin. A study at Western

Michigan University found that chlorphyrifos (Dursban), another pesticide commonly used in external flea-control products, causes birth defects of the brain, ears, eyes, feet, genitalia, heart, nipples, palate, and teeth of humans. I don't care how flea-infested your home is, it's not worth that kind of risk. Even if you're not pregnant or about to be, it should be clear that these pesticides are not good for you.

There is abundant evidence from hundreds, or probably thousands, of studies done worldwide that the type of pesticides being used on pets have the potential to cause your pets, your children, and yourself a long list of problems, including allergies, asthma, blood poisoning, damage to glands (such as the thyroid), disorders of the nerves and the brain, disruption of the reproductive system, heavy-metal toxicity, liver damage, skin problems (such as rashes), such acute symptoms as seizures, vomiting, and a variety of cancers (especially leukemia). That is quite a list. Are these pesticides you would want to bathe in, ingest, spray all over your body, or wear around your neck? I hope not. Please don't expose your dog to them.

The effectiveness of flea collars, pills, powders, shampoos, sprays, and spot-on drugs is also very limited. Flea collars kill the fleas when they go under the collar on the way to the dog's eyes for water. Unless your dog has a severe infestation, the fleas will be getting enough moisture from the skin and won't need to be traveling to your dog's head. The shampoos kill the adult fleas on your dog only until she jumps out of the bathtub and picks up more. You have to keep the sprays, powders, and spot-on drugs on your dog at all times, which is unpleasant and toxic for you, your children, and your dog. The pills only work if the female flea bites your dog. Knowing there are thousands of fleas waiting for your dog to come out and play, the FDA recommends that the pills be used along with external flea control, in effect asking you to expose your dog to pesticides both internally and externally.

There are herbal flea-control products that can be used until my program of nutritional flea control starts to work. I do not *ever* recommend flea collars. Aromatic essential oils from plants, such as rosemary, in doses strong enough to repel fleas on a flea collar, can be irritating to your dog's skin. I don't like putting anything so close to a dog's eyes, ears, mouth, and nose on a constant, twenty-four-hour basis, and since their effectiveness is so limited, why bother?

Herbal flea shampoos will leave a fragrance on your dog that is undesirable to fleas. Look for shampoos containing bergamot, citronella, eucalyptus, geranium, juniper, lavender, pine cedar, or rosemary. You can kill all the fleas on your dog by working the shampoo up into a lather and massaging your dog for about fifteen minutes. Your dog will enjoy the massage; it's great for her skin, and you will drown the fleas. For those of you with bathtubs, here's a tip for avoiding a battle at bath time: Before you put your dog in the bathtub, fill a plastic pitcher full of water that is as warm as you can get it without being hot. Have you ever noticed that your dog doesn't really start fighting until you turn the water on? Preparing the warm water before your dog is in the bathtub avoids the stress of the running water until you can get your dog relaxed. Once you get your dog in the bathtub, start pouring this warm water on her, add shampoo, and give her a good massage. The very warm water causes the dog to become totally relaxed and your only problem will be keeping your dog standing. A woman who had to put on her bathing suit and close the shower curtain to bathe her excitable Golden Retriever tried this and has since retired her bathing suit.

## NATURAL FLEA CONTROL

The way to prevent a severe case of fleas is to catch them early when there are only a few. Be sure to include a quick check for fleas in your monthly health check. Look on the stomach, leg pits, on the back, and near the tail. As you look for fleas, also look for flea feces. Flea feces, also known as flea dirt, are black and each is about the size of a poppy seed. To confirm that it is flea dirt, and not dirt from your backyard, put some on a paper towel and put a few drops of water on it. If it dissolves into red blood it is flea dirt.

If you find fleas on your dog, the first task is to rid your dog and house of the fleas. The second task will be to make your dog undesirable to the fleas, so you will not be constantly battling them. Your best defense is a good offense, so concentrate on prevention.

If you do find some fleas on your dog, bathe and massage her with a natural herbal shampoo, as described above, to be sure all the fleas are dead. If your dog is allergic to the flea saliva and has chewed her skin raw, bring her to your veterinarian. There she will receive a steroid shot, which will stop her from itching and biting, thereby giving the skin a chance to heal and buying some comfortable time for your dog until you can bring her back to health. Oatmeal shampoo is also good to help relieve the itching.

If your dog only has a couple of fleas, you do not have to worry about a house infestation. You will know your house is infested if the fleas are biting you as well as your dog.

If your home is infested with fleas, here is a recipe for getting rid of them. Mix and sprinkle around:

1 1/2 pounds diatomaceous earth

1 1/2 pounds natural borax

1 cup salt

The diatomaceous earth contains tiny particles with sharp spines that puncture the outer covering, or exoskeleton, of the flea. The borax and salt absorb all the moisture from the flea and make the cracks and crevices dry and undesirable. Diatomaceous earth does not kill the eggs or larvae in their cocoon, so it will take anywhere from a few weeks to months of weekly treatments and vacuuming to rid your house of all the adults, larvae, and eggs.

Buy the diatomaceous earth and natural borax at a garden store, not a pool store. The diatomaceous earth at the pool store has a high crystalline silica content that is dangerous to you and your dog. Look for diatoma-ceous earth with a crystalline silica content that is less than three percent. Pour some of the mixture into your vacuum cleaner bag and thoroughly vacuum all carpeting. Clean your dog's bedding, your bedding and cur-tains. Sprinkle the mixture into any cracks and crevices that your dog can't get into, such as behind furniture, closets, or in a spare bedroom. If the infestation is really bad, you can sprinkle it onto your carpeting and upholstery, let it sit for a day or two, and then vacuum it up. Needless to say, it's best if you are elsewhere while the powder sits. These powders aren't poisonous, but it's not wise to breathe any type of powder for hours on end.

If you don't have time for all that, there is a company (*see* Resources in back) that will come to your home and apply a sodium-polyborate powder (similar to the diatomaceous earth, borax, and salt mixture) that rids your home of fleas in two to six weeks and your home is guaranteed to be flea-free for one year.

Next, we want to make your dog undesirable to the fleas with our nutri-tional program. As with all new things you introduce to your dog, intro-duce each facet gradually, carefully watching for any adverse reactions.

Unprocessed brewer's yeast (not nutritional yeast) is readily available at your health food store and some pet stores. It is packed full of B vita-mins, which will enhance your dog's overall health. Vitamin $B_1$ (thia-mine) will repel fleas, mosquitoes, and ticks. As with all supplements here, give half the daily dose with the morning meal and half with the evening meal. Give one tablespoon per day for a small dog (under 20 pounds), two tablespoons a day for a medium dog (20–50 pounds), three tablespoons a day for a large dog (50–100 pounds) and four tablespoons a day for a giant dog (over 100 pounds).

If your dog shows any adverse reactions to brewer's yeast, such as itching or diarrhea, give her a yeast-free B-complex supplement.

Daily dosages for a B-complex supplement for adult dogs:

| | Small Dog | Medium Dog | Large Dog | Giant Dog |
|---|---|---|---|---|
| Thiamin (B$_1$) | 1 mg | 2 mg | 3 mg | 4 mg |
| Riboflavin (B$_2$) | 1 mg | 2 mg | 3 mg | 4 mg |
| Niacin (B$_3$) | 1 mg | 2 mg | 3 mg | 4 mg |
| Pantothenic Acid (B$_5$) | 1 mg | 2 mg | 3 mg | 4 mg |
| Pyridoxine (B$_6$) | 1 mg | 2 mg | 3 mg | 4 mg |
| Cobalamin (B$_{12}$) | 1 mcg | 2 mcg | 3 mcg | 4 mcg |
| Biotin | 1 mcg | 2 mcg | 3 mcg | 4 mcg |
| Folic Acid | 1 mcg | 2 mcg | 3 mcg | 4 mcg |

Garlic, one of my favorite nutrients for humans and pets, is intolerable to fleas. Give your dog a half to two cloves a day, depending on size, using whole fresh cloves, liquid, or powder. Fresh cloves can be irritating to the stomach, so if you use them, be sure to give them with plenty of food. The fleas are repelled by the odor of the garlic, so the odorless garlic that comes in pill form won't work. If you too are repelled by the smell of garlic, don't worry—you won't smell it unless your dog gives you a big kiss, or yawns in your face right after she's eaten. Garlic is also excellent for your dog's overall health. It is antibacterial and antiviral, boosts the immune system, relieves respiratory problems, strengthens the heart, and works as an intestinal cleaner and parasite preventive.

Black-walnut hulls come in capsule form at most health food stores and will repel fleas, ticks, and mosquitoes. Give small and medium dogs (up to 50 pounds) one capsule a day, large dogs (50–100 pounds) two capsules a day and giant dogs (over 100 pounds) three capsules a day. Double the dose if you live in an area, or will be traveling to an area where Lyme disease or heartworm is a threat. Lyme disease is carried by ticks, and heartworm is carried by mosquitoes. If you are not sure whether

Lyme disease or heartworm is a threat, call a local veterinarian or the state's veterinary medical association.

If you are looking for the convenience of one-stop shopping and quicker meal preparation for your dog, there are very tasty supplements that work very well. (*See* Resources in back.)

As an additional precaution against bringing fleas into the house, run a flea comb through your dog before she comes in the house. The flea comb pulls any fleas out of the hair and will also keep your dog's hair mat-free, which is an important part of maintaining your dog's health. Most veterinarians and pet stores carry flea combs.

None of these supplements listed are instant answers to your flea problem. Bloodsucking predators smell the blood before they dive in for a meal, and although these supplements cause the blood to take on an odor the fleas don't like, this will take, on average, four to six weeks. If your dog is in poor health and exposed to a lot of fleas, it will take longer. Keep your focus on the light at the end of the tunnel, which is a flea-free household forever. If your winters are cold and you only have to worry about fleas a few months out of the year, start your dog on flea prevention two months before flea season starts.

# 7

## Understanding Homeopathy

Homeopathic remedies can heal many of your dog's health problems quickly, without invasive methods or drug side effects. You can use homeopathy to treat your dog for a wide variety of common ailments. For more complicated problems, it's best to seek out an experienced homeopathic practitioner. Many homeopaths treat both people and animals, and many holistic veterinarians use at least some homeopathy.

### THE ORIGIN AND DEVELOPMENT OF HOMEOPATHY

Homeopathy is a type of medicine developed in the 1800s by a German scientist named Dr. Samuel Hahnemann. He is particularly known for creating an extensive *Materia Medica* (materials of medicine), a list of homeopathic remedies and the symptoms they could cause or cure. In the late 1800s, veterinary homeopathy was established by Baron von Boenninghausen, and by the early 1900s homeopathic remedies formulated specifically for animals had become available.

Homeopathic remedies may be of animal, mineral, or plant origin and they are prescribed for every conceivable type of illness, including mental and emotional conditions.

## How Homeopathy Works

Dr. Hahnemann discovered that whatever ailment a substance caused in a normal or large dose, it could also cure those symptoms when given in such infinitesimally small doses that not even a molecule of the original substance could be found in it. For example, in normal doses arsenic is a poison, but in homeopathic doses it can be given to treat a wide variety of symptoms, many of which resemble some stage of arsenic poisoning. An internal dose of the plant arnica causes what Dr. Hahnemann describes as ". . . conditions upon the system quite similar to those resulting from injuries, falls, blows, contusions." In homeopathic doses, arnica is one of the most commonly used remedies for treating bruises, muscle soreness, and sprains and strains.

In Dr. Hahnemann's words, "Every medicine which, among the symptoms it can cause in a healthy body, reproduces those most present in a given disease, is capable of curing the disease in the swiftest, most thorough and most enduring fashion." That elaborate description is now commonly known as "like cures like."

One way to describe how homeopathy works is that it helps stimulate the body to marshal its resources to heal very specific symptoms. For that reason, a homeopathic doctor will ask extremely detailed questions about the symptoms of an ailment. For example, is it better or worse at different times of the day, or when it's hot or cold, or with or without pressure? Does the person avoid sunshine or darkness, crave hot or cold drinks, or have great sensitivity to loud noises? All of the hundreds of remedies described in Hahnemann's *Materia Medica* list these types of symptoms, and a good homeopath is familiar with most of them.

In the nearly 200 years since testing homeopathic remedies began, Dr. Hahnemann and his successors have also found that the more they diluted the remedies and then activated them (by shaking), the more potent they became. The remedies are diluted to either a 10-times potency which is noted as $x$ on the label, or 100-times potency which is noted as $C$ on the label. A *1x* on the label of a liquid remedy would mean that 1 drop of the remedy was added to nine drops of alcohol and shaken. It would become *2x* if one drop of the *1x* remedy were added to nine drops of alcohol and shaken. A *C* potency is likewise one drop of the remedy added to 99 drops of alcohol and shaken.

Homeopathic remedies come in sugar pills, alcohol-based tinctures, or in creams for external applications.

## WORKING WITH A HOMEOPATH

The homeopath evaluates the whole animal, so the more information regarding your dog's life that you can provide, the more precise the remedy that is chosen. Successful treatment with homeopathic remedies relies on a detailed description of the illness. Some of the questions you might be asked include:

- When did you first notice the symptoms?
- Have there been any changes in your dog's nature or attitude?
- Were there any special circumstances when it started, such as a change in diet, a death in the family (including another dog), moving, new rugs, or a new lawn-care company?

In the case of diarrhea, vomiting, nasal or anal discharge, for example, specific descriptions are needed. It will be unpleasant, but you need to be able to describe the color and consistency of discharges, along with anything in the liquid, such as blood, food, grass, or objects.

It is important to know if weather, heat, cold, rest, or motion seems to affect the symptoms. Have water intake or appetite increased or decreased? Does your dog have an unusual need for warmth or cold? Have his sleep habits changed?

It can be helpful if you know the mother's history. Did she have any serious illnesses or trauma before or during pregnancy?

Discuss all your thoughts, no matter how insignificant they may seem, and don't be afraid to start your sentence with, "I thought this was really weird . . ." That may be just what your homeopath is looking for.

## USING HOMEOPATHIC REMEDIES

Homeopathic remedies cost very little, they work quickly, and you never have to struggle to get a pill down your dog's throat. For an acute or immediate problem, remedies can be given every hour to two hours depending on symptoms, or they can simply be added to your dog's drinking water.

Homeopathic remedies come either as a very small sugar pill, which can be placed under the lip or on the tongue, a liquid, or a cream. The tablets dissolve in a matter of seconds. If possible, do not give the remedies fifteen minutes before, or one hour after, food.

The dosages for people are also applicable to dogs. Read the label and follow dosage instructions. You can stop using the remedy when the symptoms begin to change, and only resume using it if the symptoms reappear. More is *not* better with homeopathic remedies. In the Resources section at the back of the book, you will find some very useful homeopathic products made specifically for pets, which can narrow your choices from a confusing array of hundreds of possible remedies to a few that are known to work well for specific ailments in dogs.

## HOMEOPATHIC REMEDIES FOR COMMON AILMENTS

There are a wide variety of common dog ailments you can treat with homeopathic remedies. For example, if your dog is playing and suddenly starts limping, it's a pretty good guess he has a bruise or strain. (If he's not putting any weight on it after an hour or so, or is whining or crying, it's obviously broken or dislocated, and you need to take him straight to the vet.) Arnica, rhus tox, and ruta are wonderful homeopathic remedies for bruises, sprains, and strains, and they can be put on externally as a cream or given internally as a liquid or sugar pill.

Here are some remedies to keep in your dog's medicine cabinet (and most likely yours as well) that can be used to treat simple, non-life-threatening symptoms.

## Symptoms

**Aconite** can be used to treat a sudden onset of fever, inflammation, or infection in the initial stages.

**Apis mellifica** is for allergic reactions that cause swelling, such as bee stings or hives. Use with any swelling that is shiny red in appearance and will momentarily indent when you press on it.

**Arnica montana** should always be within arm's reach. Arnica montana is used for bruising, fever, hemorrhage, injuries, muscle soreness, and a high sensitivity to pain to the point where your dog doesn't want to be touched. Recovery from surgery can be accelerated by giving your dog arnica before and after surgery. In addition to being sold in tablet form for internal use, arnica is available in gel, lotion, or ointment for external use on injuries that are not to painful to touch.

**Bryonia** is useful for both constipation and diarrhea.

**Calendula officinalis** works as an antiseptic as well as for relieving pain. You can use calendula cream to treat minor cuts and scrapes, to prevent infection, and promote healing, and you can also use it internally for promoting healing in somewhat more serious wounds.

**Hepar sulphuris** is useful for bacterial infections, hot spots, inflammation, and when there is evidence of pus (thick yellowish-white fluid) with sensitivity and a tendency toward repeated infections.

**Hypericum perforatum** is useful as a cream for treating nerve damage, such as that awful moment when your dog hesitates as you go through the door and gets his tail or toe caught. It is most useful when there is a shooting pain present.

Use **Ledum palustre** internally if the wound had dirt in it or your dog was bitten by a wild animal and tetanus is a concern. Ledum can be used for any type of puncture wound, and before, during, and after surgery.

**Nux vomica** is helpful if your dog has bloating and gas that is worse after eating. The dog that needs nux vomica may also be constipated with ineffective urgings, or have indigestion and irritability. These dogs sometimes also have diarrhea and vomiting.

**Pyrogenium** works well for pets with infected wounds, some abscesses, and septic conditions, especially if accompanied by a high fever.

**Rhus toxicodendron** is useful for aches and pains in the joints, commonly diagnosed as arthritis, rheumatism, or old age, as well as sprains or strains. If damp weather tends to cause lameness in your dog, give rhus toxicodendron preventively whenever the humidity is high. Rhus tox can also be used for rashes.

**Ruta graveolens** is useful for sprains, strains, and the dislocation of a joint. Sprains are a result of torn or stretched ligaments or tendons, while strains are caused by stretched or torn muscles. Sprains and strains are usually the result of sudden, quick movements and cause temporary pain and swelling around a joint. The symptoms of a sprain or strain (lameness, painful swollen joints) will also be seen if there is a broken bone. If the lameness is severe, or if your dog can't put weight on the joint, there may be a broken bone.

**Symphytum** is very useful if your pet has broken a bone and has already had it set. It has often been noted to dramatically speed up bone healing. Three to four doses of this remedy during the the healing process will be sufficient. Please don't over-treat with this remedy.

**Thuja occidentalis** is used to counteract the side effects of vaccinations. If you can't avoid multiple vaccines, give one daily dose for each vaccine. For example, if your dog has had three vaccines, give one dose of thuja for three days. Never vaccinate your dog if he is under stress or is ill.

## Emotional and Behavioral Symptoms

Many dogs and cats have emotional and behavioral problems that, despite all your patience and loving care, you can not seem to cure. Many veterinarians have seen dramatic results with homeopathic remedies. Dr. Stephen Day, author of *The Homeopathic Treatment of Small Animals, Principals and Practice*, treated a Cocker Spaniel that had been sick and depressed since his lifelong companion, a ten-year-old female, had died. Conventional treatment had cured each symptom, only to find another one appearing. Dr. Day treated the dog with ignatia for the sadness and grief. After a few treatments, the dog had a full recovery and is now back to his old self.

Here are some remedies for simple, short-term, emotional and behavioral symptoms that can be treated at home:

**Aconitum napellus** for dogs who love to go for a ride in the car, but may become uneasy when it involves a long car trip to a strange place. To help ease the fear of traveling, give a tablet one hour before traveling and another tablet just before you leave. If your dog becomes nervous again during your trip, give as needed. Aconite can be used anytime your dog has experienced a sudden shock or is anxious and restless.

**Baryta carbonica** is useful for the dog that is overly shy and timid without aggressiveness.

**Chamomilla** is used when there is irritability due to pain. It is used during recovery from an illness, teething, or for a mother that has pain after giving birth. Chamonilla does not affect the source of the pain, it helps alleviate the grumpiness from being in pain. Chamonilla should also be on your shopping list with the bowls, leash, and collar when you adopt a new puppy. It does wonders to stop incessant chewing.

**Cocculus** is good to use if your dog loves the car, boat, plane, or train but suffers from motion sickness.

**Gelsemium** alleviates fear in anticipation of an event or after a fright if your dog is shaky or lethargic. This is for those dogs who start shaking before the weatherman knows a thunderstorm is coming, or who somehow know you are taking them to the veterinarian.

**Ignatia.** The Cocker Spaniel that Dr. Day treated with Ignatia for loss of a loved one is one example of its many uses. Ignatia can also be used when stress appears at the time of the event, rather than in anticipation. Ignatia is also used for such symptoms as separation anxiety, stress at the groomer or vet's office, and nervousness in the show ring.

**Pitric Acid** is useful for male dogs who are overly obsessed with sex, and **Platina Metallicum** is useful for female dogs obsessed with sex.

**Rescue Remedy** is a remedy for extreme situations, such as fear, stress, trauma, and unconsciousness, and should never be far from your dog. There are combination homeopathic remedies made specifically for pets in distress, and there is a Bach flower remedy called Rescue Remedy that is very effective for dogs in distress as well as people. Bach flower remedies are flower essences that assist in physical healing by keeping the emotional state in balance. Rescue Remedy is a combination of five flower remedies: Cherry plum, clematis, impatiens, rock rose, and star of Bethlehem.

These remedies are invaluable in an emergency situation, to buy some time until you can get medical help for your dog. They can help keep your dog from going into shock, which can mean the difference between death and a full recovery. These same remedies can also be used for stressful situations that are not emergencies, such as separation anxiety, show-ring jitters, and thunderstorms.

# 8

## Natural Prevention and Treatment of Common Dog Diseases

These days dogs rarely die from old age; they die prematurely from cancer, heart disease, kidney failure, liver disease, and gastric bloat and torsion. As the lifespan of people has been climbing over the years, the expected lifespan for dogs has been decreasing. While advanced medical technology and better nutrition have made major contributions to peoples' increased lifespan, advances in veterinary medicine have not been accompanied by better nutrition for dogs. A few months ago, I was in an animal hospital that was selling a dry dog food with peanut hulls as one of the ingredients. Clearly conventional veterinarians can't be depended on to educate people about the nutritional needs of their dogs, so dog owners need to educate themselves and bring that knowledge back to their veterinarians.

One way to start educating yourself about how to significantly delay the onset of illnesses that can shorten your dog's life is to follow my nutritional guidelines. They will help you keep your dog at optimal health in all phases of life and life situations.

In this chapter, you will learn about the top five causes of death in dogs, what causes these illnesses, and how you can nutritionally support your dog to prevent them.

## KIDNEY FAILURE

Your dog, just like you, has two kidneys located behind and below the rib cage. These organs are involved in the formation and excretion of urine and the balance of water and electrolytes. Kidneys extract water, mineral salts, toxins, and other waste products from the blood and send it to the bladder for elimination. They then take the purified water, mix in the perfect balance of electrolytes, such as calcium, chloride, phosphorous, potassium, and sodium, and put it back into the bloodstream.

A dog is considered to have kidney failure when 65–75 percent of both kidneys are not functioning. Kidney disease (as compared to kidney failure) is rarely diagnosed in dogs because the loss of kidney function is usually not symptomatic until the dog experiences kidney failure.

Kidney failure can be caused by:

- All infections, including gums, skin, and teeth;
- An imbalance of electrolytes;
- Any kind of trauma, such as an accident;
- Anything that affects the flow of blood, such as high or low blood pressure, and heart disease;
- Dehydration;
- A poor diet;
- A severe illness, such as cancer;
- Toxins, such as pesticides.

Additionally, over time a diet too high in acid, phosphorous, sodium, or protein, or a diet low in potassium, can also cause kidney failure.

Breeds prone to kidney failure are the American Cocker Spaniel, Basenji, Beagle, Brittany Spaniel, Chow Chow, Doberman Pinscher,

German Shepherd, Lhasa Apso, Norwegian Elkhound, Samoyed, and Standard Poodle.

Breeds prone to abnormally developing kidneys, which can lead to kidney failure, are the Doberman Pinscher, Miniature Dachshund, Miniature Schnauzer, Shih Tzu, Soft-Coated Wheaten Terrier, and Standard Dachshund.

Kidney failure is a critical condition which must be immediately treated by a veterinarian. Long-term successful treatment of kidney failure is labor-intensive for you and your veterinarian. A strong commitment of time and money is required to keep a dog healthy after it has had kidney failure. Special meals have to be prepared, along with daily supplements and frequent trips to the veterinarian. Nothing can be taken for granted with a dog that has had kidney failure.

### Mandy's Congenital Kidney Failure Reversed with Intensive Natural Treatments

Mandy, a six-month-old Springer Spaniel, was in total kidney failure and given a few weeks to live by a conventional veterinarian. She came to Dr. Beverly Cappel-King with vomiting, diarrhea, breath that smelled like a mixture of bad fish and ammonia, and was so weak she could barely walk. Dr. King's diagnosis was that Mandy was in kidney failure as a result of renal dysplasia, a congenital kidney disease. (If you have a dog like Mandy who is born with abnormal kidneys, early detection is crucial.)

Dr. King immediately put Mandy on intravenous therapy, which included fluids, vitamin C, and B-complex vitamins. Over the next two weeks, she also used homeopathic remedies, special supplements, an herbal formula called Essiac to help flush out the liver and kidneys, Chinese herbs, and some acupuncture to stimulate the kidneys. She gave Mandy's owners instructions for home-cooked meals and a dandelion and parsley tea, which they gave her two or three times a day to help flush her kidneys. Mandy made a full recovery and has been maintaining her healthy kidneys for a year-and-a-half.

Dr. King carefully monitors Mandy, and the owners are vigilant in keeping her on a strict diet, which includes liver (it is easy to digest), small portions of other meats, cheese, eggs, and lots of grains and vegetables. Mandy drinks a variety of fluids, and dandelion and parsley are added to her food, all to keep her kidneys flushed. When she gets tired of drinking homemade chicken broth, clam broth, and water from tuna fish, they offer her melted ice cream. Aside from being a fluid, when it is melted, ice cream is high in fat, does not have a lot of protein, which Mandy has to stay away from, and is high in carbohydrates and sugar, which give her energy.

Mandy also takes kidney supplements, which contain raw kidney, high doses of the B-complex vitamins, and vitamins A and C, along with a supplement of essential fatty acids.

The key to preventing kidney failure in the first place is to keep your whole dog healthy. If your dog is exposed to a lot of pesticides, the kidneys will be stressed as they work to detoxify the blood. If you have a dog that is prone to kidney problems, be sure to read the chapters on building a strong immune system, and making homemade food.

Symptoms of failing kidneys are diarrhea, dry coat, increased thirst, lack of appetite, lethargy, urinating, vomiting, and breath that smells like ammonia and/or rotten fish.

## HEART DISEASE

The heart is a complex muscle that gives your dog life by pumping nutrient- and oxygen-enriched blood throughout her body. The heart, human and animal, has four chambers called the right atrium and right ventricle, and the left atrium and left ventricle. The right and left chambers are separated by a wall of muscle. Each of the four chambers has a valve that controls the flow of blood into and out of the heart. The valves open, letting blood flow through and then close tightly to force the blood forward and at the same time prevent any backflow of blood.

The most common type of heart disease in dogs is degeneration of the valves, known as congestive heart disease, heart murmur, leaky valve, or valvular heart disease. Other common types of heart disease in dogs are arrhythmias, bacterial infections, cardiomyopathy, and pericardial disease.

## Arrhythmias

An arrhythmia is an irregular heartbeat, usually seen as unusually fast or slow. A heart beating too fast or too slow can result in severe weakness and collapse. You can check your dog's heartbeat by lightly pressing your fingers over your dog's heart, which is located in her chest just below her front legs. The heartbeat can also be felt on the femoral artery, which is inside the back leg at the very top where it meets the body. Depending on her age, size, and activity level, your dog's heart rate can vary tremendously. A large dog that is sleeping will have a heart rate of about 30 beats per minute, while a small, excited dog's heart rate can climb to over 200 beats per minute. Heart rate at a normal activity level can be anywhere from 60–140 beats per minute.

## Bacterial Infections

The most common sources of bacterial infections in dogs are diseased gums or teeth. If your dog has rotting gums or teeth, it is only a matter of time before the infection in her mouth will spread throughout her body, infecting her organs, including the heart. Raw bones once or twice a week are an inexpensive way to keep your dog's gums and teeth healthy and clean.

## Cardiomyopathy

Cardiomyopathy is a deterioration of the heart muscle that leaves the heart unable to efficiently pump blood through the dog's body. Cardiomyopathy is rarely seen in mixed breed dogs. Over 90 percent of recorded cases have occurred in the Boxer, Cocker Spaniel, Doberman

Pinscher, German Shepherd, Golden Retriever, great Dane, Irish Wolfhound, and Saint Bernard.

## Pericardial Disease

Pericardial disease is an accumulation of fluid between the heart and the pericardial sac which surrounds the heart. Pericardial disease is usually caused by a bacterial infection, or cancer of the sac or the outer surface of the heart.

## Congenital and Acquired Heart Disease

Heart disease can either be congenital or acquired. Congenital heart disease occurs when a puppy is born with a defect in the heart, which may or may not be hereditary and is most commonly seen in purebred dogs. If caught early, many types of congenital heart disease can be corrected with surgery.

Acquired heart disease develops over time and can be caused by a slow degeneration of the heart, an infection invading the heart, a weak immune system, stress, or cancer. With proper nutrition and exercise, acquired heart disease can be prevented or the onset delayed.

Most heart problems, acquired or congenital, involve an erratic flow of blood which can be detected simply by an experienced person listening to your dog's heart with a stethoscope. As the heart disease progresses and the heart functions less efficiently, there will be a buildup of fluid in the abdominal cavity, lungs, beneath the skin, and in the space between the lungs and the chest wall. The severity of the buildup of fluids is an indication of how much the heart disease has progressed. Symptoms of heart disease, such as coughing, fainting, intolerance for exercise, and shallow rapid breathing, are primarily caused by the fluid buildup. Early detection is the key to preventing serious heart problems.

Breeds prone to congenital heart disease are the border Terrier, English

Bulldog, Irish Setter, Italian Greyhound, Keeshound, Standard Schnauzer, and Toy Poodle. If you adopt a puppy of any of these breeds, have your veterinarian listen to her heart carefully so you can catch any problems early.

Breeds prone to acquired heart disease are the American Cocker Spaniel, Beagle, Bearded Collie, Boxer, Cavalier King Charles Spaniel, Doberman Pinscher, German Shepherd, German Short-Haired Retriever, Golden Retriever, Great Dane, Irish Wolfhound, Miniature Poodle, Miniature Schnauzer, Newfoundland, Rottweiler, Saint Bernard, Smooth Fox Terrier, Sussex Spaniel, and Wirehaired Fox Terrier.

If heart disease is diagnosed early, it can be treated with adjustments in your dog's exercise routine, a salt-free home-cooked diet, and some heart-healthy supplements. If your dog has advanced heart disease, the most successful treatment involves a combination of conventional and complementary medicine. It is best to do as much as you can naturally before you give drugs to an already sick dog.

### Natural Supplements and Diet Come to Beau's Rescue

A Doberman named Beau is a perfect example of the dramatic effect that natural supplements can have on your dog's health. Beau was in heart failure when he went to a conventional veterinarian. His lungs and abdomen were full of fluid and he couldn't tolerate the slightest exertion. The doctor put him on the drugs digitalis, lasix, and vasotex, which made Beau feel a little better, but he still couldn't go up or down the stairs or romp with his friends. The owner brought Beau to Dr. Beverly Cappel-King and she prescribed the natural supplements CoQ$_{10}$, dimethylglycine (DMG), L-carnitine, taurine, and vitamin E. She also gave the owners instructions for making salt-free home-cooked meals. Beau had a miraculous recovery and is now running up and down the stairs and playing and running with his friends.

It is important to closely monitor a dog with heart disease and work closely with your veterinarian. If the disease has not progressed too far, you can usually treat your dog with natural supplements alone, with great success, which is preferable to expensive drugs that always have negative side effects.

If your dog is on a diuretic drug, such as lasix, to control fluid buildup, she will need extra minerals to replace those flushed out by the diuretics. You can add a liquid mineral supplement from your health food store, or find one that she will chew at your pet store. (*See also* Resources in back.)

To maintain a healthy heart, your dog needs the same things you do:
- A daily vitamin-mineral supplement;
- A slim, trim body;
- A toxin-free environment;
- Clean air and water;
- Daily exercise; and
- Good nutrition.

If you follow my nutritional guidelines for food and a multivitamin-mineral supplement in Part One, you're most of the way towards providing your dog with a good foundation for a healthy heart.

If your dog has heart disease, develops heart disease, or is at high risk for heart disease, here are some nutrients that are essential to the proper functioning of the heart.

### Vitamin B

Low levels of vitamins $B_{12}$, $B_6$, and folic acid will result in dangerously high levels of homocysteine in your dog's blood. Homocysteine is an amino acid that is a waste product of methionine, an amino acid that is important in maintaining your dog's metabolism. High levels of homocysteine will damage your dog's blood vessels, causing her heart to work much harder to pump blood throughout her body. As with all things animate and inanimate, if the heart is forced to continuously work beyond its normal capacity it is going to wear out sooner. The B-complex vitamins work intricately together and are all essential for your dog's health, so I recommend that you supplement with a B-complex rather than individual B vitamins.

## Vitamin C

Vitamin C is an antioxidant that keeps the arteries clear, the blood clean, and reduces blood pressure. If your dog has heart disease, be sure the vitamin C is sodium-free, and check to see if your dog can tolerate additional vitamin C with the bowel-tolerance test. If your dog isn't already receiving the following recommended daily dose, start with this, and if her stools remain normal, gradually increase the dose. If she develops diarrhea or gas, the dose is too high. Back off to the last dose that doesn't cause diarrhea or gas and use that as your daily dose of vitamin C for your dog.

Approximate daily dosages are:

- 500–1,000 mg for small dogs;
- 1,000–2,000 mg for medium and large dogs;
- 2,000–4,000 mg for giant dogs.

## Vitamin E

Dr. Wendell Belfield, author of *How To Have A Healthier Dog*, believes that vitamin E is the key to a healthy heart. Dr. Belfield has found that many symptoms of heart disease, such as coughing and intolerance to exercise, greatly improve with vitamin-E supplementation. If your dog has heart disease, it is important to give her vitamin E every day. Dr. Belfield has also found that dogs whose owners skipped a few days of their vitamin-E supplements had the symptoms of heart disease return very quickly. I have found that the easiest way to remember my dog's supplements is to fit them into my daily routine—he gets his supplements right after each meal.

Vitamin E is also great for the prevention of heart disease. Because of the high incidence of heart disease in dogs, I recommend all dogs receive vitamin E supplements every day in their multivitamin-mineral. If you need to give more, vitamin E is available in liquid or powder form. Recommended daily doses for all dogs are:

- 100 IU for small dogs;
- 200 IU for medium and large dogs;
- 400 IU for giant dogs.

Check to be sure that your daily multivitamin-mineral supplement gives your dog the dosages recommended in Chapter 3.

### Magnesium

Vitamin E is at the top of the list for heart-healthy vitamins and magnesium is at the top of the list for heart-healthy minerals. Magnesium is involved in almost every process in your dog's body, including the absorption of nutrients, the maintenance of blood vessels, and normal heart rhythm and valve function. Proper nutrition is useless if your dog can't properly absorb the nutrients from her food. Without strong, clean blood vessels, your dog's heart won't be able to efficiently pump blood throughout her body. A magnesium deficiency can also be the cause of arrhythmias (irregular heartbeat). Magnesium, like vitamin C, can cause diarrhea if it's not in a chelated form, meaning bound to another substance. Magnesium needs calcium to be properly absorbed, so buy magnesium in combination with calcium in the chelated forms of magnesium citrate, magnesium gluconate, or magnesium glycinate.

Be sure your dog's multivitamin-mineral supplement includes magnesium at the following daily doses:

- 50 mg for small and medium dogs;
- 100 mg for large and giant dogs.

If she has heart disease, try an additional supplement in the same dosage.

## Coenzyme Q10 (CoQ$_{10}$)

Coenzyme Q$_{10}$ is a safe, non-toxic nutrient that is vital to life. Without CoQ$_{10}$, your dog's cells wouldn't work properly. CoQ$_{10}$ strengthens the heart and the immune system, and lowers blood pressure. Stress and illness deplete your dog's body of CoQ$_{10}$, and as she ages she will produce less CoQ$_{10}$. The highest concentrations are in the heart and the liver, which means that if those organs are diseased they will more readily deplete your dog's body of CoQ$_{10}$. CoQ$_{10}$ comes as a powder, in a capsule, or in a gel capsule. I recommend the gel capsules, which are more potent. If your dog has heart disease or is prone to heart disease, give her daily dosages of:

- 10 mg for small and medium dogs;
- 30 mg for large and giant dogs.

The best nutritional sources for CoQ$_{10}$ are beef heart and liver.

## Garlic

Garlic helps keep your dog's blood and blood vessels clean, and helps reduce blockages that may already exist.

Garlic is also proven to lower blood pressure. If you walk into a doctor's office, the first thing they do is take your blood pressure. Nobody takes a dog's blood pressure, however, because there's no quick, easy way to do it, but I'm sure it's an important risk factor for dogs just as it is with people.

Garlic is heart healthy and will also help your dog eliminate any parasites, both internally and externally. One-half to two cloves a day, depending on the size of your dog, will drive away fleas and kill internal worms (it doesn't kill heartworm).

If you give your dog fresh garlic cloves, which I recommend, mix it in with her meal. Fresh garlic can be irritating to an empty stomach. The other forms of garlic, such as powder, flakes, or the aged garlic found in capsules are all beneficial too, but fresh, raw garlic has the most benefit.

## CANCER

Standing in the veterinarian's office with a sick dog and hearing the word *cancer* generates more fear in dog owners than any other diagnosis. People tend to remember those who died of cancer rather than its many survivors. If caught early, cancer doesn't have to be a death sentence. If you don't want to go the conventional route with chemotherapy and radiation (they haven't proven to cure cancer in dogs), holistic veterinarians use natural remedies to bring your dog's body back into balance and give it the strength to fight the cancer.

---

### Holistic Treatments Banish Butter's Jawbone Cancer

A Golden Retriever named Butter is one of the many dogs that holistic veterinarian Dr. Beverly Cappel-King has successfully treated for cancer. Butter had bone cancer of the upper jaw that had invaded the palate and jaw by the left upper canine tooth so severely that the tooth had been moved out of place. The cancerous mass was bigger than a quarter and caused such severe swelling that Butter couldn't chew on that side and her lip didn't close properly.

Dr. King put Butter on shark cartilage, a proanthocyanidin bioflavanoid (such as grapeseed extract or pycnogenal), the herbal formula Essiac, vitamins, homeopathic remedies, and a special diet of homemade food. In six months, Butter went into remission, and over a year later Butter's tumor is gone and she is a healthy, happy dog. Butter's owner reports that the process of caring for Butter and making her meals created an even stronger bond between them. They are inseparable and both of them have found a whole new love for life.

---

Unfortunately, not every dog who gets cancer has the benefit of Dr. Cappel-King's treatment. One in four dogs develop cancer and approximately 50 percent of dogs over ten die from cancer. The most common locations for cancer in dogs are the bones, lymph nodes, mammary glands, mouth, skin, and organs involved in the formation of blood. The most common types of cancerous tumors in dogs are adenocarcinomas (cancer of the glandular tissue), lymphomas (cancer of lymphocytes, which are critical to the immune system), and osteosarcomas (bone cancer).

Some of the symptoms of cancer are:

- An abnormal growth or lump;
- A sore that doesn't heal;
- Difficulty eating, swallowing, urinating, or defecating;
- Lack of appetite or energy;
- Lameness or stiffness.

These are all symptoms that tend to be ignored for a few days or a few months by owners because, they say, "otherwise the dog seems fine." It is important to bring your dog to the veterinarian if you see any changes in health or appearance, especially in older dogs.

Breeds prone to one or two types of cancer are the Beagle, Boxer, Bull Terrier, Collie, Dalmatian, Doberman Pinscher, English Bulldog, German Short-Haired Retriever, Golden Retriever, Great Dane, Greyhound, Keeshond, Labrador Retriever, Miniature and Toy Poodle, Pug, Saint Bernard, Samoyed, standard Schnauzer, Vizsla, Weirmaraner, and Whippet.

Breeds prone to numerous types of cancer are the American Cocker Spaniel, Border Terrier, Boston Terrier, English Springer Spaniel, German Shepherd, and Scottish Terrier.

Exactly how cancer gets out of control is still debatable, but a lot is known about its causes. In very simple terms, cancer occurs when damaged cells multiply out of control and destroy healthy cells in the process. Cancer occurs most often in older dogs, and is caused by a combination of factors, such as exposure to toxins and stress, genetics, and poor diet, that leads over time to an overload of damaged cells and a deterioration of the immune system. A dog with a healthy immune system is least likely to get cancer, and boosting the function of the immune system is the best way to control cancer.

Chemotherapy and radiation may kill a cancer in the short term, but in the long-term the dog's body is severely weakened and its chances of survival are diminished.

The best prevention program for cancer is to give your dog healthy, natural food, a daily vitamin-mineral supplement, clean water, plenty of exercise, a pesticide-free environment, and of course plenty of love. Try to keep the carbohydrates to 20–30 percent of your dog's diet, and remember to factor in any carbohydrate-based cookies. Carbohydrates are broken down into simple sugars, which are then absorbed into the bloodstream. They are your dog's first source of energy. The second source of energy is fat. If your dog has too many carbohydrates, none of the fat in her diet will be burned, and the leftover carbohydrates that aren't used for energy will produce an overabundance of sugar. Not only will the excess sugar pack on the pounds, but sugar is the primary source of energy for cancerous cells. If you have a breed that has a higher risk of cancer, be sure she is getting the following cancer-fighting vitamins and minerals daily. If she is on my daily multivitamin-mineral program, she's already getting what she needs of these nutrients.

## Vitamin C

The pioneer of vitamin C studies and two-time Nobel Prize winner Linus Pauling was adamant in his conviction that vitamin C plays an important role in both the prevention and treatment of cancer. Almost thirty years ago, scientists at the National Cancer Institute found he was right. The pioneer of vitamin C studies and two-time Nobel Prize winner Linus Pauling was adamant in his conviction that vitamin C plays an important role in both the prevention and treatment of cancer. Almost thirty years ago, scientists at the National Cancer Institute found he was right

Vitamin C boosts the immune system, is a powerful antioxidant, and has been proven to reduce the risk of cancer and improve the health of people with cancer. I recommend that all dogs have a vitamin C supplement every day.

The daily dosage for an adult dog is:
- 500–1,000 mg for small dogs;
- 1,000–2,000 mg for medium and large dogs;
- 2,000–4,000 mg for giant dogs.

## Vitamin E

Vitamin E is a powerful antioxidant that protects cells from damage, boosts the immune system, and has proven anticancer effects. Dr. N.H. Lambert, a veterinarian in Ireland, has found that vitamin E stops the growth of tumors in dogs and that, in some cases, the tumors have even become smaller. I recommend that all dogs get a vitamin-E supplement every day. The daily dose is:
- 100 IU for small dogs;
- 200 IU for medium and large dogs;
- 400 IU for giant dogs.

## Beta-Carotene

Beta-carotene is a powerful antioxidant that boosts the immune system and will reduce your dog's risk of cancer. Beta-carotene also has the unique ability to convert to vitamin A, another anticancer nutrient, as the body needs it.

If your dog is prone to cancer, be sure to give her the dark green, orange, and yellow fruits and vegetables, which are rich in beta-carotene.

A beta-carotene supplement should always be given with a vitamin E supplement, as they work together. The recommended dosage for all dogs is 15 IU.

## Selenium

Selenium is a trace mineral that acts as an antioxidant. It stimulates the immune system and has strong anticancer effects. Population studies have shown that people living in areas where the soil is depleted of selenium have higher rates of cancer, while populations living in selenium-rich soil have lower rates of cancer.

Check your dog's multivitamin-mineral supplement to be sure she is getting enough selenium:

- 25 mcg for small dogs;
- 50 mcg for all dogs over 20 pounds.

## LIVER DISEASE

The liver is your dog's largest organ. It is located between the diaphragm and the stomach and does at least 500 different jobs involving detoxification of drugs and toxins, the digestive system, removal of waste from the blood, metabolism, temperature and circulation regulation, and the storage and dispersal of nutrients.

In dogs, liver disease, like kidney disease, doesn't tend to show obvious symptoms until the disease has progressed to a serious condition. A primary symptom of liver disease is jaundice, where the whites of the eyes turn yellow and the urine is tea-colored, but there are many other symptoms, including an accumulation of fluid in the abdomen, bad breath, constipation, diarrhea, ear infections, excessive thirst, lethargy, loss of appetite, red itchy eyes, skin problems, vomiting, and weight loss. Since these symptoms are similar to many other health problems, this makes it difficult to diagnose and treat early. The best way to keep this important organ healthy is to have it checked each year through a simple blood test.

The most common forms of liver disease in dogs are chronic hepatitis, a viral infection that causes inflammation of the liver, and hepatic necrosis, a deterioration of liver cells or tissues. Liver disease can be a symptom of another illness, such as cancer, an infection, an intestinal disorder, or a virus. It can also be caused by drugs, an immune-mediated response, nutrition-absorption problems, nutritional deficiencies, or toxins. In most cases, liver disease results from the cumulative effects of being exposed to a combination of liver stressors over a long period of time.

Breeds prone to liver disease are the Australian Cattle Dog, Bedlington Terrier, Bernese Mountain Dog, Boxer, Cairn Terrier, Chihuahua, Doberman Pinscher, Golden Retriever, Irish Wolfhound, Keeshond, Labrador Retriever, Maltese, Miniature Schnauzer, Pomeranian, Pug, Saint Bernard, Samoyed, Shetland Sheepdog, Shih Tzu, Toy Poodle, West Highland White Terrier, and Yorkshire Terrier.

If treated aggressively and naturally with the help of a good holistic vet, even a seriously diseased liver can be restored back to health.

A Doberman Pinscher named Sam and his owner are proof. Sam has a condition that is common in Dobermans, Bedlington Terriers, and West Highland White Terriers in which the body is unable to metabolize copper. As a result, the copper builds up in the liver, poisoning it, and causing it to fail. Sam was brought to Dr. Beverly Cappel-King with liver failure and was immediately put on oral doses of zinc to remove the copper from the liver. Sam was also taken off food for a couple of days and put on an intravenous solution that contained glucose and an electrolyte solution. Sam's therapy also included the B-vitamins, the herb milk thistle (silymarin), some glandular supplements containing adrenal and liver extracts, along with a copper-free vitamin-mineral supplement. Over the next couple of weeks, Sam's liver returned to its normal size, he put on some weight and the luster in his coat returned. A few months later, he took a turn for the worse and Dr. King found there was a tumor in Sam's liver. She put him back on the regimen that had restored his liver a few months earlier, along with high doses of antioxidants. The antioxidants help flush out the liver, they protect the tiny blood vessels called capillaries from breaking down and bleeding, and they improve circulation. Dr. King also put Sam on a combination of herbs that have proven successful for her in treating cancer. The tumor shrank over a period of four months and Sam became a healthy, happy dog. He lived four more years until he died at the ripe old age of fourteen.

Keeping your dog in optimal health will keep her liver in optimal health. If your dog has to take medications over a long period of time, has had a high exposure to toxins, or has spent her life on a low-quality diet, there is no doubt that her liver has suffered.

## Supplements for Liver Health

Milk thistle and alpha lipoic acid are both nutrients that can help restore the health of the liver.

Milk thistle is a member of the daisy family and contains silymarin, a flavonoid that enhances liver function, stimulates production of new cells, and has antioxidant properties that protect the liver cells from damage. Daily doses for milk thistle are:

- One-half capsule for small dogs;
- 1 capsule for medium and large dogs;
- 2 capsules for giant dogs.

For maintenance of a healthy liver, I recommend milk thistle (silymarin) for a month each year for all dogs over six-years-old.

Alpha lipoic acid is an antioxidant that is a potent promoter of glutathione. Glutathione (GSH), a major antioxidant and detoxifying agent, is found in highest concentrations in the liver, which is the primary organ in charge of detoxifying the body. If your dog has been, or is, on any medications for an extended period of time, I recommend supplementing with alpha lipoic acid at the following daily doses:

- 50 mg for small dogs;
- 100 mg for medium dogs;
- 200 mg for large dogs;
- 300 mg for giant dogs.

Bupleurum is a Chinese herb that helps clean the liver and stimulate regrowth. Give the following doses:

- 300–500 mg twice a day for small and medium dogs;
- 500–800 mg twice a day for large dogs;
- 800–1600 mg twice a day for giant dogs.

Dandelion and yarrow are herbs that help to increase bile flow, flushing fatty buildup in the liver.

A liver glandular or organic liver will act as an overall supplement to help support the liver.

## GASTRIC BLOAT AND TORSION

Gastric bloat and torsion, also know as gastric dilation/volvulus (GDV), is a life-threatening condition that is primarily found in large and giant deep-chested dogs. Gastric bloat is the result of air and gas building up in the dog's stomach causing the stomach to swell and, in most cases, causing the torsion or twisting of the stomach. The swelling and twisting of the stomach cuts off blood circulation to the stomach and other organs by putting pressure on them. If this happens, your dog will go into shock, and all the organs, including the heart, will start to shut down from lack of blood. Another danger with gastric bloat and torsion is that of the stomach rupturing and spilling toxins and bacteria into the bloodstream.

The one common denominator in the many theories about what causes gastric bloat and torsion is diet. A team of researchers from Purdue University found that dogs who eat smaller meals, dogs who are slow eaters, and calm, relaxed dogs have less risk for bloat than stressed dogs who quickly gulp a big meal. The researchers found that, contrary to popular belief, vigorous exercise is not a precipitating factor, but stress is. They also found that dogs described as happy are less likely to experience bloat than dogs described as fearful.

Breeds that are more prone to gastric bloat and torsion are the Basset Hound, Bernese Mountain Dog, Bloodhound (leading cause of death), Borzoi, Bouvier des Flandres, Boxer, Briard, Bullmastiff,

Chinese Shar-Pei, Chow Chow, Doberman Pinscher, English Setter, German Shepherd, Gordon Setter, Great Dane, Greyhound, Irish Setter, Labrador Retriever, mastiff, Russian Wolfhound, Saint Bernard, Scottish Deerhound, Standard Poodle, and Weirmaraner.

Dogs experiencing gastric bloat and torsion will suddenly be panting, whining, and restless. Their breathing will become labored and they will start arching their back. They may also drool and try to vomit, and the stomach will become visibly distended and firm. If you suspect that your dog may be experiencing gastric bloat and/or torsion, it is an emergency situation that needs to be treated immediately.

Here are some guidelines that may reduce the risk of gastric bloat and torsion.

- Feed a high-quality diet.
- Feed several smaller meals rather than one large one.
- Do not feed an excited or stressed dog.
- Do not feed one hour before or after vigorous exercise. (Although the Purdue researchers found this not to be a cause, many breeders do feel it is an important factor.)
- Do not let an excited or stressed dog drink large quantities of water.

# 9

# Natural Remedies for
# Common Ailments

I t's inevitable that your dog will have minor ailments and accidents. Here you will learn what to keep in your medicine cabinet for those occasions. You will also learn what to do in case of trauma and shock, and how to prevent or delay the progression of some of the more common ailments that all dogs, including mixed breeds, are highly prone to.

## ACCIDENTS

For minor accidents, such as cuts, scrapes and burns, clean the wound thoroughly and use a zinc ointment or Dr. Cappel-King's herbal cream on the wound for faster healing. Zinc is important for healthy skin and has antibacterial properties. Dr. Cappel-King's herbal cream is easy to make and is great for pets and people too.

---

### Dr. Beverly Cappel-King's Herbal Cream

1. In a 16-ounce jar, put one cup of fresh St. John's Wort flowers and one cup of fresh marigolds.
2. Fill the jar with olive oil, cover, and put in a dark place for ten days.

> The olive oil should now be bright orange—if not, leave it in the dark until it turns color.
>
> 3. Strain the flowers from the olive oil with a fine strainer or cheesecloth.
> 4. Add 4 ounces of melted beeswax and the liquid from a vitamin E capsule to the mixture.
> 5. Store in a dark place, preferably the medicine cabinet where you keep your other remedies.

Try to keep your dog from licking the wound long enough for the salve to be absorbed into the skin. If you can't keep your dog from licking, wrap the wound and change it twice a day. I have found that the self-sticking bandaging gauze works well and doesn't tear the hair out when you take it off. If that fails, your veterinarian will have a neck brace or cone that will prevent your dog from getting to the wound. If you watch your dog for a while after the wound is bandaged and gently tell him *no* when he starts to lick or chew, that is often enough. Unless he's very uncomfortable, he'll probably leave it alone once he knows what you want from him.

For more serious wounds and burns go to the vet. She or he will be able to clean and bandage the wound in a way that will prevent infection.

If your dog is badly injured and you can keep him from going into shock, it will speed his recovery. A dog that is in a stupor, with glazed eyes, pale gums and tongue, and a slow pulse, is in shock. Make him as comfortable as possible, cover him with a blanket (progressed shock will cause your dog to become cold), talk very calmly to him, tell him what is going on, and get him to a veterinarian as soon as possible. If your dog has a serious accident, immediately give him a homeopathic remedy for trauma and shock or Rescue Remedy (*see* Chapter 8). I keep Rescue Remedy in my house and car for any type of traumatic event, and give it to people and animals. The dosage instructions on the label apply to people and pets. If your dog has been in a serious accident, it would also be very traumatic for you, so remember to take some of the Rescue Remedy yourself.

For serious injuries that will take time to heal, support your dog's body by increasing his multivitamin-mineral supplement by one-third and double his dose of vitamin E. Increase his vitamin C to bowel tolerance and when you change the bandage, reapply the the zinc ointment or herbal cream to the wound.

For pain, you can use a buffered aspirin every eight hours. For dogs less than twenty pounds, use buffered baby aspirin, for medium and large dogs, use one buffered aspirin, and for giant dogs, you can use two buffered aspirin every eight hours. Do *not* use ibuprofen or acetaminophen. For external pain, calendula is a homeopathic ointment that works as an antiseptic, relieves pain, and will promote healing. Use calendula instead of the zinc ointment or herbal cream if your dog is in pain.

If your dog is stressed, use liquid valerian, kava, or a homeopathic remedy to calm him. Valerian and kava are herbal remedies that have a calming effect. Kava is also an effective analgesic, or painkiller. You can find both at your local health food store. They come in liquid form, as tinctures, or in capsules. In the liquid form, they can be put directly on the tongue, and in the capsule form, pull the capsule apart, empty out enough to create the proper dose, and wrap it in food or put it down his throat as you would any other pill. Most tinctures contain alcohol and some dogs detest the taste of alcohol, so a capsule in food would be the easiest and least stressful approach for those dogs. For small dogs, use one quarter the recommended dose, and for medium, large, and giant dogs use half the recommended dose for people. The dosages for homeopathic remedies are the same for people and pets.

If your dog is put on antibiotics, with each meal, be sure to give him a heaping spoonful of plain yogurt (low-fat for overweight dogs) that contains active cultures, or buy a probiotics supplement in the refrigerated section of your health food store.

(For more information, *see* Chapters 3 for vitamins C and E, 4 for zinc, 5 for probiotics and recovering from illness, and 8 for homeopathic remedies and Rescue Remedy.)

## ALLERGIES

The most common symptom of allergies is itchy, red skin and licking the paws. In time the itching will lead to raw skin, which can then become susceptible to a bacterial infection. More severe allergies can cause dogs, like people, to start sneezing and have red, runny eyes, a runny nose, and post-nasal drip. Symptoms of post-nasal drip are wheezing or labored breathing.

Breeds prone to allergies are the Beagle, Bichon Frise, Boston Terrier, Boxer, Chinese Shar-Pei, Dalmatian, German Shepherd, Golden Retriever, Irish Setter, Labrador Retriever, Lhasa Apso, Miniature Schnauzer, Poodle, Pug, Sealyham Terrier, Smooth Fox Terrier, Soft-Coated Wheaten Terrier, West Highland White Terrier, and Wirehaired Fox Terrier. West Highland White Terriers seem to have a particularly high incidence of allergies. When I spoke to Dr. Beverly Cappel-King about dog allergies, she was treating at least 50 Westies for allergies.

Dogs most often have inhalant allergies, which are caused by one or more of a seemingly infinite number of particles in the air, such as air pollution, chemical sprays, cigarette smoke, dust, grasses, molds, pollen, trees, and including household cleaners, pesticides used on your lawn, and so-called air fresheners. Your dog's immune system is designed to clean up the air it breathes. When the particles are inhaled, the immune system goes into action to neutralize any it finds offensive. An allergic reaction occurs when the immune system fails to neutralize the allergen, and overreacts by releasing substances called histamines, which cause inflammation and itching.

It is important to treat allergies as soon as they appear. If left untreated they can slowly weaken the immune system, causing it to overreact to potential allergens. Pretty soon a dog that is allergic to one or two things may become allergic to dozens.

One of the most important steps in ridding your dog of allergies is to get all the chemicals out of his life. Eliminate all air fresheners, chemical cleaners, chemical flea sprays, collars, lawn pesticides, and shampoos. When you clean his bedding, and yours, be sure that your laundry detergent is free of perfumes and dyes, and avoid using fabric softener.

If you have ever had hives or poison ivy, you know how maddening the itching can be, so do all you can to relieve your dog's itching. A bath in a mild shampoo that contains aloe, oatmeal, and/or tea tree oil can help. If the itching continues after the bath, apply tea tree oil, calendula ointment, or witch hazel to the area that's itching. If you have pure tea tree oil, use a 1–1 dilution. For example, mix a tablespoon tea tree oil with a tablespoon water. For hot spots or a bacterial infection, the homeopathic remedies apis mellifica or hepar sulphuris can be helpful. Both are available at your health food store and you can use the instructions for humans. If the wounds are raw or open, clean them with *Betadine* or peroxide, and put on *Baby Gold Bond* powder. The cornstarch in the *Baby Gold Bond* will help dry the sore, and the zinc helps speed healing. If your dog is still itching after all these efforts, don't hesitate to go to your veterinarian for some steroid therapy—just remember that this is a *short-term* solution. Steroids are an immune suppressant and used long-term can cause brittle bones, increased urination, and weight gain.

High-quality chemical-free foods, preferably in the form of home-cooked meals, will alleviate allergies in many dogs. If there are any foods your dog has been eating every day for months, such as his favorite treat, he may have developed an allergy to one or more of the ingredients. A lot of dogs are allergic to beef and dairy products, so experiment with different types of meat, such as fish, lamb, liver, pork, rabbit, or venison, and, if you need to, eliminate all dairy products.

Vitamin C and quercetin have antihistamine properties and are excellent for allergies.

Daily doses for quercetin are:

- 100–150 mg three times daily for small dogs;
- 150–300 mg three times daily for medium and large dogs;
- 500 mg two to three times daily for giant dogs.

For skin allergies, you can try methylsulfonyl methane (MSM), an organic sulfur supplement that softens the cells, making them more permeable and allowing toxins, such as allergens, to be flushed from the cells more efficiently. MSM comes in tablet or powder form and can be found at your health food store. Recommended daily doses are:

- 250 mg for small dogs;
- 500 mg for medium dogs;
- 1,000 mg for large and giant dogs.

If your dog has flea allergies (bites himself raw from one flea bite) and they are seasonal, be sure to start your dog on flea control a month before flea season starts.

(*See* Chapter 6 for more information on allergies. *See also* Chapters 1 on high-quality commercial dog food and home-cooked meals, 3 on vitamin C, 7 on flea allergies and natural flea-control products, and Resources in back.)

## ARTHRITIS

The most common form of arthritis in dogs is osteoarthritis. Osteoarthritis is a degenerative joint disease that attacks the cartilage, which cushions the joints, leading to inflammation and pain. Cartilage does deteriorate simply through the aging process and a lifetime of use, but its deterioration can be accelerated by excessive exercise, free-radical damage, poor nutrition, or a previous injury to the joint.

Arthritis is common in all breeds of dogs, including mixed breeds. Large and giant dogs are more prone to arthritis than medium and small dogs. The added weight of larger dogs causes more wear and tear to their joints.

If your dog gets up very slowly, seems stiff or lame when he walks, is reluctant to climb stairs or jump in the car, he may have arthritis. Those can also be symptoms of other illnesses, such as hip dysplasia or Lyme disease, so have your dog diagnosed by a veterinarian before you treat him.

Vitamin C plays a major role in healthy tissue and will help to protect cartilage from further deterioration. If your dog has arthritis and his daily multivitamin-mineral supplement doesn't meet my recommended daily doses for vitamin C, buy a powder supplement and increase his dose to bowel tolerance. Once or twice a year gradually increase his vitamin C to bowel tolerance, which will tell you if his need for vitamin C has increased. If he is sick or stressed, he will need more vitamin C.

Prostaglandins and leukotrienes are made by your body in response to inflammation. Vitamin E inhibits some prostaglandins, and omega-3 fatty acids suppress the production of leukotriene $B_4$. If your dog has arthritis, you can double the recommended daily dose of vitamin E and selenium, and add some fish rich in omega-3 fatty acids, such as anchovies, salmon, sardines, or tuna, to his diet a few times a week.

Alfalfa and yucca are great anti-inflammatory nutrients. Both are available for pets (*see* Resources in back). Read the label for dosage instructions.

Glucosamine is great for building cartilage and connective tissue back on the joints. Start with 500 mg per day for all sizes of dogs and, if needed, increase to 500 mg twice a day. Glucosamine can take a few months to have its effect, so be patient.

It is also important to feed a high-quality chemical-free food. Home-cooked meals are preferable as long as you avoid foods that can aggravate arthritis, such as vegetables from the nightshade family (eggplant, peppers, potato, tomato), cheese, corn, eggs, oats, processed meats, and wheat.

(*See* Chapters 3 and 4 for more information on vitamins C and E and the mineral selenium.)

## CATARACTS

All breeds of dogs, including mixed breeds, are highly prone to cataracts. They can be congenital (present at birth), juvenile (onset from birth to six years), or, most commonly, age-related (onset after 6 years). To reduce the risk of adopting a purebred dog with congenital or juvenile cataracts, look for a breeder who routinely provides Canine Eye Registration Foundation (CERF) certification. Age-related cataracts is a degenerative disease in older dogs that causes the lens of the eye to become cloudy, preventing light from entering the eye, and causing a partial or total loss of vision. If you look into the eyes of a dog with cataracts, you will see a whitish film in the eye.

A lifestyle free of toxins, a diet of fresh, chemical-free foods, and a multivitamin-mineral supplement containing plenty of antioxidants will prevent or delay the onset of cataracts. For all dogs, I recommend daily supplementation with the antioxidant vitamins C and E to help prevent cataracts.

Orange and yellow fruits and vegetables, such as cantaloupe, carrots (you can shred them), squash, and yams, contain high levels of carotenoids, nutrients that protect the eyes from ultraviolet light and keep blood vessels strong.

Alpha lipoic acid is an antioxidant that has been successfully used to prevent cataracts in laboratory animals, and it improves blood flow through the tiny blood vessels in the eyes. If your dog has been diagnosed with cataracts, use alpha lipoic acid as follows:

- 50 mg for small dogs;
- 100 mg for medium dogs;
- 200 mg for large dogs;
- 300 mg for giant dogs.

It is also important to avoid toxic eye irritants, such as car exhaust, fumes from bug repellents and household cleaners, lawn pesticides, and scented products such as air fresheners, fabric softeners, and laundry detergents. Try not to let your dog ride in the car with his head out the window because the dust and debris will be driven into his eyes at a high rate of speed, causing inflammation and damage to the eyeball. (*See* Chapters 3 and 4 for more information on vitamins and minerals.)

## CONSTIPATION

A healthy, well-exercised dog has at least two bowel movements a day. Walking your dog at about the same time in the morning and the evening will easily produce that.

If your dog goes twenty-four hours without a bowel movement, he is constipated and needs some help. Psyllium seed husk is a natural, gentle form of fiber and bulk that is easy to add to your dog's food because it has no taste. Buy it in pure form at your natural health food store and feed 1 teaspoon for every 20 pounds of your dog's weight. For example, a 10-pound dog would get ½ teaspoon, a 40-pound dog would get 2 teaspoons, and a 60-pound dog would get 3 teaspoons per day. Add at least one cup of water for every teaspoon of psyllium. Too much psyllium, especially without adequate liquid, can cause a serious bowel impaction, so please do not overdose your dog on fiber.

If the psyllium isn't helpful and the constipation continues for more than a couple of days, it's time to seek veterinary help.

## DIARRHEA

If your dog has continuous diarrhea for longer than twenty-four hours, or if there is blood or mucous in the stools, it is important to bring him to your veterinarian to determine the underlying cause.

Occasional short bouts of diarrhea with a known cause can be treated with a diet that is easy to digest and has plenty of liquids. First, place your dog on a fast (no food, plenty of water) for twelve hours, or twenty-four hours for more severe cases. Following the fast, put your dog back on food slowly, feeding three to four small meals for a day or two. After the diarrhea stops, which should be within twelve hours, you can slowly add your dog's regular diet back into the meals. Use cottage cheese or organic liver for protein, add well-cooked brown rice, minced or shredded vegetables, and plenty of homemade chicken or beef broth. Dr. Beverly Cappel-King has had great success feeding the following recipe to dogs with diarrhea.

To boiling water, add:

1 medium white potato

1 medium sweet potato

2-inch piece of turnip

2-inch piece of leek

Cook until soft. Mash together and serve.

If your dog has chronic or frequently recurring bouts of diarrhea and your veterinarian can't find a medical reason, it is most likely a nutritional problem. Very slowly switch him to home-cooked meals, using well-cooked grains and raw meat and vegetables. The home-cooked meals will be easier to digest because the raw food contains live enzymes that help with digestion.

If your dog is on antibiotics, give him probiotics from the refrigerated section of your health food store or a heaping spoonful of plain yogurt with active cultures (low-fat for overweight dogs) with each meal. The active cultures in the yogurt are probiotics and will keep the good intestinal bacteria alive and prevent diarrhea. Give probiotics while your dog is on the antibiotics and continue them for one week after your dog is off the antibiotics.

(*See* Chapters 1 for more information on home-cooked meals and fresh foods, and 5 for details on probiotics.)

## DIGESTIVE PROBLEMS

Digestive problems can be caused by a large number of factors, such as allergies, diabetes, a foreign object in the intestine, kidney disease, or liver disease. Digestive problems can also be caused by food allergies, a lack of digestive enzymes, malabsorption, nutrient deficiencies, or nutrient imbalances. The symptoms of digestive problems are as varied as the causes. They range from constipation, diarrhea, lack of appetite, nausea, or an overabundant appetite, to all types of skin and skeletal problems. Repeated swallowing is a sign of nausea. Nux vomica is a homeopathic remedy used for bloating, indigestion and nausea. Give 1–2 pellets, 3–4 times a day. Pillcuring is a Chinese herb that is also effective for an upset stomach. Give three pills, three times a day. Nux vomica and pillcuring are available at your health food store. If your dog is older and has digestive problems, he probably just needs food that is easier to digest. If your dog has chronic digestive problems, see your veterinarian to rule out any life-threatening conditions.

Once again, feeding home-cooked meals, including raw meat and raw vegetables along with a multivitamin-mineral supplement, will solve the vast majority of digestive problems. For severe digestive problems, stick to foods that are easily digested.

If your dog is still experiencing digestive problems after a couple of months on home-cooked meals, add some digestive enzymes to his food. You can find digestive enzymes at a health food store. Some pet stores may have digestive enzymes for dogs or see Resources in back. If you buy digestive enzymes for people, use one-quarter the recommended dose for small and medium dogs and one-half the recommended dose for large and giant dogs.

(*See* Chapters 1, 3, and 4 for more information on home-cooked meals and fresh foods, vitamins, and minerals.)

## HIP DYSPLASIA

Hip dysplasia is an abnormal development of the hip, which causes the hip joint to rub on the socket, causing pain, inflammation, and a deterioration of the bones. In severe cases, the hip will slip in and out of place.

Symptoms such as abnormal gait, difficulty getting up, and lameness will manifest by the time the dog is two years old.

Breeds prone to hip dysplasia are the Afghan hound, Airedale Terrier, Akita, Alaskan Malamute, American Cocker Spaniel, Bearded Collie, Australian Cattle Dog, Australian Shepherd, Belgian Malinois, Belgian Sheepdog, Bernese Mountain Dog, Bloodhound, Border Collie, Bouvier des Flandres, Briard, Bullmastiff, Chesapeake Bay Retriever, Chinese Shar-Pei, Chow Chow, Clumber Spaniel, Collie, Coonhound, Dalmatian, Dandie Dinmont Terrier, Doberman Pinscher, English Bulldog, English Setter, English Springer Spaniel, Flat-Coated Retriever, German Shepherd, German Short-Haired Retriever, German Wirehaired Pointer, Giant Schnauzer, Golden Retriever, Great Dane, Great Pyrenees, Hungarian Puli, Irish Setter, Irish Wolfhound, Komondor, Kuvasz, Maltese, Neapolitan Mastiff, Newfoundland, Norwegian Elkhound, Old English Sheepdog, Otter Hound, Pointer, Pug, Rhodesian Ridgeback, Rottweiler, Russian Wolfhound, Saint Bernard, Samoyed, Shetland Sheepdog, Siberian Husky, Standard Poodle, Tibetan Mastiff, Vizsla, Weirmaraner, Welsh Springer Spaniel, and Wirehaired Pointing Griffon.

Vitamin C is important in the prevention of hip dysplasia. (*See* Chapter 3 on vitamin C for details.)

Once a dog has hip dysplasia, the best you can do is to make him comfortable and attempt to stop the progression. Regular exercise can help postpone the degeneration of the hip for years, because the muscles will support the hip joint.

To care for a dog with hip dysplasia, see the above instructions for arthritis. Although hip dysplasia and arthritis originate from different causes, the end results of bone deterioration and loss of cartilage in the joints is the same. As with arthritis, the needs of a dog with hip dysplasia are strong bones, strong muscles to support the bones, and maintenance of the fluid and cartilage in the joints.

## SEIZURES

Most dogs that get seizures have a magnesium deficiency and low thyroid (hypothyroidism).

Breeds prone to seizures are the American Cocker Spaniel, Australian Cattle Dog, Basset Hound, Beagle, Belgian Malinois, Belgian Sheepdog, Belgian Tervuren, Bichon Frise, Border Collie, Collie, Dachshund, English Setter, English Springer Spaniel, German Shepherd, Golden Retriever, Greyhound, Irish Setter, Italian Greyhound, Keeshond, Labrador Retriever, Norfolk Terrier, Norwich Terrier, Pembroke Welsh Corgi, Pointer, Poodle, Pug, Saint Bernard, Schnauzer, Standard Manchester Terrier, and Vizsla.

Under the supervision of a veterinarian, you should be able to significantly cut down on seizure medication by adding magnesium supplements to your dog's diet. Dr. Beverly Cappel-King puts all dogs with seizures on magnesium and consistently sees a decrease in the frequency and intensity of their seizures.

Go to bowel tolerance (dog experiences diarrhea or gas) and then cut back until the diarrhea stops. Start with doses of:

- 10 mg for small dogs;
- 20 mg for medium dogs;
- 50 mg for large dogs;
- 75 mg for giant dogs.

A simple blood test can tell you if your dog has hypothyroidism (underactive thyroid) or hyperthyroidism (overactive thyroid). Ask your veterinarian for the natural thyroid supplements, such as Armour (also called desiccated thyroid or USP thyroid), rather than synthetic, and be sure your dog is getting his daily dose of selenium. Selenium works with the thyroid hormone, enabling it to work more efficiently.

(*See* Chapter 4 for more information on magnesium and selenium.)

## SKIN PROBLEMS

Skin problems, such as bald spots, constant scratching, and rashes, are the number one chronic condition in dogs. Dr. Beverly Cappel-King finds that the majority of skin problems are caused by hypothyroidism, or low thyroid. The symptoms of hypothyroidism can range from subtle changes, such as a dry, brittle, sparse coat, lethargy, and weight gain, to the more obvious blackening of the skin in the groin, greasy skin, lick granulomas on the legs, and muscle weakness. A simple blood test can tell you if your dog has thyroid problems.

Ask your veterinarian for the natural, rather than synthetic thyroid, such as Armour (also called desiccated thyroid or USP thyroid) or Thyro Complex, a combination of adrenal, pituitary thyroid, and kelp, and be sure your dog is getting his daily dose of selenium. Selenium works with the thyroid hormone, enabling it to work more efficiently.

Skin problems are sometimes caused by an inability to absorb certain nutrients. Alaskan Malamutes, bull Terriers, and Siberian huskies are prone to a genetic condition in which they have a decreased capacity for zinc absorption from the intestines.

The huskies and Malamutes will be fine if they are put on a zinc supplement. Your veterinarian will give you the proper dosages and will adjust the dosages as your dog ages. Bull Terriers are prone to a more complicated form of this condition and they do not usually respond to zinc supplementation.

Doberman Pinschers, German Shepherds, German Shorthaired Pointers, Great Danes, and Labrador Retrievers are also prone to skin problems from a zinc deficiency. The deficiency can be caused by a zinc-deficient diet, parasites, or by oversupplementation of nutrients that interfere with the absorption of zinc, such as calcium, copper, and iron.

Skin problems can also be caused by a wide range of ailments and pests, such as allergies, autoimmune diseases, bacterial infections, cancer of the skin, fleas, fungal infections, lice, mange, mites, ticks, certain viruses, and yeast infections. To narrow down this long list, see your veterinarian, and start by eliminating the most common problems, keeping in mind that your dog's allergies may be caused by a combination of such things as allergies and hypothyroidism.

If your dog is pest-free and doesn't have a medical reason for the skin problems, such as allergies, hypothyroidism, or a zinc deficiency, then the skin problems are most likely caused by nutritional and/or environmental factors.

Start feeding your dog home-cooked meals, including plenty of fresh, live foods and a multivitamin-mineral supplement every day. Eliminate all the toxins from his life, including all chemicals and pesticides.

Depending on the severity of the problems, within a few months you will have a vibrant, energetic dog with a beautiful shiny coat.

(*See* Chapters 3 and 4 for more information on vitamins and minerals, and earlier in this chapter for information on allergies.)

## GUM AND TOOTH DISEASE

Plaque and tartar buildup leads to tooth decay and gum disease. If left untreated, the bacteria can cause heart-valve and kidney infections. If your dog has bad breath, there's a good chance he has gum disease.

Keep your dog's teeth clean and gums healthy with marrow bones once or twice a week and raw meat at least once a day. The enzymes in raw meat give your dog's teeth a daily cleaning, while the marrow bone will get the tough spots and keep his jaws strong. If the marrow bones at your butcher or local grocery store are too big for your dog, ask the butcher to cut them. Don't be afraid to give a little dog a fairly big bone.

## VOMITING

If, on rare occasions, your dog vomits some yellow bile, a small object (such as a piece of bone or stick), gets carsick, or vomits from stress, you don't need to be overly concerned. Just be sure he has plenty of fresh, clean water close by when it happens. If you know the cause, such as over-eating, you can use Kaopectate or Pepto Bismol to help alleviate the vomiting. Give the children's dose for all sizes of dogs. If your dog won't lap it up, use a baster, large syringe, or for small dogs a large dropper, being careful *not* to go back as far as the throat when you put it in the mouth.

Vomiting blood, foul smelling material, projectile vomiting, and continuous vomiting or retching are serious conditions that need to be treated by a veterinarian.

If your dog vomits occasionally, seems lethargic, and has a dull, dry coat, there is an underlying disorder, possibly diabetes, a liver or kidney problem, or worms, that needs to be treated.

If your dog has frequent bouts of vomiting and your veterinarian doesn't know the cause, it is most likely something in his food and/or environment. Slowly switch your dog to a chemical-free commercial food or home-cooked meals, along with a multivitamin-mineral supplement. If there is no improvement in a month, eliminate all dairy products and try different forms of protein, such as lamb, liver, or venison. It is also important to eliminate all chemicals from your dog's life, including flea and housecleaning products, and lawn applications.

(*See* Chapter 1 for more information on home-cooked meals, fresh foods, and commercial dog food.)

## OVERALL HEALTH

The Lycium Goji berry is a tiny red berry that the people of Central Asia have been using for centuries to maintain a long and healthy life. It is believed that the Goji berry contains an amazing variety of nutrients that support the entire body. It has been shown to contain properties that sustain the blood, bones, digestion, heart, kidneys, liver, muscles, and vision. You can use Goji-berry juice as a daily preventive or to help your dog rebound from health problems. When Dudley, my eleven-year-old Bichon Frise, was attacked by a coyote, I had been giving him Goji each morning for about a year. His veterinarian was amazed at how quickly he recovered from his wounds. I have heard countless other wonderful stories from owners who feel that Goji has greatly enhanced the quality of their dog's life.

Give the following daily dosages of the juice:

- 1 tablespoon for small dogs;
- 2 tablespoons for medium dogs;
- 3 tablespoons for large dogs;
- 4 tablespoons for giant dogs.

Try to find a Goji-berry juice that is 100 percent juice without any additives, including water.

## PART THREE

# THE DOG HIT PARADE

# 10

## Breed–Specific Health Problems

The process of adopting a dog starts with deciding whether you want a mixed-breed dog or a purebred dog. Mixed-breed dogs, also known as mutts, mongrels, and Heinz 57s, are just as the names imply—a mixture of breeds. Mixed-breed dogs have a significantly larger genetic background than purebred dogs, so they are not as prone to health problems as purebred dogs. Purebred dogs are *man-made* dogs whose genetic background is limited by the breed and the specific line within the breed that is created by the breeder. Purebreds can easily become inbred, which exaggerates both positive traits and weaknesses, for example a predisposition to illness.

Mixed-breed dogs, although generally healthier than purebred dogs, have high incidences of the most common health problems. If you have a mixed-breed dog and can connect her to a specific breed, or breeds, such as a German Shepherd mix or a Labrador Retriever and Golden Retriever mix, familiarize yourself with the health problems for the breed(s) your dog is related to.

To add a little confusion to your choice of dogs, the man-made, mixed-breed, or crossbred dog is quickly gaining in popularity and availability. The Cockapoo, a Cocker Spaniel and Poodle mix, was one of the first crossbred dogs to be sold by breeders. Now there are dozens of mixes, most of which are a Poodle blend. There is the Goldendoodle, Labradoodle, Maltipoo, Schnoodle, Shihpoo, and the Puggle, a mix of a Pug and a Beagle. The Poodle has gained popularity for cross breeding because it comes in many sizes and colors and has the reputation of being a hypoallergenic, shed-free dog. People are being sold on the idea of having a dog, such as a Golden Retriever, that is hypoallergenic and doesn't shed, hence the Goldendoodle. Please be aware that there is no such thing as a non- allergenic dog and that all dogs shed. Poodles don't have a dense undercoat, which means they have less hair, therefore less to be allergic to. The hair also sheds and grows differently than most of the dogs we think of as allergenic shedders, such as the Golden Retriever. The hair shed tends to stay under the coat until it is brushed out, and the hair keeps growing until it is cut. Most people keep their Poodle's hair short, which also helps keep the allergens to a minimum, along with the grooming that is required every four to six weeks. The best way to avoid developing an allergy to your dog is to keep her well brushed and in optimal health. If you adopt a crossbred dog, try to avoid those that involve two dogs with a large number of breed-specific health problems in common.

The breed-specific health problems listed below range from very rare to very common. They include birth defects and developmental abnormalities, as well as diseases that develop over the years from a combination of genetic predisposition, poor nutrition, and immune-suppressing agents, such as yearly revaccinations and environmental toxins.

The importance of becoming familiar with your dog's potential health problems begins when you start looking for that very special dog to join your family, and continues into your dog's later years.

If you are interested in a purebred or crossbred puppy, this list gives you the general health information for the breed so you can ask the breeder specific questions about the health of the puppy's ancestors.

One of the keys to successfully treating an illness is early detection. If you are trying to diagnose an illness, bring the list for your breed(s) to your veterinarian. There may be an uncommon health problem specific to your breed that your veterinarian hasn't considered.

This list also gives you the tools for the most successful treatment, which is prevention.

# Purebred Giant—Over 100 Pounds

## ANATOLIAN SHEPHERD (KARABASH)

*Anesthetic sensitivity*: A serious condition in which a dog is very sensitive to anesthesia. In many cases the dog is also sensitive to medications and flea-control products that contain pesticides.

*Eye abnormalities*: The Anatolian Shepherd is prone to a rolling in of the eyelid(s).

*Gastric bloat and torsion*: Gastric bloat is a swelling of the stomach from excess gas and is usually followed by gastric torsion, a twisting of the stomach. Gastric torsion will result in death if not treated immediately.

*Hip dysplasia*: An abnormal development of the hip joint(s).

*Hypothyroidism*: A common disease of thyroid-hormone deficiency. The thyroid regulates your dog's metabolism. A large number of skin problems in dogs are caused by thyroid disease.

## BORZOI (RUSSIAN WOLFHOUND)

*Blood-clotting disorders*: The Borzoi is prone to a blood-clotting disorder due to a deficiency of coagulation factor I.

*Calcinosis*: Hard lumps of calcium salt deposits in the skin.

*Cataract*: In older dogs the lens of the eye becomes cloudy, causing a partial or total loss of vision.

*Gastric bloat and torsion*: Gastric bloat is a swelling of the stomach from excess gas and is usually followed by gastric torsion, a twisting of the stomach. Gastric torsion will result in death if not treated immediately.

*Hip dysplasia*: An abnormal development of the hip joint(s).

*Hygroma:* A thick-walled, fluid-filled sac usually found on the elbows.

*Progressive retinal atrophy* **(PRA):** A deterioration of the retina, which can cause blindness.

*Teeth abnormalities:* The number, placement, or development of the teeth is not normal.

*Thyroid disease:* The Borzoi is prone to thyroiditis and hypothyroidism. Thyroiditis is an inflammation of the thyroid, which very often leads to hypothyroidism. Hypothyroidism is a common disease of thyroid-hormone deficiency. The thyroid regulates your dog's metabolism. A large number of skin problems in dogs are caused by thyroid disease.

*Von Willebrand's disease:* Abnormal blood-clotting defect involving both platelet and coagulation function (factor VIII).

## BULLMASTIFF

*Cleft palate:* A birth defect in which the roof of the mouth doesn't grow properly, leaving a hole from the roof of the mouth into the nose.

*Eye abnormalities:* The Bullmastiff is prone to abnormally growing eyelashes, a rolling in of the eyelid(s), a protruding of the third eyelid(s), malformed retina, and a developmental condition in which the iris, which regulates the amount of light entering the eye, doesn't form properly.

*Gastric bloat and torsion:* Gastric bloat is a swelling of the stomach from excess gas and is usually followed by gastric torsion, a twisting of the stomach. Gastric torsion will result in death if not treated immediately.

*Glaucoma:* Pressure on the retina from excess fluid in the eyeball, which causes partial or total loss of vision.

*Hip dysplasia:* An abnormal development of the hip joint(s).

*Hypothyroidism:* A common disease of thyroid-hormone deficiency. The thyroid regulates your dog's metabolism. A large number of skin problems in dogs are caused by thyroid disease.

*Neck vertebrae malformation:* An abnormal development of the vertebrae in the neck that causes nerve damage. Some dogs walk with a pronounced flexion of the knee, similar to a high-stepping horse.

*Osteochondritis dissecans*: Inflammation of the cartilage in the joints. A form of arthritis.

*Osteochondrosis*: An abnormal development of joint cartilage. Most commonly found in the shoulder, elbow, and knee.

*Progressive retinal atrophy* (**PRA**): A slow deterioration of the retina, leading to blindness.

*Teeth abnormalities*: The number, placement, or development of the teeth is not normal.

*Vaginal hyperplasia*: An increase in the number of cells in the tissues of the vagina, possibly indicating a precancerous condition.

## GREAT DANE

*Acne*: Pimples and blackheads on the chin and lips of young dogs.

*Ataxia*: A progressive loss of coordination.

*Bone disease*: Diseases of the bone caused by a metabolic dysfunction.

*Calcinosis*: Hard lumps of calcium salt deposits in the skin.

*Cancer*: The Great Dane is prone to bone cancer.

*Cataract*: In older dogs the lens of the eye becomes cloudy, causing a partial or total loss of vision.

*Cerebellar hypoplasia*: Underdevelopment of a part of the brain called the cerebellum. The cerebellum gives your dog balance, coordination, and posture.

*Cervical spondylosis*: A degenerative disease of the neck vertebrae.

*Deafness*: A partial or total loss of hearing.

*Degenerative myelopathy*: A progressive deterioration of the spinal cord.

*Demodectic mange*: A skin disease in which canine mites are living in the skin, causing itching, loss of hair, and skin infections. Usually found on the face and front legs.

*Dermoid cyst*: A skin-like growth usually seen on the back.

*Eye abnormalities*: The great Dane is prone to abnormally growing eyelashes, rolling in or out of the eyelid(s), abnormal growing retina(s), and a protruding third eyelid(s).

**Gastric bloat and torsion:** Gastric bloat is a swelling of the stomach from excess gas and is usually followed by gastric torsion, a twisting of the stomach. Gastric torsion will result in death if not treated immediately.

**Glaucoma:** Pressure on the retina from excess fluid in the eyeball, which causes partial or total loss of vision.

**Heart disease:** Developmental abnormality of the mitral valve, and cardiomyopathy, or weakened heart muscles.

**Hemeralopia:** A disorder of the retina causing blindness during the day with partial sight in dim light.

**Hip dysplasia:** An abnormal development of the hip joint(s).

**Histiocytoma:** A tumor that forms beneath the skin.

**Hygroma:** A thick-walled, fluid-filled sac usually found on the elbows.

**Hypertrophic osteodystrophy:** A painful inflammation of the bones along with development of bony growths, found in fast-growing giant breeds.

**Lick granuloma (acral lick dermatitis):** Inflammation or infection of the skin from excessive licking. Usually found on the leg or paw.

**Muscular dystrophy:** A progressive muscle disorder, which causes a wasting of the muscles. It is an inherited disease with symptoms of difficulty eating and swallowing, slow growth, and weakness.

**Neck vertebrae malformation:** An abnormal development of the vertebrae in the neck that causes nerve damage. Some dogs walk with a pronounced flexion of the knee, similar to a high-stepping horse.

**Osteochondritis dissecans:** Inflammation of the cartilage in the joints. A form of arthritis.

**Osteochondrosis:** An abnormal development of joint cartilage. Most commonly found in the shoulder, elbow, and knee.

**Progressive retinal atrophy (PRA):** A slow deterioration of the retina, leading to blindness.

**Thyroid disease:** The great Dane is prone to thyroiditis, lymphocytic thyroiditis, and hypothyroidism. Thyroiditis and lymphocytic thyroiditis are autoimmune diseases that lead to hypothyroidism, a common disease of thyroid-hormone deficiency. The thyroid regulates your dog's metabolism. A large number of skin problems in dogs are caused by thyroid disease.

*Von Willebrand's disease*: Abnormal blood-clotting defect involving both platelet and coagulation function (factor VIII).

## GREAT PYRENEES

*Blood-clotting disorders*: The Great Pyrenees is prone to blood-clotting disorders due to a deficiency of coagulation factors IX or XI.

*Cataract*: In older dogs the lens of the eye becomes cloudy, causing a partial or total loss of vision.

*Deafness*: A partial or total loss of hearing.

*Demodectic mange*: A skin disease in which canine mites are living in the skin, causing itching, loss of hair, and skin infections. Usually found on the face and front legs.

*Eye abnormalities*: The Great Pyrenees is prone to a rolling out or in of the eyelid(s).

*Hip dysplasia*: An abnormal development of the hip joint(s).

*Hot spots*: A bacterial skin infection that progresses into severe inflammation from excessive licking and chewing.

*Hypothyroidism*: A common disease of thyroid-hormone deficiency. The thyroid regulates your dog's metabolism. A large number of skin problems in dogs are caused by thyroid disease.

*Osteochondritis dissecans*: Inflammation of the cartilage in the joints. A form of arthritis.

*Osteochondrosis*: An abnormal development of joint cartilage. Most commonly found in the shoulder, elbow, and knee.

*Progressive retinal atrophy (PRA)*: A slow deterioration of the retina, leading to blindness.

*Swimmer puppies*: A developmental condition caused by a weakness of the muscles that puppies use to pull their legs together. Newborns are unable to put their feet under them to walk.

*Teeth abnormalities*: The number, placement, or development of the teeth is not normal.

*Thrombocytopenia*: An abnormal decrease in the number of blood platelets. Blood platelets play a role in blood clotting. Symptoms are tiny hemorrhages in the skin and mucous membranes.

*Vaginal hyperplasia*: An increase in the number of cells in the tissues of the vagina, possibly indicating a precancerous condition.

## GREATER SWISS MOUNTAIN DOG

*Osteochondritis dissecans*: Inflammation of the cartilage in the joints. A form of arthritis.

*Osteochondrosis*: An abnormal development of joint cartilage. Most commonly found in the shoulder, elbow, and knee.

*Platelet disorders*: The Greater Swiss Mountain Dog is prone to functional abnormalities and an abnormal decrease in the number of blood platelets. Blood platelets play a role in blood clotting.

## IRISH WOLFHOUND

*Cataract*: In older dogs the lens of the eye becomes cloudy, causing a partial or total loss of vision.

*Eye abnormalities*: The Irish Wolfhound is prone to a rolling in of the eyelid(s).

*Heart disease*: Cardiomyopathy, or weakened heart muscles.

*Hip dysplasia*: An abnormal development of the hip joint(s).

*Hygroma*: A thick-walled, fluid-filled sac usually found on the elbows.

*Hypertrophic osteodystrophy*: A painful inflammation of the bones along with development of bony growths, found in fast-growing giant breeds.

*Hypothyroidism*: A common disease of thyroid-hormone deficiency. The thyroid regulates your dog's metabolism. A large number of skin problems in dogs are caused by thyroid disease.

*Liver abnormalities*: The Irish Wolfhound is prone to an abnormal formation of blood vessels in the liver.

*Osteochondritis dissecans*: Inflammation of the cartilage in the joints. A form of arthritis.

*Osteochondrosis*: An abnormal development of joint cartilage. Most commonly found in the shoulder, elbow, and knee.

*Von Willebrand's disease*: Abnormal blood-clotting defect involving both platelet and coagulation function (factor VIII).

## KOMONDOR

*Cataract*: In older dogs the lens of the eye becomes cloudy, causing a partial or total loss of vision.

*Eye abnormalities*: The Komondor is prone to a rolling in of the eyelid(s).

*Hip dysplasia*: An abnormal development of the hip joint(s).

*Hypothyroidism*: A common disease of thyroid-hormone deficiency. The thyroid regulates your dog's metabolism. A large number of skin problems in dogs are caused by thyroid disease.

*Skin disease*: The Komondor is prone to all types of skin disease.

## KUVASZ

*Cataract*: In older dogs the lens of the eye becomes cloudy, causing a partial or total loss of vision.

*Eye abnormalities*: The Kuvasz is prone to a rolling in of the eyelid(s).

*Eosinophilic panosteitis*: An inflammatory bone disease found in fast-growing puppies, which is accompanied by increased eosinophils, a type of white blood cell.

*Hip dysplasia*: An abnormal development of the hip joint(s).

*Hypertrophic osteodystrophy*: A painful inflammation of the bones along with development of bony growths, found in fast-growing giant breeds.

*Hypothyroidism*: A common disease of thyroid-hormone deficiency. The thyroid regulates your dog's metabolism. A large number of skin problems in dogs are caused by thyroid disease.

*Osteochondritis dissecans*: Inflammation of the cartilage in the joints. A form of arthritis.

*Osteochondrosis*: An abnormal development of joint cartilage. Most commonly found in the shoulder, elbow, and knee.

*Von Willebrand's disease*: Abnormal blood-clotting defect involving both platelet and coagulation function (factor VIII).

## MASTIFF

*Corneal dystrophy*: An inherited degenerative condition in which the cornea of the eye becomes cloudy or opaque.

*Eye abnormalities*: The Mastiff is prone to a rolling out or in of the eyelid(s) and abnormal development of the retina(s).

*Gastric bloat and torsion*: Gastric bloat is a swelling of the stomach from excess gas and is usually followed by gastric torsion, a twisting of the stomach. Gastric torsion will result in death if not treated immediately.

*Hypothyroidism*: A common disease of thyroid-hormone deficiency. The thyroid regulates your dog's metabolism. A large number of skin problems in dogs are caused by thyroid disease.

*Osteochondritis dissecans*: Inflammation of the cartilage in the joints. A form of arthritis.

*Osteochondrosis*: An abnormal development of joint cartilage. Most commonly found in the shoulder, elbow, and knee.

*Progressive retinal atrophy (PRA)*: A slow deterioration of the retina, leading to blindness.

*Vaginal hyperplasia*: An increase in the number of cells in the tissues of the vagina, possibly indicating a precancerous condition.

## NEAPOLITAN MASTIFF

*Cataract*: In older dogs the lens of the eye becomes cloudy, causing a partial or total loss of vision.

*Dermoid cyst*: A skin-like growth usually seen on the back.

*Eye abnormalities*: The Neapolitan Mastiff is prone to a rolling out or in of the eyelid(s).

*Hip dysplasia*: An abnormal development of the hip joint(s).

*Hypertrophic osteodystrophy*: A painful inflammation of the bones along with development of bony growths, found in fast-growing giant breeds.

*Hypothyroidism*: A common disease of thyroid-hormone deficiency. The thyroid regulates your dog's metabolism. A large number of skin problems in dogs are caused by thyroid disease.

*Osteochondritis dissecans*: Inflammation of the cartilage in the joints. A form of arthritis.

*Progressive retinal atrophy (PRA)*: A slow deterioration of the retina, leading to blindness.

## NEWFOUNDLAND

*Cataract*: In older dogs the lens of the eye becomes cloudy, causing a partial or total loss of vision.

*Dermoid cyst*: A skin-like growth usually seen on the back.

*Elbow dysplasia*: An abnormal development of the elbow joint(s).

*Eye abnormalities*: The Newfoundland is prone to a rolling out or in of the eyelid(s) and a protruding third eyelid(s).

*Heart disease*: Cardiomyopathy, or weakened heart muscles, developmental abnormalities of the heart, and valve disease.

*Hip dysplasia*: An abnormal development of the hip joint(s).

*Immune-mediated hemolytic anemia (IMHA)*: Anemia resulting from an immune system mediated destruction of the red blood cells.

*Osteochondritis dissecans*: Inflammation of the cartilage in the joints. A form of arthritis.

*Osteochondrosis*: An abnormal development of joint cartilage. Most commonly found in the shoulder, elbow, and knee.

*Thrombocytopenia*: An abnormal decrease in the number of blood platelets. Blood platelets play a role in blood clotting. Symptoms are tiny hemorrhages in the skin and mucous membranes.

*Thyroid disease*: The Newfoundland is prone to thyroiditis, lymphocytic thyroiditis, and hypothyroidism. Thyroiditis and lymphocytic thyroiditis are autoimmune diseases that lead to hypothyroidism, a common disease of thyroid-hormone deficiency. The thyroid regulates your dog's metabolism. A large number of skin problems in dogs are caused by thyroid disease.

**Von Willebrand's disease:** Abnormal blood-clotting defect involving both platelet and coagulation function (factor VIII).

## ROTTWEILER

**Addison's disease:** A disease in which the adrenal glands secrete an insufficient amount of cortisone, a steroid hormone.

**Cataract:** In older dogs the lens of the eye becomes cloudy, causing a partial or total loss of vision.

**Diabetes mellitus:** A disease caused by an insufficient production or use of insulin.

**Elbow dysplasia:** An abnormal development of the elbow joint(s).

**Eosinophilic panosteitis:** An inflammatory bone disease found in fast-growing puppies, which is accompanied by increased eosinophils, a type of white blood cell.

**Eye abnormalities:** The Rottweiler is prone to abnormally growing eyelashes, abnormal development of the retina(s), and a rolling in or out of the eyelid(s).

**Heart disease:** A constriction of the valve between the heart and the aorta.

**Hip dysplasia:** An abnormal development of the hip joint(s).

**Immune-mediated hemolytic anemia (IMHA):** Anemia resulting from an immune system mediated destruction of the red blood cells.

**Malabsorption:** A condition in which the small intestine doesn't absorb nutrients properly.

**Pigmentation abnormalities:** A lack of color in the skin.

**Progressive retinal atrophy (PRA):** A slow deterioration of the retina, leading to blindness.

**Thrombocytopenia:** An abnormal decrease in the number of blood platelets. Blood platelets play a role in blood clotting. Symptoms are tiny hemorrhages in the skin and mucous membranes.

*Thyroid disease:* The Rottweiler is prone to thyroiditis, lymphocytic thyroid-itis, and hypothyroidism. Thyroiditis and lymphocytic thyroiditis are auto-immune diseases that lead to hypothyroidism, a common disease of thyroid-hormone deficiency. The thyroid regulates your dog's metabolism. A large number of skin problems in dogs are caused by thyroid disease.

*Von Willebrand's disease:* Abnormal blood-clotting defect involving both platelet and coagulation function (factor VIII).

## SAINT BERNARD

*Blood-clotting disorders:* The Saint Bernard is prone to blood-clotting disor-ders due to a deficiency of coagulation factors I, VIII, or IX.

*Bone disease:* Diseases of the bone caused by a metabolic dysfunction.

*Cancer:* The Saint Bernard is prone to bone cancer.

*Cataract:* In older dogs the lens of the eye becomes cloudy, causing a partial or total loss of vision.

*Dermoid cyst:* A skin-like growth usually seen on the back.

*Ehler's-Danlos syndrome:* A connective-tissue disease in which the skin is very fragile and is easily cut or bruised.

*Epilepsy:* A brain disorder in which the dog experiences seizures (convulsions).

*Eye abnormalities:* The Saint Bernard is prone to a rolling in or out of the eyelid(s), abnormally growing eyelashes, and a protruding third eyelid(s).

*Gastric bloat and torsion:* Gastric bloat is a swelling of the stomach from excess gas and is usually followed by gastric torsion, a twisting of the stomach. Gastric torsion will result in death if not treated immediately.

*Heart disease:* The Saint Bernard is prone to cardiomyopathy, or weakened heart muscles.

*Hip dysplasia:* An abnormal development of the hip joint(s).

*Hypothyroidism:* A common disease of thyroid-hormone deficiency. The thyroid regulates your dog's metabolism. A large number of skin problems in dogs are caused by thyroid disease.

*Liver abnormalities:* The Saint Bernard is prone to an abnormal formation of blood vessels in the liver.

*Osteochondritis dissecans*: Inflammation of the cartilage in the joints. A form of arthritis.

*Osteochondrosis*: An abnormal development of joint cartilage. Most commonly found in the shoulder, elbow, and knee.

*Pigmentation abnormalities*: A lack of color in the skin.

*Vaginal hyperplasia*: An increase in the number of cells in the tissues of the vagina, possibly indicating a precancerous condition.

*Von Willebrand's disease*: Abnormal blood-clotting defect involving both platelet and coagulation function (factor VIII).

## SCOTTISH DEERHOUND

*Cataract*: In older dogs the lens of the eye becomes cloudy, causing a partial or total loss of vision.

*Eosinophilic panosteitis*: An inflammatory bone disease found in fast-growing puppies, which is accompanied by increased eosinophils, a type of white blood cell.

*Gastric bloat and torsion*: Gastric bloat is a swelling of the stomach from excess gas and is usually followed by gastric torsion, a twisting of the stomach. Gastric torsion will result in death if not treated immediately.

*Hypertrophic osteodystrophy*: A painful inflammation of the bones along with development of bony growths, found in fast-growing giant breeds.

*Hypothyroidism*: A common disease of thyroid-hormone deficiency. The thyroid regulates your dog's metabolism. A large number of skin problems in dogs are caused by thyroid disease.

*Osteochondritis dissecans*: Inflammation of cartilage in the joints. A form of arthritis.

*Osteochondrosis*: An abnormal development of joint cartilage. Most commonly found in the shoulder, elbow, and knee.

## TIBETAN MASTIFF

*Elbow dysplasia*: An abnormal development of the elbow joint(s).

*Hip dysplasia*: An abnormal development of the hip joint(s).

*Hypertrophic osteodystrophy*: A painful inflammation of the bones along with development of bony growths, found in fast-growing giant breeds.

*Osteochondritis dissecans*: Inflammation of the cartilage in the joints. A form of arthritis.

*Thyroid disease*: The Tibetan Mastiff is prone to thyroiditis, lymphocytic thyroiditis, and hypothyroidism. Thyroiditis and lymphocytic thyroiditis are autoimmune diseases that lead to hypothyroidism, a common disease of thyroid-hormone deficiency. The thyroid regulates your dog's metabolism. A large number of skin problems in dogs are caused by thyroid disease.

*Von Willebrand's disease*: Abnormal blood-clotting defect involving both platelet and coagulation function (factor VIII).

# Purebred Large—50-100 Pounds

## AFGHAN HOUND

*Anesthetic sensitivity*: A serious condition in which a dog is very sensitive to anesthesia. In many cases the dog is also sensitive to medications and flea-control products that contain pesticides.

*Blood-clotting disorders*: The Afghan Hound is prone to a blood-clotting disorder due to a deficiency of coagulation factor VIII.

*Cataract*: In older dogs the lens of the eye becomes cloudy, causing a partial or total loss of vision.

*Corneal dystrophy*: An inherited degenerative condition in which the cornea of the eye becomes cloudy or opaque.

*Degenerative myelopathy*: A progressive deterioration of the spinal cord.

*Elbow dysplasia*: An abnormal development of the elbow joint(s).

*Eye abnormalities*: The Afghan Hound is prone to a protruding third eyelid(s) and retinal dysplasia, an abnormal development of the retina(s).

*Glaucoma*: Pressure on the retina from excess fluid in the eyeball, which causes partial or total loss of vision.

*Hip dysplasia*: An abnormal development of the hip joint(s).

*Hypothyroidism*: A common disease of thyroid-hormone deficiency. The thyroid regulates your dog's metabolism. A large number of skin problems in dogs are caused by thyroid disease.

*Narcolepsy*: A neurological disorder in which the dog suddenly falls asleep.

*Osteochondritis dissecans*: Inflammation of the cartilage in the joints. A form of arthritis.

*Osteochondrosis*: An abnormal development of joint cartilage. Most commonly found in the shoulder, elbow, and knee.

*Pemphigus erythematosus*: An autoimmune skin disease.

*Progressive retinal atrophy (PRA)*: A slow deterioration of the retina, leading to blindness.

*Vertebra malformation*: A condition in which only half the vertebra is formed.

*Von Willebrand's disease*: Abnormal blood-clotting defect involving both platelet and coagulation function (factor VIII).

## AIREDALE TERRIER

*Antibody (type IgA) deficiency*: A deficiency in the production of the type IgA antibody, causing a weakened immune system.

*Blood-clotting disorders*: The Airedale Terrier is prone to a blood-clotting disorder due to a deficiency of coagulation factor IX.

*Cerebellar hypoplasia*: Underdevelopment of a part of the brain called the cerebellum. The cerebellum gives your dog balance, coordination, and posture.

*Corneal dystrophy*: An inherited degenerative condition in which the cornea of the eye becomes cloudy or opaque.

*Eye abnormalities*: The Airedale Terrier is prone to abnormally growing eyelashes, abnormal development of the retina(s), and a rolling in of the eyelid(s).

*Growth-hormone-responsive dermatosis*: Skin disorder caused by a deficiency of growth hormones.

*Hip dysplasia*: An abnormal development of the hip joint(s).

*Hot spots*: A bacterial skin infection that progresses into severe inflammation from excessive licking and chewing.

*Hypothyroidism*: A common disease of thyroid-hormone deficiency. The thyroid regulates your dog's metabolism. A large number of skin problems in dogs are caused by thyroid disease.

*Lick granuloma (acral lick dermatitis)*: Inflammation or infection of the skin from excessive licking. Usually found on the leg or paw.

*Narcolepsy*: A neurological disorder in which the dog suddenly falls asleep.

*Pannus*: Progressive immune-mediated disease in which there is a growth of tissue over the cornea, causing inflammation and possible blindness.

*Progressive retinal atrophy (PRA)*: A slow deterioration of the retina, leading to blindness.

*Umbilical hernia*: A tear in the muscle wall of the stomach where the umbilical cord was.

*Von Willebrand's disease*: Abnormal blood-clotting defect involving both platelet and coagulation function (factor VIII).

## AKITA

*Cataract*: In older dogs the lens of the eye becomes cloudy, causing a partial or total loss of vision.

*Corneal dystrophy*: An inherited degenerative condition in which the cornea of the eye becomes cloudy or opaque.

*Cushing's disease (hyperadrenocorticism)*: A condition in which the adrenal glands secrete too much cortisol. Cortisol is a steroid hormone which regulates carbohydrate, fat, and protein metabolism.

*Eye abnormalities*: The Akita is prone to a rolling in of the eyelid(s) and a protruding third eyelid(s).

*Glaucoma*: Pressure on the retina from excess fluid in the eyeball, which causes partial or total loss of vision.

*Glycogen storage disease*: An inability to store and use the complex carbohydrate glycogen, which is primarily stored in the liver and muscle.

*Hip dysplasia*: An abnormal development of the hip joint(s).

*Hot spots*: A bacterial skin infection that progresses into severe inflammation from excessive licking and chewing.

*Immune-mediated hemolytic anemia (IMHA)*: Anemia resulting from an immune system mediated destruction of the red blood cells.

*Malabsorption*: A condition in which the small intestine does not absorb nutrients properly.

*Osteochondritis dissecans*: Inflammation of the cartilage in the joints. A form of arthritis.

*Osteochondrosis*: An abnormal development of joint cartilage. Most commonly found in the shoulder, elbow, and knee.

*Pemphigus foliaceous*: An autoimmune skin disease.

*Progressive retinal atrophy (PRA)*: A slow deterioration of the retina, leading to blindness.

*Thyroid disease*: The Akita is prone to thyroiditis, lymphocytic thyroiditis, and hypothyroidism. Thyroiditis and lymphocytic thyroiditis are autoimmune diseases that lead to hypothyroidism, a common disease of thyroid-hormone deficiency. The thyroid regulates your dog's metabolism. A large number of skin problems in dogs are caused by thyroid disease.

*Umbilical hernia*: A tear in the muscle wall of the stomach where the umbilical cord was.

*Von Willebrand's disease*: Abnormal blood-clotting defect involving both platelet and coagulation function (factor VIII).

## ALASKAN MALAMUTE

*Anemia with chondrodysplasia*: An abnormal development of cartilage and red blood cells.

*Blood-clotting disorders*: The Alaskan Malamute is prone to blood-clotting disorders due to a deficiency of coagulation factors VII, VIII, or IX.

*Cataract*: In older dogs the lens of the eye becomes cloudy, causing a partial or total loss of vision.

*Corneal dystrophy*: An inherited degenerative condition in which the cornea of the eye becomes cloudy or opaque.

*Corneal ulcer*: A deterioration of the cornea.

*Diabetes mellitus:* A disease caused by an insufficient production or use of insulin.

*Eye abnormalities:* The Alaskan Malamute is prone to abnormal development of the eye(s).

*Glaucoma:* Pressure on the retina from excess fluid in the eyeball, which causes partial or total loss of vision.

*Hemeralopia:* A disorder of the retina causing blindness during the day with partial sight in dim light.

*Hereditary kidney hypoplasia:* A condition in which the dog is born with immature kidneys that never develop completely.

*Hip dysplasia:* An abnormal development of the hip joint(s).

*Hypothyroidism:* A common disease of thyroid-hormone deficiency. The thyroid regulates your dog's metabolism. A large number of skin problems in dogs are caused by thyroid disease.

*Immune-mediated hemolytic anemia (IMHA):* Anemia resulting from an immune system mediated destruction of the red blood cells.

*Narcolepsy:* A neurological disorder in which the dog suddenly falls asleep.

*Osteochondritis dissecans:* Inflammation of the cartilage in the joints. A form of arthritis.

*Osteochondrosis:* An abnormal development of joint cartilage. Most commonly found in the shoulder, elbow, and knee.

*Progressive retinal atrophy (PRA):* A slow deterioration of the retina, leading to blindness.

*Von Willebrand's disease:* Abnormal blood-clotting defect involving both platelet and coagulation function (factor VIII).

*Zinc-responsive dermatosis:* A skin disease caused by a zinc deficiency.

## AMERICAN FOXHOUND

*Deafness:* A partial or total loss of hearing.

*Osteochondrosis (spinal):* An abnormal development of the vertebrae.

*Thrombocytopathy:* The small blood cells that are needed to control bleeding are dysfunctional.

## BEARDED COLLIE

*Addison's disease:* A disease in which the adrenal glands secrete an insufficient amount of cortisone, a steroid hormone.

*Cataract:* In older dogs the lens of the eye becomes cloudy, causing a partial or total loss of vision.

*Corneal dystrophy:* An inherited degenerative condition in which the cornea of the eye becomes cloudy or opaque.

*Eye abnormalities:* The bearded collie is prone to abnormal development of the retina(s).

*Hip dysplasia:* An abnormal development of the hip joint(s).

*Hypothyroidism:* A common disease of thyroid-hormone deficiency. The thyroid regulates your dog's metabolism. A large number of skin problems in dogs are caused by thyroid disease.

*Progressive retinal atrophy* (**PRA**): A slow deterioration of the retina, leading to blindness.

## BELGIAN SHEEPDOG

*Cataract:* In older dogs the lens of the eye becomes cloudy, causing a partial or total loss of vision.

*Epilepsy:* A brain disorder in which the dog experiences seizures (convulsions).

*Eye abnormalities:* The Belgian Sheepdog is prone to abnormal development of the retina(s).

*Hip dysplasia:* An abnormal development of the hip joint(s).

*Hypothyroidism:* A common disease of thyroid-hormone deficiency. The thyroid regulates your dog's metabolism. A large number of skin problems in dogs are caused by thyroid disease.

*Muscular dystrophy:* A progressive muscle disorder that causes a wasting of the muscles. It is an inherited disease with symptoms of slow growth, difficulty eating and swallowing, and weakness.

*Pannus:* Progressive immune-mediated disease in which there is a growth of tissue over the cornea, causing inflammation and possible blindness.

*Progressive retinal atrophy (PRA)*: A slow deterioration of the retina, leading to blindness.

## BELGIAN TERVUREN

*Cataract*: In older dogs the lens of the eye becomes cloudy, causing a partial or total loss of vision.

*Epilepsy*: A brain disorder in which the dog experiences seizures (convulsions).

*Hypothyroidism*: A common disease of thyroid-hormone deficiency. The thyroid regulates your dog's metabolism. A large number of skin problems in dogs are caused by thyroid disease.

*Osteochondritis dissecans*: Inflammation of the cartilage in the joints. A form of arthritis.

*Osteochondrosis*: An abnormal development of joint cartilage. Most commonly found in the shoulder, elbow, and knee.

*Pannus*: Progressive immune-mediated disease in which there is a growth of tissue over the cornea, causing inflammation and possible blindness.

*Progressive retinal atrophy (PRA)*: A slow deterioration of the retina, leading to blindness.

## BERNESE MOUNTAIN DOG

*Ataxia*: A progressive loss of coordination.

*Cataract*: In older dogs the lens of the eye becomes cloudy, causing a partial or total loss of vision.

*Cerebellar degeneration/malformation*: A deterioration or malformation of a part of the brain.

*Cleft palate and/or lip*: Birth defects in which, with cleft palate, the roof of the mouth doesn't grow properly, leaving a hole from the roof of the mouth into the nose or, with cleft lip, the skin below the nose doesn't grow together.

*Eye abnormalities*: The Bernese Mountain Dog is prone to a rolling in of the eyelid(s) and abnormal development of the retina(s).

*Gastric bloat and torsion*: Gastric bloat is a swelling of the stomach from excess gas and is usually followed by gastric torsion, a twisting of the stomach. Gastric torsion will result in death if not treated immediately.

*Hepatocerebellar degeneration*: Progressive brain and liver disease of six-to-eight-week-old Bernese Mountain Dogs.

*Hip dysplasia*: An abnormal development of the hip joint(s).

*Hypothyroidism*: A common disease of thyroid-hormone deficiency. The thyroid regulates your dog's metabolism. A large number of skin problems in dogs are caused by thyroid disease.

*Liver abnormalities*: The Bernese Mountain Dog is prone to an abnormal formation of blood vessels in the liver.

*Osteochondritis dissecans*: Inflammation of the cartilage in the joints. A form of arthritis.

*Osteochondrosis*: An abnormal development of joint cartilage. Most commonly found in the shoulder, elbow, and knee.

*Progressive retinal atrophy (PRA)*: A slow deterioration of the retina, leading to blindness.

*Umbilical hernia*: A tear in the muscle wall of the stomach where the umbilical cord was.

## BLACK AND TAN COONHOUND
*Blood-clotting disorders*: The Coonhound (black and tan) is prone to a blood-clotting disorder due to a deficiency of coagulation factor IX.

*Eye abnormalities*: The Coonhound (black and tan) is prone to a rolling in or rolling out of the eyelid(s).

*Hip dysplasia*: An abnormal development of the hip joint(s).

*Osteochondritis dissecans*: Inflammation of the cartilage in the joints. A form of arthritis.

*Osteochondrosis*: An abnormal development of joint cartilage. Most commonly found in the shoulder, elbow, and knee.

## BLOODHOUND
*Eye abnormalities*: The Bloodhound is prone to a rolling in or out of the

eyelid(s), a protruding third eyelid(s), and dry eye, a condition in which the eye(s) does not produce enough liquid.

*Gastric bloat and torsion*: Gastric bloat is a swelling of the stomach from excess gas and is usually followed by gastric torsion, a twisting of the stomach. This is the leading cause of death in Bloodhounds.

*Hip dysplasia*: An abnormal development of the hip joint(s).

*Hypothyroidism*: A common disease of thyroid-hormone deficiency. The thyroid regulates your dog's metabolism. A large number of skin problems in dogs are caused by thyroid disease.

*Osteochondritis dissecans*: Inflammation of the cartilage in the joints. A form of arthritis.

*Osteochondrosis*: An abnormal development of joint cartilage. Most commonly found in the shoulder, elbow, and knee.

*Teeth abnormalities*: The number, placement, or development of the teeth is not normal.

## BLUETICK COONHOUND

*Globoid cell leukodystrophy*: Degeneration of a type of brain cell.

*Osteochondritis dissecans*: Inflammation of the cartilage in the joints. A form of arthritis.

*Osteochondrosis*: An abnormal development of joint cartilage. Most commonly found in the shoulder, elbow, and knee.

## BOUVIER DES FLANDRES

*Cataract*: In older dogs the lens of the eye becomes cloudy, causing a partial or total loss of vision.

*Cleft palate*: A birth defect in which the roof of the mouth doesn't grow properly, leaving a hole from the roof of the mouth into the nose.

*Eye abnormalities*: The Bouvier des Flandres is prone to a rolling in of the eyelid(s).

*Gastric bloat and torsion*: Gastric bloat is a swelling of the stomach from excess gas and is usually followed by gastric torsion, a twisting of the stomach. Gastric torsion will result in death if not treated immediately.

*Glaucoma*: Pressure on the retina from excess fluid in the eyeball, which causes partial or total loss of vision.

*Hip dysplasia*: An abnormal development of the hip joint(s).

*Hypothyroidism*: A common disease of thyroid-hormone deficiency. The thyroid regulates your dog's metabolism. A large number of skin problems in dogs are caused by thyroid disease.

*Osteochondritis dissecans*: Inflammation of the cartilage in the joints. A form of arthritis.

*Osteochondrosis*: An abnormal development of joint cartilage. Most commonly found in the shoulder, elbow, and knee.

*Reproductive disorders*: The Bouvier des Flandres is prone to ovarian cyst(s), experiencing complications giving birth, and endometriosis, an inflammation of the uterus.

*Umbilical hernia*: A tear in the muscle wall of the stomach where the umbilical cord was.

*Von Willebrand's disease*: Abnormal blood-clotting defect involving both platelet and coagulation function (factor VIII).

## BOXER

*Acne*: Pimples and blackheads on the chin and lips of young dogs.

*Allergies*: The Boxer is prone to all types of allergies.

*Blood-clotting disorders*: The Boxer is prone to blood-clotting disorders due to a deficiency of coagulation factors II or VIII.

*Cancer*: The Boxer is prone to skin cancer and a rare form of cancer in which the mast cells become cancerous. The mast cell secretes histamine in response to allergens.

*Cataract*: In older dogs the lens of the eye becomes cloudy, causing a partial or total loss of vision.

*Corneal ulcer*: A deterioration of the cornea.

*Cushing's disease (hyperadrenocorticism)*: A condition in which the adrenal glands secrete too much cortisol. Cortisol is a steroid hormone which regulates carbohydrate, fat, and protein metabolism.

**Demodectic mange:** A skin disease in which canine mites are living in the skin, causing itching, loss of hair, and skin infections. Usually found on the face and front legs.

**Dermoid cyst:** A skin-like growth usually seen on the back.

**Ehler's-Danlos syndrome:** A connective-tissue disease in which the skin is very fragile and is easily cut or bruised.

**Eye abnormalities:** The Boxer is prone to a rolling in of the eyelid(s), abnormally growing eyelashes, and a protruding third eyelid(s).

**Fainting:** A sudden, brief state of unconsciousness.

**Gastric bloat and torsion:** Gastric bloat is a swelling of the stomach from excess gas and is usually followed by gastric torsion, a twisting of the stomach. Gastric torsion will result in death if not treated immediately.

**Heart disease:** The Boxer is prone to cardiomyopathy, or weakened heart muscles, developmental abnormalities of the heart, and valve disease.

**Histiocytoma:** A tumor that forms beneath the skin.

**Incontinence:** Loss of control of urination and bowel movements.

**Liver abnormalities:** The Boxer is prone to an abnormal formation of blood vessels in the liver.

**Osteochondritis dissecans:** Inflammation of the cartilage in the joints. A form of arthritis.

**Osteochondrosis:** An abnormal development of joint cartilage. Most commonly found in the shoulder, elbow, and knee.

**Progressive retinal atrophy (PRA):** A slow deterioration of the retina, leading to blindness.

**Spondylosis:** A malformation of the vertebrae.

**Teeth abnormalities:** The number, placement, or development of the teeth is not normal.

**Thyroid disease:** The Boxer is prone to thyroiditis, lymphocytic thyroiditis, and hypothyroidism. Thyroiditis and lymphocytic thyroiditis are autoimmune diseases that lead to hypothyroidism, a common disease of thyroid-hormone deficiency. The thyroid regulates your dog's metabolism. A large number of skin problems in dogs are caused by thyroid disease.

*Ulcerative colitis:* A chronic inflammation of the colon that results in the formation of ulcers in the colon.

*Urinary stones:* A hard mass of magnesium-ammonium-phosphate stones or crystals in the urinary tract.

*Vaginal hyperplasia:* An increase in the number of cells in the tissues of the vagina, possibly indicating a precancerous condition.

*Von Willebrand's disease:* Abnormal blood-clotting defect involving both platelet and coagulation function (factor VIII).

## BRIARD

*Cancer:* The Briard is prone to cancer of the lymphatic system.

*Cataract:* In older dogs the lens of the eye becomes cloudy, causing a partial or total loss of vision.

*Eosinophilic panosteitis:* An inflammatory bone disease found in fast-growing puppies, which is accompanied by increased eosinophils, a type of white blood cell.

*Gastric bloat and torsion:* Gastric bloat is a swelling of the stomach from excess gas and is usually followed by gastric torsion, a twisting of the stomach. Gastric torsion will result in death if not treated immediately.

*Hip dysplasia:* An abnormal development of the hip joint(s).

*Hypothyroidism:* A common disease of thyroid-hormone deficiency. The thyroid regulates your dog's metabolism. A large number of skin problems in dogs are caused by thyroid disease.

*Progressive retinal atrophy (PRA):* A slow deterioration of the retina, leading to blindness.

*Von Willebrand's disease:* Abnormal blood-clotting defect involving both platelet and coagulation function (factor VIII).

## BULL TERRIER

*Acrodermatitis:* A zinc deficiency caused by an inability to utilize and store zinc properly.

*Boils:* A deep infection of the skin.

*Cancer:* The Bull Terrier is prone to skin cancer and a rare form of cancer in which the mast cells become cancerous. The mast cell secretes histamine in response to allergens.

*Deafness*: A partial or total loss of hearing.

*Eye abnormalities*: The bull Terrier is prone to a rolling in or out of the eyelid(s), and a condition where the lens in the eye slips out of place.

*Hernia*: A rupture of the wall of an internal organ in the groin area.

*Osteochondritis dissecans*: Inflammation of the cartilage in the joints. A form of arthritis.

*Osteochondrosis*: An abnormal development of joint cartilage. Most commonly found in the shoulder, elbow, and knee.

*Umbilical hernia*: A tear in the muscle wall of the stomach where the umbilical cord was.

## CHESAPEAKE BAY RETRIEVER

*Cataract*: In older dogs the lens of the eye becomes cloudy, causing a partial or total loss of vision.

*Eye abnormalities*: The Chesapeake Bay Retriever is prone to abnormally growing eyelashes, a rolling in of the eyelid(s), a protruding third eyelid(s), and an abnormal development of the retina(s).

*Hip dysplasia*: An abnormal development of the hip joint(s).

*Osteochondritis dissecans*: Inflammation of the cartilage in the joints. A form of arthritis.

*Osteochondrosis*: An abnormal development of joint cartilage. Most commonly found in the shoulder, elbow, and knee.

*Progressive retinal atrophy (PRA)*: A slow deterioration of the retina, leading to blindness.

*Von Willebrand's disease*: Abnormal blood-clotting defect involving both platelet and coagulation function (factor VIII).

## COLLIE

*Blood-clotting disorders*: The Collie is prone to a blood-clotting disorder due to a deficiency of coagulation factor VIII.

***Bullous pemphigoid:*** An autoimmune disease in which painful blisters form just beneath the skin.

***Cancer:*** The Collie is prone to bladder cancer.

***Cataract:*** In older dogs the lens of the eye becomes cloudy, causing a partial or total loss of vision.

***Cerebellar abiotrophy:*** Malformation of the neurons in the cerebellum. The cerebellum is the part of the brain that gives your dog balance, coordination, and posture.

***Collie eye anomaly:*** An inherited disorder in which the narrow shape of the head causes the eyes to be malformed.

***Corneal dystrophy:*** An inherited degenerative condition in which the cornea of the eye becomes cloudy or opaque.

***Cyclic hematopoiesis:*** An inherited condition of gray collies in which, periodically, a type of white blood cell is not produced.

***Deafness:*** A partial or total loss of hearing.

***Demodectic mange:*** A skin disease in which canine mites are living in the skin, causing itching, loss of hair, and skin infections. Usually found on the face and front legs.

***Epilepsy:*** A brain disorder in which the dog experiences seizures (convulsions).

***Eye abnormalities:*** The Collie is prone to a rolling in of the eyelid(s), abnormally growing eyelashes, malformed optic nerve(s), and abnormal development of the retina(s).

***Hernia:*** A rupture of the wall of an internal organ in the groin area.

***Hip dysplasia:*** An abnormal development of the hip joint(s).

***Histiocytoma:*** A tumor that forms beneath the skin.

***Hypothyroidism:*** A common disease of thyroid-hormone deficiency. The thyroid regulates your dog's metabolism. A large number of skin problems in dogs are caused by thyroid disease.

***Keratitis:*** Inflammation of the cornea.

***Osteochondritis dissecans:*** Inflammation of the cartilage in the joints. A form of arthritis.

*Osteochondrosis*: An abnormal development of joint cartilage. Most commonly found in the shoulder, elbow, and knee.

*Progressive retinal atrophy* (**PRA**): A slow deterioration of the retina, leading to blindness.

*Skin disorders*: The collie is prone to autoimmune skin disease, skin disease of the nose, and an inflammation of the skin and muscles.

*Umbilical hernia*: A tear in the muscle wall of the stomach where the umbilical cord was.

*Von Willebrand's disease*: Abnormal blood-clotting defect involving both platelet and coagulation function (factor VIII).

## CHOW CHOW

*Behavioral abnormalities*: A whole range of abnormal behavior patterns, such as aggression and panic disorders.

*Cataract*: In older dogs the lens of the eye becomes cloudy, causing a partial or total loss of vision.

*Cerebellar hypoplasia*: Underdevelopment of a part of the brain called the cerebellum. The cerebellum gives your dog balance, coordination, and posture.

*Cleft palate*: A birth defect in which the roof of the mouth doesn't grow properly, leaving a hole from the roof of the mouth into the nose.

*Demodectic mange*: A skin disease in which canine mites are living in the skin, causing itching, loss of hair, and skin infections. Usually found on the face and front legs.

*Elbow dysplasia*: An abnormal development of the elbow joint(s).

*Epiphyseal dysplasia*: Abnormal development of the long bone.

*Eye abnormalities*: The Chow Chow is prone to a rolling in or out of the eyelid(s) and abnormally growing eyelashes.

*Gastric bloat and torsion*: Gastric bloat is a swelling of the stomach from excess gas and is usually followed by gastric torsion, a twisting of the stomach. Gastric torsion will result in death if not treated immediately.

*Glaucoma*: Pressure on the retina from excess fluid in the eyeball, which causes partial or total loss of vision.

*Growth-hormone-responsive dermatosis*: Skin disorder caused by a deficiency of growth hormones.

*Hip dysplasia*: An abnormal development of the hip joint(s).

*Malabsorption*: A condition in which the small intestine does not absorb nutrients properly.

*Muscular dystrophy*: A progressive muscle disorder that causes a wasting of the muscles. It is an inherited disease with symptoms of slow growth, difficulty eating and swallowing, and weakness.

*Osteochondritis dissecans*: Inflammation of the cartilage in the joints. A form of arthritis.

*Osteochondrosis*: An abnormal development of joint cartilage. Most commonly found in the shoulder, elbow, and knee.

*Pannus*: A progressive immune-mediated disease in which there is a growth of tissue over the cornea, causing inflammation and possible blindness.

*Pemphigus foliaceous*: An autoimmune skin disease.

*Progressive retinal atrophy (PRA)*: A slow deterioration of the retina, leading to blindness.

*Thyroid disease*: The Chow Chow is prone to thyroiditis, lymphocytic thyroiditis, and hypothyroidism. Thyroiditis and lymphocytic thyroiditis are autoimmune diseases that lead to hypothyroidism, a common disease of thyroid-hormone deficiency. The thyroid regulates your dog's metabolism. A large number of skin problems in dogs are caused by thyroid disease.

## CLUMBER SPANIEL

*Eye abnormalities*: The Clumber Spaniel is prone to a rolling in or out of the eyelid(s).

*Hip dysplasia*: An abnormal development of the hip joint(s).

*Jaw abnormality*: The lower jaw is longer than the upper jaw.

*Teeth abnormalities*: The number, placement, or development of the teeth is not normal.

## CURLEY-COATED RETRIEVER

*Cataract*: In older dogs the lens of the eye becomes cloudy, causing a partial or total loss of vision.

*Ehler's-Danlos syndrome*: A connective-tissue disease in which the skin is very fragile and is easily cut or bruised.

*Eye abnormalities*: The Curley-Coated Retriever is prone to a rolling in of the eyelid(s) and abnormally growing eyelashes.

*Progressive retinal atrophy (PRA)*: A slow deterioration of the retina, leading to blindness.

## DALMATIAN

*Allergies*: The Dalmatian is prone to all types of allergies.

*Blue eyes*: An adverse reaction to the adenovirus type 1 (hepatitis virus) vaccine, which causes a bluish discoloration to the cornea. Use adenovirus type 2 vaccine.

*Boils*: A deep infection of the skin.

*Cancer*: Skin cancer.

*Deafness*: A partial or total loss of hearing.

*Demodectic mange*: A skin disease in which canine mites are living in the skin, causing itching, loss of hair, and skin infections. Usually found on the face and front legs.

*Eye abnormalities*: The Dalmatian is prone to a rolling in of the eyelid(s) and abnormally growing eyelashes.

*Folliculitis*: Inflammation of the hair follicle(s).

*Glaucoma*: Pressure on the retina from excess fluid in the eyeball, which causes partial or total loss of vision.

*Globoid cell leukodystrophy*: Degeneration of a type of brain cell.

*Hip dysplasia*: An abnormal development of the hip joint(s).

*Hypothyroidism*: A common disease of thyroid-hormone deficiency. The thyroid regulates your dog's metabolism. A large number of skin problems in dogs are caused by thyroid disease.

*Osteochondritis dissecans*: Inflammation of the cartilage in the joints. A form of arthritis.

*Osteochondrosis*: An abnormal development of joint cartilage. Most commonly found in the shoulder, elbow, and knee.

*Pannus*: A progressive immune-mediated disease in which there is a growth of tissue over the cornea, causing inflammation and possible blindness.

*Progressive retinal atrophy* (**PRA**): A slow deterioration of the retina, leading to blindness.

*Uric-acid-excretion abnormality*: The Dalmatian is prone to having an abnormally high amount of uric acid in the urine, which causes urinary stones.

*Urinary stones*: A hard mass of magnesium-ammonium-phosphate stones or crystals in the urinary tract.

## DOBERMAN PINSCHER

*Acanthosis nigricans*: A rare skin disease characterized by dark skin, hair loss, and inflammation of the skin. Primarily found in the armpits.

*Acne*: Pimples and blackheads on the chin and lips of young dogs.

*Antibody (type IgM) deficiency*: A deficiency of antibody production during the initial response of the immune system to an antigen.

*Behavioral abnormalities*: A whole range of abnormal behavior patterns, such as aggression and panic disorders.

*Blood-clotting disorders*: The Doberman Pinscher is prone to a blood-clotting disorder due to a deficiency of coagulation factor VIII.

*Cancer*: The Doberman Pinscher is prone to bone cancer and hemangiosarcoma, which is a cancer of blood vessels involving the liver, skin, or spleen.

*Cataract*: In older dogs the lens of the eye becomes cloudy, causing a partial or total loss of vision.

*Ciliary dyskinesia*: A condition in which the ciliated cells (hairlike cells lining the respiratory tract) are deformed and rigid. Causes pneumonia and other respiratory difficulties.

*Copper metabolism abnormality*: An inability to utilize and store copper properly. Results in liver disease if not treated.

*Craniomandibular osteopathy*: Abnormally dense bones in the face and the jaw.

*Demodectic mange*: A skin disease in which canine mites are living in the skin, causing itching, loss of hair, and skin infections. Usually found on the face and front legs.

*Eosinophilic panosteitis*: An inflammatory bone disease found in fast-growing puppies, which is accompanied by increased eosinophils, a type of white blood cell.

*Eye abnormalities*: The Doberman Pinscher is prone to abnormal development of the eye(s) and a rolling in of the eye(s).

*Fainting*: A sudden, brief state of unconsciousness.

*Folliculitis*: Inflammation of the hair follicle(s).

*Gastric bloat and torsion*: Gastric bloat is a swelling of the stomach from excess gas and is usually followed by gastric torsion, a twisting of the stomach. Gastric torsion will result in death if not treated immediately.

*Heart disease*: The Doberman Pinscher is prone to cardiomyopathy, or weakened heart muscles, and a deterioration of the electrical system of the heart.

*Hip dysplasia*: An abnormal development of the hip joint(s).

*Immune-mediated hemolytic anemia* (*IMHA*): Anemia resulting from an immune system mediated destruction of the red blood cells.

*Incontinence*: Loss of control of urination and bowel movements.

*Kidney disease*: The Doberman Pinscher is prone to abnormally developed kidney(s).

*Lick granuloma* (*acral lick dermatitis*): Inflammation or infection of the skin from excessive licking. Usually found on the leg or paw.

*Narcolepsy*: A neurological disorder in which the dog suddenly falls asleep.

*Neck vertebrae malformation*: An abnormal development of the vertebrae in the neck that causes nerve damage. Some dogs walk with a pronounced flexion of the knee, similar to a high-stepping horse.

*Osteochondritis dissecans*: Inflammation of the cartilage in the joints. A form of arthritis.

*Osteochondrosis*: An abnormal development of joint cartilage. Most commonly found in the shoulder, elbow, and knee.

*Pigmentation abnormalities*: A lack of color in the skin.

*Progressive retinal atrophy (PRA)*: A slow deterioration of the retina, leading to blindness.

*Teeth abnormalities*: The number, placement, or development of the teeth is not normal.

*Thrombosis*: The formation of a blood clot(s) in a blood vessel or the heart.

*Thyroid disease*: The Doberman Pinscher is prone to thyroiditis, lymphocytic thyroiditis, and hypothyroidism. Thyroiditis and lymphocytic thyroiditis are autoimmune diseases that lead to hypothyroidism, a common disease of thyroid-hormone deficiency. The thyroid regulates your dog's metabolism. A large number of skin problems in dogs are caused by thyroid disease.

*Ulcerative colitis*: A chronic inflammation of the colon that results in the formation of ulcers in the colon.

*Von Willebrand's disease*: Abnormal blood clotting defect involving both platelet and coagulation function (factor VIII).

## ENGLISH BULLDOG

*Acne*: Pimples and blackheads on the chin and lips of young dogs.

*Cancer*: The English Bulldog is prone to cancer of the brain, spinal cord, and anus.

*Cataract*: In older dogs the lens of the eye becomes cloudy, causing a partial or total loss of vision.

*Cleft palate and/or lip*: Birth defects in which, with cleft palate, the roof of the mouth doesn't grow properly, leaving a hole from the roof of the mouth into the nose or, with cleft lip, the skin below the nose doesn't grow together.

*Dystocia*: Complications giving birth.

*Eye abnormalities*: The English Bulldog is prone to abnormally growing eyelashes, a rolling in or out of the eyelid(s), and dry eye, a condition in which the eye(s) does not produce enough liquid.

*Heart disease*: The English Bulldog is prone to abnormal growth of the mitral valve(s) and malfunctioning valves.

*Hip dysplasia*: An abnormal development of the hip joint(s).

*Hydrocephalus*: The accumulation of fluid in the brain.

*Hypothyroidism*: A common disease of thyroid-hormone deficiency. The thyroid regulates your dog's metabolism. A large number of skin problems in dogs are caused by thyroid disease.

*Pyloric stenosis*: A constriction of the opening of the lower end of the stomach.

*Skin disease*: The English Bulldog is prone to infections on the face and tail due to excessive skin folds, inflammation of the hair follicle(s), deep infections in the skin (boils), and demodectic mange, a skin disease in which canine mites are living in the skin, causing itching, loss of hair, and skin infections. This is usually found on the face and front legs.

*Spina bifida*: A developmental abnormality in which the vertebrae fail to encircle the spinal cord.

*Teeth abnormalities*: The number, placement, or development of the teeth is not normal.

*Trachea hypoplasia*: Incomplete development of the trachea.

*Vaginal hyperplasia*: An increase in the number of cells in the tissues of the vagina, possibly indicating a precancerous condition.

*Vertebra malformation*: A condition in which only half the vertebra is formed.

*Von Willebrand's disease*: Abnormal blood-clotting defect involving both platelet and coagulation function (factor VIII).

## ENGLISH FOXHOUND

*Deafness*: A partial or total loss of hearing.

*Osteochondrosis (spinal)*: An abnormal development of the vertebrae.

## ENGLISH SETTER

*Blood-clotting disorders*: The English Setter is prone to a blood-clotting disorder due to a deficiency of coagulation factor VIII.

*Cataract*: In older dogs the lens of the eye becomes cloudy, causing a partial or total loss of vision.

*Craniomandibular osteopathy*: Abnormally dense bones in the face and the jaw.

*Deafness*: A partial or total loss of hearing.

*Eclampsia*: Convulsions during or after whelping.

*Eye abnormalities*: The English Setter is prone to a rolling in or out of the eyelid(s) and dry eye, a condition in which the eye(s) does not produce enough liquid.

*Gastric bloat and torsion*: Gastric bloat is a swelling of the stomach from excess gas and is usually followed by gastric torsion, a twisting of the stomach. Gastric torsion will result in death if not treated immediately.

*Hip dysplasia*: An abnormal development of the hip joint(s).

*Hypoglycemia*: A low level of glucose (blood sugar) in the blood.

*Hypothyroidism*: A common disease of thyroid-hormone deficiency. The thyroid regulates your dog's metabolism. A large number of skin problems in dogs are caused by thyroid disease.

*Lipidosis*: An accumulation of lipids (fats) in the nerves.

*Neuronal ceroid-lipofuscinosis*: An accumulation of fatty pigments in the brain.

*Osteochondritis dissecans*: Inflammation of the cartilage in the joints. A form of arthritis.

*Osteochondrosis*: An abnormal development of joint cartilage. Most commonly found in the shoulder, elbow, and knee.

*Progressive retinal atrophy (PRA)*: A slow deterioration of the retina, leading to blindness.

*Von Willebrand's disease*: Abnormal blood-clotting defect involving both platelet and coagulation function (factor VIII).

## FLAT-COATED RETRIEVER

*Cataract*: In older dogs the lens of the eye becomes cloudy, causing a partial or total loss of vision.

*Eye abnormalities*: The Flat-Coated Retriever is prone to a rolling in or out of the eyelid(s) and abnormally growing eyelashes.

*Hip dysplasia*: An abnormal development of the hip joint(s).

*Hypothyroidism*: A common disease of thyroid-hormone deficiency. The thyroid regulates your dog's metabolism. A large number of skin problems in dogs are caused by thyroid disease.

*Progressive retinal atrophy (PRA)*: A slow deterioration of the retina, leading to blindness.

## GERMAN SHEPHERD

*Allergies*: The German Shepherd is prone to all types of allergies.

*Antibody (type IgA) deficiency*: A deficiency in the production of the type IgA antibody, causing a weakened immune system.

*Behavioral abnormalities*: A whole range of abnormal behavior patterns, such as aggression and panic disorders.

*Blood-clotting disorders*: The German Shepherd is prone to blood-clotting disorders due to a deficiency of coagulation factors VIII or IX.

*Calcinosis*: Hard lumps of calcium salt deposits in the skin.

*Cancer*: The German Shepherd is prone to bone cancer and hemangiosarcoma, a cancer of the blood vessels involving the liver, skin, or spleen.

*Cataract*: In older dogs the lens of the eye becomes cloudy, causing a partial or total loss of vision.

*Cleft palate and/or lip*: Birth defects in which, with cleft palate, the roof of the mouth doesn't grow properly, leaving a hole from the roof of the mouth into the nose or, with cleft lip, the skin below the nose doesn't grow together.

*Corneal dystrophy*: An inherited degenerative condition in which the cornea of the eye becomes cloudy or opaque.

*Cutaneous vasculopathy*: A puppy disease characterized by swollen footpads that lose their color, and lesions and crusting on the ear(s) and tail.

*Degenerative myelopathy*: A progressive deterioration of the spinal cord.

*Dermoid cyst*: A skin-like growth usually seen on the back.

*Ehler's-Danlos syndrome*: A connective-tissue disease in which the skin is very fragile and is easily cut or bruised.

*Elbow dysplasia*: An abnormal development of the elbow joint(s).

*Eosinophilic panosteitis*: An inflammatory bone disease found in fast-growing puppies, which is accompanied by increased eosinophils, a type of white blood cell.

*Epilepsy*: A brain disorder in which the dog experiences seizures (convulsions).

*Esophageal disorder*: Spasms in the muscles of the esophagus.

*Eye abnormalities*: The German Shepherd is prone to a protruding third eyelid(s), abnormal development of the eye(s), a rolling in of the eyelid(s), a protruding third eyelid(s), and a disorder where the lens in the eye(s) slips out of place.

**Gastric bloat and torsion**: Gastric bloat is a swelling of the stomach from excess gas and is usually followed by gastric torsion, a twisting of the stomach. Gastric torsion will result in death if not treated immediately.

*Glycogen storage disease*: An inability to store and use the complex carbohydrate glycogen, which is primarily stored in the liver and muscle.

**Heart disease**: Cardiomyopathy, or weakened heart muscles, and a malfunctioning valve(s).

**Hereditary kidney hypoplasia**: A condition in which the dog is born with immature kidneys that never develop completely.

*Hip dysplasia*: An abnormal development of the hip joint(s).

*Incontinence*: Loss of control of urination and bowel movements.

*Keratoacanthoma*: Non-cancerous skin tumor usually found on the face.

*Keratitis*: Inflammation of the cornea.

*Lymphedema*: An accumulation of fluid in the tissues due to a disorder of the lymphatic system.

*Malabsorption*: A condition in which the small intestine does not absorb nutrients properly.

*Myasthenia gravis*: An autoimmune disease characterized by progressive muscle fatigue and generalized weakness resulting from the impaired transmission of nerve impulses.

*Osteochondritis dissecans*: Inflammation of the cartilage in the joints. A form of arthritis.

*Osteochondrosis*: An abnormal development of joint cartilage. Most commonly found in the shoulder, elbow, and knee.

*Pancreatic insufficiency*: A digestive-enzyme deficiency.

*Pannus*: Progressive immune-mediated disease in which there is a growth of tissue over the cornea, causing inflammation and possible blindness.

*Progressive retinal atrophy* **(PRA)**: A slow deterioration of the retina, leading to blindness.

*Silica uroliths*: Bladder stones formed primarily from silicone.

*Skin disease*: The German Shepherd is prone to deep infections in the skin (boils), autoimmune diseases of the skin, infections of the nose and ear(s), and seborrhea, which is characterized by scaly, crusty, and greasy skin.

*Systemic lupus erythematosus*: An autoimmune disease characterized by blood abnormalities, organ disorders, and skin infections.

*Thyroid disease*: The German Shepherd is prone to thyroiditis, lymphocytic thyroiditis, and hypothyroidism. Thyroiditis and lymphocytic thyroiditis are autoimmune diseases that lead to hypothyroidism, a common disease of thyroid-hormone deficiency. The thyroid regulates your dog's metabolism. A large number of skin problems in dogs are caused by thyroid disease.

*Ulcerative colitis*: A chronic inflammation of the colon that results in the formation of ulcers in the colon.

*Von Willebrand's disease*: Abnormal blood-clotting defect involving both platelet and coagulation function (factor VIII).

## GERMAN SHORTHAIRED POINTER

*Acral mutilation*: Mutilation of the feet and legs from excessive licking. Seen in pointing breeds that are born without pain sensation.

*Addison's disease*: A disease in which the adrenal glands secrete an insufficient amount of cortisone, a steroid hormone.

*Cancer*: The German Shorthaired Pointer is prone to cancer of the fibrous tissues and skin cancer.

*Cataract:* In older dogs the lens of the eye becomes cloudy, causing a partial or total loss of vision.

*Corneal dystrophy:* An inherited degenerative condition in which the cornea of the eye becomes cloudy or opaque.

*Eye abnormalities:* The German Shorthaired Pointer is prone to a rolling in of the eyelid(s) and a protruding third eyelid(s).

*Hip dysplasia:* An abnormal development of the hip joint(s).

*Hypothyroidism:* A common disease of thyroid-hormone deficiency. The thyroid regulates your dog's metabolism. A large number of skin problems in dogs are caused by thyroid disease.

*Lipidosis:* An accumulation of lipids (fats) in the nerves.

*Lymphedema:* An accumulation of fluid in the tissues due to a disorder of the lymphatic system.

*Neuronal ceroid-lipofuscinosis:* An accumulation of fatty pigments in the brain.

*Osteochondritis dissecans:* Inflammation of the cartilage in the joints. A form of arthritis.

*Osteochondrosis:* An abnormal development of joint cartilage. Most commonly found in the shoulder, elbow, and knee.

*Pannus:* Progressive immune-mediated disease in which there is a growth of tissue over the cornea, causing inflammation and possible blindness.

*Progressive retinal atrophy (PRA):* A slow deterioration of the retina, leading to blindness.

*Subaortic stenosis:* A constriction of the valve between the heart and the aorta.

*Thrombocytopathy:* A dysfunction of the small blood cells that are needed to control bleeding.

*Von Willebrand's disease:* Abnormal blood-clotting defect involving both platelet and coagulation function (factor VIII).

## GERMAN WIREHAIRED POINTER

*Cataract:* In older dogs the lens of the eye becomes cloudy, causing a partial or total loss of vision.

*Eye abnormalities:* The German Wirehaired Pointer is prone to a rolling in of the eyelid(s) and abnormal development of the retina(s).

*Hip dysplasia:* An abnormal development of the hip joint(s).

*Osteochondritis dissecans:* Inflammation of the cartilage in the joints. A form of arthritis.

*Osteochondrosis:* An abnormal development of joint cartilage. Most commonly found in the shoulder, elbow, and knee.

*Subcutaneous cyst:* A fluid-filled sac located just beneath the skin.

*Von Willebrand's disease:* Abnormal blood-clotting defect involving both platelet and coagulation function (factor VIII).

## GIANT SCHNAUZER

*Cataract:* In older dogs the lens of the eye becomes cloudy, causing a partial or total loss of vision.

*Eosinophilic panosteitis:* An inflammatory bone disease found in fast-growing puppies, which is accompanied by increased eosinophils, a type of white blood cell.

*Eye abnormalities:* The Giant Schnauzer is prone to abnormal development of the retina(s).

*Glaucoma:* Pressure on the retina from excess fluid in the eyeball, which causes partial or total loss of vision.

*Hip dysplasia:* An abnormal development of the hip joint(s).

*Hypertrophic osteodystrophy:* A painful inflammation of the bones along with development of bony growths, found in fast-growing giant breeds.

*Immune-mediated hemolytic anemia (IMHA):* Anemia resulting from an immune system mediated destruction of the red blood cells.

*Osteochondritis dissecans:* Inflammation of the cartilage in the joints. A form of arthritis.

*Osteochondrosis:* An abnormal development of joint cartilage. Most commonly found in the shoulder, elbow, and knee.

*Progressive retinal atrophy (PRA):* A slow deterioration of the retina, leading to blindness.

*Seborrhea*: A skin disease characterized by raw, scaling skin and an excess of sebum (oil-like substance), which causes a rancid body odor.

*Thrombocytopenia*: An abnormal decrease in the number of blood platelets. Blood platelets play a role in blood clotting. Symptoms are tiny hemorrhages in the skin and mucous membranes.

*Thyroid disease*: The Giant Schnauzer is prone to thyroiditis, lymphocytic thyroiditis, and hypothyroidism. Thyroiditis and lymphocytic thyroiditis are autoimmune diseases that lead to hypothyroidism, a common disease of thyroid-hormone deficiency. The thyroid regulates your dog's metabolism. A large number of skin problems in dogs are caused by thyroid disease.

*Vitamin B$_{12}$-responsive malabsorption*: A condition in which puppies have an inability to absorb vitamin B$_{12}$, which is characterized by chronic anemia, low white blood cell counts, and metabolites (methylmalonic acid) in the urine.

## GOLDEN RETRIEVER

*Allergies*: The Golden Retriever is prone to all types of allergies.

*Blood-clotting disorders*: The Golden Retriever is prone to a blood-clotting disorder due to a deficiency of coagulation factor VIII.

*Cancer*: The Golden Retriever is prone to cancer of the blood vessels involving the liver, skin, or spleen (hemangiosarcoma), and cancer of the lymphatic system.

*Cataract*: In older dogs the lens of the eye becomes cloudy, causing a partial or total loss of vision.

*Corneal dystrophy*: An inherited degenerative condition in which the cornea of the eye becomes cloudy or opaque.

*Elbow dysplasia*: An abnormal development of the elbow joint(s).

*Epilepsy*: A brain disorder in which the dog experiences seizures (convulsions).

*Eye abnormalities*: The Golden Retriever is prone to abnormally developing eye(s), a rolling in or out of the eyelid(s), malformation of the optic nerve, and abnormally growing eyelashes.

*Heart disease*: Cardiomyopathy, or weakened heart muscles, and malfunctioning valve(s).

*Immune-mediated hemolytic anemia* (*IMHA*): Anemia resulting from an immune system mediated destruction of the red blood cells.

*Hip dysplasia*: An abnormal development of the hip joint(s).

*Liver abnormalities*: The Golden Retriever is prone to an abnormal formation of blood vessels in the liver.

*Muscular dystrophy*: A progressive muscle disorder that causes a wasting of the muscles. It is an inherited disease with symptoms of slow growth, difficulty eating and swallowing, and weakness.

*Myasthenia gravis*: An autoimmune disease characterized by progressive muscle fatigue and generalized weakness resulting from the impaired transmission of nerve impulses.

*Osteochondritis dissecans*: Inflammation of the cartilage in the joints. A form of arthritis.

*Osteochondrosis*: An abnormal development of joint cartilage. Most commonly found in the shoulder, elbow, and knee.

*Pigmentation abnormalities*: A lack of color in the skin.

*Progressive retinal atrophy* (*PRA*): A slow deterioration of the retina, leading to blindness.

*Skin disease*: The Golden Retriever is prone to bacterial skin infections that cause excessive licking and chewing and progress into severe inflammation (hot spots), deep infections of the skin (boils), inflammation of the hair follicle(s), and an inflammation or infection of the skin from excessive licking (lick granuloma).

*Thyroid disease*: The Golden Retriever is prone to thyroiditis, lymphocytic thyroiditis, and hypothyroidism. Thyroiditis and lymphocytic thyroiditis are autoimmune diseases that lead to hypothyroidism, a common disease of thyroid-hormone deficiency. The thyroid regulates your dog's metabolism. A large number of skin problems in dogs are caused by thyroid disease.

*Von Willebrand's disease*: Abnormal blood-clotting defect involving both platelet and coagulation function (factor VIII).

## GORDON SETTER

*Cataract:* In older dogs the lens of the eye becomes cloudy, causing a partial or total loss of vision.

*Cerebellar abiotrophy:* Malformation of the neurons in the cerebellum. The cerebellum is the part of the brain that gives your dog balance, coordination, and posture.

*Eye abnormalities:* The Gordon Setter is prone to dry eye, a condition in which the eye(s) does not produce enough liquid, a rolling in of the eyelid(s), and abnormal development of the retina(s).

*Gastric bloat and torsion:* Gastric bloat is a swelling of the stomach from excess gas and is usually followed by gastric torsion, a twisting of the stomach. Gastric torsion will result in death if not treated immediately.

*Hip dysplasia:* An abnormal development of the hip joint(s).

*Hypothyroidism:* A common disease of thyroid-hormone deficiency. The thyroid regulates your dog's metabolism. A large number of skin problems in dogs are caused by thyroid disease.

*Osteochondritis dissecans:* Inflammation of the cartilage in the joints. A form of arthritis.

*Osteochondrosis:* An abnormal development of joint cartilage. Most commonly found in the shoulder, elbow, and knee.

*Progressive retinal atrophy* (PRA): A slow deterioration of the retina, leading to blindness.

## GREYHOUND

*Anesthetic sensitivity:* A serious condition in which a dog is very sensitive to anesthesia. In many cases the dog is also sensitive to medications and flea-control products that contain pesticides.

*Blood-clotting disorders:* The Greyhound is prone to a blood-clotting disorder due to a deficiency of coagulation factor VIII.

*Cancer:* The Greyhound is prone to bone cancer.

*Cataract:* In older dogs the lens of the eye becomes cloudy, causing a partial or total loss of vision.

*Corneal dystrophy*: An inherited degenerative condition in which the cornea of the eye becomes cloudy or opaque.

*Dystocia*: Complications giving birth.

*Ehler's-Danlos syndrome*: A connective-tissue disease in which the skin is very fragile and is easily cut or bruised.

*Epilepsy*: A brain disorder in which the dog experiences seizures (convulsions).

*Esophageal disorder*: Spasms in the muscles of the esophagus.

*Eye abnormalities*: The Greyhound is prone to abnormally growing eye-lashes, the lens in the eye slipping out of place, and optic nerve malformation.

*Gastric bloat and torsion*: Gastric bloat is a swelling of the stomach from excess gas and is usually followed by gastric torsion, a twisting of the stomach. Gastric torsion will result in death if not treated immediately.

*Hygroma*: A thick-walled, fluid-filled sac usually found on the elbows.

*Hypothyroidism*: A common disease of thyroid-hormone deficiency. The thyroid regulates your dog's metabolism. A large number of skin problems in dogs are caused by thyroid disease.

*Osteochondritis dissecans*: Inflammation of the cartilage in the joints. A form of arthritis.

*Osteochondrosis*: An abnormal development of joint cartilage. Most commonly found in the shoulder, elbow, and knee.

*Pannus*: Progressive immune-mediated disease in which there is a growth of tissue over the cornea, causing inflammation and possible blindness.

*Progressive retinal atrophy (PRA)*: A slow deterioration of the retina, leading to blindness.

*Von Willebrand's disease*: Abnormal blood-clotting defect involving both platelet and coagulation function (factor VIII).

## IRISH WATER SPANIEL

*Cataract*: In older dogs the lens of the eye becomes cloudy, causing a partial or total loss of vision.

*Hip dysplasia*: An abnormal development of the hip joint(s).

*Hypothyroidism:* A common disease of thyroid-hormone deficiency. The thyroid regulates your dog's metabolism. A large number of skin problems in dogs are caused by thyroid disease.

*Hypotrichosis:* An abnormally small amount of hair growth.

*Progressive retinal atrophy* (**PRA**): A slow deterioration of the retina, leading to blindness.

*Teeth abnormalities:* The number, placement, or development of the teeth is not normal.

*Von Willebrand's disease:* Abnormal blood-clotting defect involving both platelet and coagulation function (factor VIII).

## KEESHOND

*Cancer:* The Keeshond is prone to skin cancer.

*Cataract:* In older dogs the lens of the eye becomes cloudy, causing a partial or total loss of vision.

*Cushing's disease (hyperadrenocorticism):* A condition in which the adrenal glands secrete too much cortisol. Cortisol is a steroid hormone which regulates carbohydrate, fat, and protein metabolism.

*Diabetes mellitus:* A disease caused by an insufficient production or use of insulin.

*Epilepsy:* A brain disorder in which the dog experiences seizures (convulsions).

*Eye abnormalities:* The Keeshond is prone to abnormally growing eyelashes and a rolling out of the eyelid(s).

*Glaucoma:* Pressure on the retina from excess fluid in the eyeball, which causes partial or total loss of vision.

*Heart disease:* Abnormal development of the aorta, valve(s), and ventricle(s).

*Hereditary kidney hypoplasia:* A condition in which the dog is born with immature kidneys that never develop completely.

*Hypothyroidism:* A common disease of thyroid-hormone deficiency. The thyroid regulates your dog's metabolism. A large number of skin problems in dogs are caused by thyroid disease.

*Keratoacanthoma:* Non-cancerous skin tumor usually found on the face.

*Liver abnormalities:* The Keeshond is prone to an abnormal formation of blood vessels in the liver.

*Progressive retinal atrophy (PRA):* A slow deterioration of the retina, leading to blindness.

*Sebaceous cyst:* A fluid-filled sac in the sebaceous gland.

*Skin disease:* The Keeshond is prone to skin problems, which clear up if the dog is neutered, and a skin disease caused by a deficiency of growth hormones.

*Von Willebrand's disease:* Abnormal blood-clotting defect involving both platelet and coagulation function (factor VIII).

## LABRADOR RETRIEVER

*Addison's disease:* A disease in which the adrenal glands secrete an insufficient amount of cortisone, a steroid hormone.

*Allergies:* The Labrador Retriever is prone to all types of allergies.

*Behavioral abnormalities:* A whole range of abnormal behavioral patterns, such as aggression and panic disorders.

*Blood-clotting disorders:* The Labrador Retriever is prone to blood-clotting disorders due to a deficiency of coagulation factors VIII or IX.

*Cancer:* The Labrador Retriever is prone to skin cancer.

*Cataract:* In older dogs the lens of the eye becomes cloudy, causing a partial or total loss of vision.

*Craniomandibular osteopathy:* Abnormally dense bones in the face and the jaw.

*Deafness:* A partial or total loss of hearing.

*Diabetes mellitus:* A disease caused by an insufficient production or use of insulin.

*Elbow dysplasia:* An abnormal development of the elbow joint(s).

*Epilepsy:* A brain disorder in which the dog experiences seizures (convulsions).

*Eye abnormalities:* The Labrador Retriever is prone to abnormally growing eyelashes, a rolling in or out of the eyelid(s), an abnormal development of the eye(s), and an abnormal development of the retina(s).

**Gastric bloat and torsion:** Gastric bloat is a swelling of the stomach from excess gas and is usually followed by gastric torsion, a twisting of the stomach. Gastric torsion will result in death if not treated immediately.

**Hip dysplasia:** An abnormal development of the hip joint(s).

**Hot spots:** A bacterial skin infection that progresses into severe inflammation from excessive licking and chewing.

**Hypertrophic osteodystrophy:** A painful inflammation of the bones along with development of bony growths, found in fast-growing giant breeds.

**Hypoglycemia:** A low level of glucose (blood sugar) in the blood.

**Hypothyroidism:** A common disease of thyroid-hormone deficiency. The thyroid regulates your dog's metabolism. A large number of skin problems in dogs are caused by thyroid disease.

**Lick granuloma (acral lick dermatitis):** Inflammation or infection of the skin from excessive licking. Usually found on the leg or paw.

**Liver abnormalities:** The Labrador Retriever is prone to an abnormal formation of blood vessels in the liver.

**Muscular dystrophy:** A progressive muscle disorder that causes a wasting of the muscles. It is an inherited disease with symptoms of slow growth, difficulty eating and swallowing, and weakness.

**Muscle-fiber deficiency:** A deficiency in form and/or function of a specific type of muscle fiber.

**Narcolepsy:** A neurological disorder in which the dog suddenly falls asleep.

**Osteochondritis dissecans:** Inflammation of the cartilage in the joints. A form of arthritis.

**Osteochondrosis:** An abnormal development of joint cartilage. Most commonly found in the shoulder, elbow, and knee.

**Progressive retinal atrophy (PRA):** A slow deterioration of the retina, leading to blindness.

**Prolapsed rectum:** The rectum slips outside the anus.

**Prolapsed uterus:** The uterus slips into the vaginal canal or through the vaginal opening.

*Seborrhea*: A skin disease characterized by raw, scaling skin and an excess of sebum (oil-like substance), which causes a rancid body odor.

*Shoulder dysplasia*: Abnormal development of the shoulder joint(s).

*Teeth abnormalities*: The number, placement, or development of the teeth is not normal.

*Von Willebrand's disease*: Abnormal blood-clotting defect involving both platelet and coagulation function (factor VIII).

*Wrist subluxation*: The wrist bones are loose and become partially dislocated.

## OLD ENGLISH SHEEPDOG

*Addison's disease*: A disease in which the adrenal glands secrete an insufficient amount of cortisone, a steroid hormone.

*Blood-clotting disorders*: The Old English Sheepdog is prone to a blood-clotting disorder due to a deficiency of coagulation factor IX.

*Cataract*: In older dogs the lens of the eye becomes cloudy, causing a partial or total loss of vision.

*Demodectic mange*: A skin disease in which canine mites are living in the skin, causing itching, loss of hair, and skin infections. Usually found on the face and front legs.

*Eye abnormalities*: The Old English Sheepdog is prone to a rolling in of the eyelid(s), abnormal development of the retina(s), and abnormally growing eyelashes.

*Folliculitis*: Inflammation of the hair follicle(s).

*Hip dysplasia*: An abnormal development of the hip joint(s).

*Immune-mediated hemolytic anemia (IMHA)*: Anemia resulting from an immune system mediated destruction of the red blood cells.

*Incontinence*: Loss of control of urination and bowel movements.

*Malabsorption*: A condition in which the small intestine does not absorb nutrients properly.

*Osteochondritis dissecans*: Inflammation of the cartilage in the joints. A form of arthritis.

*Osteochondrosis:* An abnormal development of joint cartilage. Most commonly found in the shoulder, elbow, and knee.

*Pigmentation abnormalities:* A lack of color in the skin.

*Progressive retinal atrophy (PRA):* A slow deterioration of the retina, leading to blindness.

*Thrombocytopenia:* An abnormal decrease in the number of blood platelets. Blood platelets play a role in blood clotting. Symptoms are tiny hemorrhages in the skin and mucous membranes.

*Thyroid disease:* The Old English Sheepdog is prone to thyroiditis, lymphocytic thyroiditis, and hypothyroidism. Thyroiditis and lymphocytic thyroiditis are autoimmune diseases that lead to hypothyroidism, a common disease of thyroid-hormone deficiency. The thyroid regulates your dog's metabolism. A large number of skin problems in dogs are caused by thyroid disease.

*Von Willebrand's disease:* Abnormal blood-clotting defect involving both platelet and coagulation function (factor VIII).

## OTTERHOUND

*Blood-clotting disorders:* The otterhound is prone to a blood-clotting disorder due to a deficiency of coagulation factor II.

*Hip dysplasia:* An abnormal development of the hip joint(s).

*Hypothyroidism:* A common disease of thyroid-hormone deficiency. The thyroid regulates your dog's metabolism. A large number of skin problems in dogs are caused by thyroid disease.

*Osteochondritis dissecans:* Inflammation of the cartilage in the joints. A form of arthritis.

*Osteochondrosis:* An abnormal development of joint cartilage. Most commonly found in the shoulder, elbow, and knee.

*Sebaceous cyst:* A fluid-filled sac in the sebaceous gland.

*Thrombocytopathy:* A dysfunction of the small blood cells that are needed to control bleeding.

*Von Willebrand's disease:* Abnormal blood-clotting defect involving both platelet and coagulation function (factor VIII).

## PHARAOH HOUND

*Allergies*: The Pharaoh Hound is prone to all types of allergies.

*Eye abnormalities*: The Pharaoh Hound is prone to abnormal development of the optic nerve(s).

*Hypothyroidism*: A common disease of thyroid-hormone deficiency. The thyroid regulates your dog's metabolism. A large number of skin problems in dogs are caused by thyroid disease.

*Thrombocytopenia*: An abnormal decrease in the number of blood platelets. Blood platelets play a role in blood clotting. Symptoms are tiny hemorrhages in the skin and mucous membranes.

## POINTER

*Acral mutilation*: Mutilation of the feet and legs from excessive licking. Seen in pointing breeds that are born without pain sensation.

*Allergies*: The pointer is prone to all types of allergies.

*Calcinosis*: Hard lumps of calcium salt deposits in the skin.

*Cataract*: In older dogs the lens of the eye becomes cloudy, causing a partial or total loss of vision.

*Corneal dystrophy*: An inherited degenerative condition in which the cornea of the eye becomes cloudy or opaque.

*Demodectic mange*: A skin disease in which canine mites are living in the skin, causing itching, loss of hair, and skin infections. Usually found on the face and front legs.

*Eosinophilic panosteitis*: An inflammatory bone disease found in fast-growing puppies, which is accompanied by increased eosinophils, a type of white blood cell.

*Epilepsy*: A brain disorder in which the dog experiences seizures (convulsions).

*Eye abnormalities*: The Pointer is prone to a rolling in of the eyelid(s).

*Hip dysplasia*: An abnormal development of the hip joint(s).

*Hypothyroidism*: A common disease of thyroid-hormone deficiency. The thyroid regulates your dog's metabolism. A large number of skin problems in dogs are caused by thyroid disease.

*Nerve disorders*: The Pointer is prone to a condition in which the nerves malfunction, causing a deterioration of the muscles and/or bone disease.

*Pannus*: Progressive immune-mediated disease in which there is a growth of tissue over the cornea, causing inflammation and possible blindness.

*Pemphigus foliaceous*: An autoimmune skin disease.

*Progressive retinal atrophy (PRA)*: A slow deterioration of the retina, leading to blindness.

*Umbilical hernia*: A tear in the muscle wall of the stomach where the umbilical cord was.

*Von Willebrand's disease*: Abnormal blood-clotting defect involving both platelet and coagulation function (factor VIII).

## RHODESIAN RIDGEBACK

*Cataract*: In older dogs the lens of the eye becomes cloudy, causing a partial or total loss of vision.

*Cerebellar abiotrophy*: Malformation of the neurons in the cerebellum. The cerebellum is the part of the brain that gives your dog balance, coordination, and posture.

*Dermoid cyst*: A skin-like growth usually seen on the back.

*Eye abnormalities*: The Rhodesian Ridgeback is prone to a rolling in of the eyelid(s).

*Hip dysplasia*: An abnormal development of the hip joint(s).

*Hypothyroidism*: A common disease of thyroid-hormone deficiency. The thyroid regulates your dog's metabolism. A large number of skin problems in dogs are caused by thyroid disease.

*Neck vertebrae malformation*: An abnormal development of the vertebrae in the neck that causes nerve damage. Some dogs walk with a pronounced flexion of the knee, similar to a high-stepping horse.

*Osteochondritis dissecans*: Inflammation of the cartilage in the joints. A form of arthritis.

*Osteochondrosis*: An abnormal development of joint cartilage. Most commonly found in the shoulder, elbow, and knee.

*Progressive retinal atrophy* (**PRA**): A slow deterioration of the retina, leading to blindness.

## SAMOYED

*Blood-clotting disorders*: The Samoyed is prone to a blood-clotting disorder due to a deficiency of coagulation factor VIII.

*Cancer*: The Samoyed is prone to cancer of the anus.

*Cataract*: In older dogs the lens of the eye becomes cloudy, causing a partial or total loss of vision.

*Corneal dystrophy*: An inherited degenerative condition in which the cornea of the eye becomes cloudy or opaque.

*Diabetes mellitus*: A disease caused by an insufficient production or use of insulin.

*Eye abnormalities*: The Samoyed is prone to a rolling in of the eyelid(s), abnormal development of the retina(s), and abnormally growing eyelashes.

*Glaucoma*: Pressure on the retina from excess fluid in the eyeball, which causes partial or total loss of vision.

*Heart disease*: Malfunctioning valves and a malformation of the dividing wall between two chambers of the heart.

*Hip dysplasia*: An abnormal development of the hip joint(s).

*Hypothyroidism*: A common disease of thyroid-hormone deficiency. The thyroid regulates your dog's metabolism. A large number of skin problems in dogs are caused by thyroid disease.

*Liver abnormalities*: The Samoyed is prone to an abnormal formation of blood vessels in the liver.

*Muscular dystrophy*: A progressive muscle disorder that causes a wasting of the muscles. It is an inherited disease with symptoms of slow growth, difficulty eating and swallowing, and weakness.

*Osteochondritis dissecans*: Inflammation of the cartilage in the joints. A form of arthritis.

*Osteochondrosis*: An abnormal development of joint cartilage. Most commonly found in the shoulder, elbow, and knee.

*Pigmentation abnormalities*: A lack of color in the skin.

*Progressive retinal atrophy (PRA)*: A slow deterioration of the retina, leading to blindness.

*Samoyed hereditary glomerulopathy*: A condition in male puppies in which the blood vessels of the kidneys become diseased, causing kidney failure. Females can be carriers, remaining healthy until they are older when they also experience kidney failure from diseased blood vessels of the kidney.

*Sebaceous cyst*: A fluid-filled sac in the sebaceous gland.

*Thrombocytopenia*: An abnormal decrease in the number of blood platelets. Blood platelets play a role in blood clotting. Symptoms are tiny hemorrhages in the skin and mucous membranes.

*Von Willebrand's disease*: Abnormal blood-clotting defect involving both platelet and coagulation function (factor VIII).

## SIBERIAN HUSKY

*Allergies*: The Siberian Husky is prone to an allergic reaction (inflamed tissue) from an accumulation of eosinophils, a type of white blood cell that functions in an allergic reaction to parasites.

*Blood-clotting disorders*: The Siberian husky is prone to a blood-clotting disorder due to a deficiency of coagulation factor VIII.

*Castration-responsive dermatosis*: A skin condition characterized by loss of hair, thickened skin, and inflammation, which responds to castration.

*Cataract*: In older dogs the lens of the eye becomes cloudy, causing a partial or total loss of vision.

*Corneal dystrophy*: An inherited degenerative condition in which the cornea of the eye becomes cloudy or opaque.

*Eye abnormalities*: The Siberian Husky is prone to a rolling in of the eyelid(s), abnormal development of the retina(s), and a condition in which the eye(s) slips out of place.

*Glaucoma*: Pressure on the retina from excess fluid in the eyeball, which causes partial or total loss of vision.

*Hip dysplasia*: An abnormal development of the hip joint(s).

*Hypothyroidism*: A common disease of thyroid-hormone deficiency. The thyroid regulates your dog's metabolism. A large number of skin problems in dogs are caused by thyroid disease.

*Osteochondritis dissecans*: Inflammation of the cartilage in the joints. A form of arthritis.

*Osteochondrosis*: An abnormal development of joint cartilage. Most commonly found in the shoulder, elbow, and knee.

*Pannus*: Progressive immune-mediated disease in which there is a growth of tissue over the cornea, causing inflammation and possible blindness.

*Pigmentation abnormalities*: A lack of color in the skin.

*Progressive retinal atrophy (PRA)*: A slow deterioration of the retina, leading to blindness.

*Skin disease*: The Siberian Husky is prone to autoimmune skin diseases and zinc-responsive dermatosis, a skin disease caused by a zinc deficiency.

*Von Willebrand's disease*: Abnormal blood-clotting defect involving both platelet and coagulation function (factor VIII).

## SPINONE ITALIANO

*Eclampsia*: Convulsions during or after whelping.

*Eye abnormalities*: The Spinone Italiano is prone to a rolling in of the eyelid(s).

## VIZSLA

*Blood-clotting disorders*: The vizsla is prone to a blood-clotting disorder due to a deficiency of coagulation factor VIII .

*Cancer*: The Vizsla is prone to hemangiosarcoma, a cancer of blood vessels involving liver, spleen, or skin, and cancer of the lymphatic system.

*Cataract*: In older dogs the lens of the eye becomes cloudy, causing a partial or total loss of vision.

*Craniomandibular osteopathy*: Abnormally dense bones in the face and the jaw.

*Demodectic mange*: A skin disease in which canine mites are living in the skin, causing itching, loss of hair, and skin infections. Usually found on the face and front legs.

*Epilepsy*: A brain disorder in which the dog experiences seizures (convulsions).

*Eye abnormalities*: The Vizsla is prone to a rolling in of the eyelid(s).

*Hip dysplasia*: An abnormal development of the hip joint(s).

*Hypothyroidism*: A common disease of thyroid-hormone deficiency. The thyroid regulates your dog's metabolism. A large number of skin problems in dogs are caused by thyroid disease.

*Jaw abnormality*: The lower jaw is longer than the upper jaw.

*Osteochondritis dissecans*: Inflammation of the cartilage in the joints. A form of arthritis.

*Osteochondrosis*: An abnormal development of joint cartilage. Most commonly found in the shoulder, elbow, and knee.

*Pigmentation abnormalities*: A lack of color in the skin.

*Progressive retinal atrophy (PRA)*: A slow deterioration of the retina, leading to blindness.

*Spinal abnormality*: Malformation of the spinal cord.

*Sterile pyogranuloma syndrome*: A non-infectious disease of the deep layers of the skin, characterized by inflammation and sores.

*Umbilical hernia*: A tear in the muscle wall of the stomach where the umbilical cord was.

## WEIRMARANER

*Alopecia*: Loss of hair.

*Antibody (type IgA) deficiency*: A deficiency in the production of the type IgA antibody, causing a weakened immune system.

*Antibody (type IgG) deficiency*: A deficiency of circulating antibodies, causing a weakened immune system.

*Antibody (type IgM) deficiency*: A deficiency of antibody production during the initial response of the immune system to an antigen.

*Blood-clotting disorders*: The Weirmaraner is prone to a blood-clotting disorder due to a deficiency of coagulation factor VIII.

*Cancer*: The Weirmaraner is prone to mastocytoma, a rare form of cancer in which the mast cells become cancerous. The mast cell secretes histamine in response to allergens.

*Corneal dystrophy*: An inherited degenerative condition in which the cornea of the eye becomes cloudy or opaque.

*Eosinophilic panosteitis*: An inflammatory bone disease found in fast-growing puppies, which is accompanied by increased eosinophils, a type of white blood cell.

*Eye abnormalities*: The Weirmaraner is prone to a rolling in of the eyelid(s), abnormally growing eyelashes, and a protruding third eyelid(s).

*Gastric bloat and torsion*: Gastric bloat is a swelling of the stomach from excess gas and is usually followed by gastric torsion, a twisting of the stomach. Gastric torsion will result in death if not treated immediately.

*Growth-hormone-responsive dermatosis*: Skin disorder caused by a deficiency of growth hormones.

*Hip dysplasia*: An abnormal development of the hip joint(s).

*Hypertrophic osteodystrophy*: A painful inflammation of the bones along with development of bony growths, found in fast-growing giant breeds.

*Hypothyroidism*: A common disease of thyroid-hormone deficiency. The thyroid regulates your dog's metabolism. A large number of skin problems in dogs are caused by thyroid disease.

*Jaw abnormality*: The lower jaw is longer than the upper jaw.

*Myasthenia gravis*: An autoimmune disease characterized by progressive muscle fatigue and generalized weakness resulting from the impaired transmission of nerve impulses.

*Progressive retinal atrophy (PRA)*: A slow deterioration of the retina, leading to blindness.

*Spinal abnormality*: Malformation of the spinal cord.

*Sterile pyogranuloma syndrome*: A non-infectious disease of the deep layers of the skin characterized by inflammation and sores.

*T-cell deficiency*: A deficiency of the T-lymphocyte cell, a type of white blood cell, resulting in a weakened immune system.

*Umbilical hernia*: A tear in the muscle wall of the stomach where the umbilical cord was.

*Vaccination reaction*: Puppies are prone to an autoimmune reaction from modified live virus vaccines.

## WIREHAIRED POINTING GRIFFON
*Hip dysplasia*: An abnormal development of the hip joint(s).

*Narcolepsy*: A neurological disorder in which the dog suddenly falls asleep.

*Otitis externa*: An inflammation of the external parts of the ear.

# Purebred Medium—20-50 Pounds

## AMERICAN COCKER SPANIEL
*Allergies*: The American Cocker Spaniel is prone to all types of allergies.

*Anasarca*: An accumulation of fluids in various tissues and body cavities in newborn puppies.

*Behavioral abnormalities*: A whole range of abnormal behavior patterns, such as aggression and panic disorders.

*Blood-clotting disorders*: The American Cocker Spaniel is prone to a blood-clotting disorder due to a deficiency of coagulation factors VIII or IX.

*Cancer*: The American Cocker Spaniel is prone to cancer of the anus, skin, and mammary glands.

*Cataract*: In older dogs the lens of the eye becomes cloudy, causing a partial or total loss of vision.

*Cleft palate and/or lip*: Birth defects in which, with cleft palate, the roof of the mouth doesn't grow properly, leaving a hole from the roof of the mouth into the nose or, with cleft lip, the skin below the nose doesn't grow together.

*Corneal dystrophy*: An inherited degenerative condition in which the cornea of the eye becomes cloudy or opaque.

*Cyclic hematopoiesis*: A condition in which, periodically, a type of white blood cell is not produced.

*Ehler's-Danlos syndrome*: A connective-tissue disease in which the skin is very fragile and is easily cut or bruised.

*Elbow dysplasia*: An abnormal development of the elbow joint(s).

*Epidermoid cyst*: A fluid-filled sac in the outermost layer of the skin.

*Epilepsy*: A brain disorder in which the dog experiences seizures (convulsions).

*Eye abnormalities*: The American Cocker Spaniel is prone to a rolling in or out of the eyelid(s), abnormally growing eyelashes, a condition in which the eye slips out of place, abnormal development of the retina(s), and a condition called dry eye in which the eye(s) does not produce enough liquid.

*Glaucoma*: Pressure on the retina from excess fluid in the eyeball, which causes partial or total loss of vision.

*Heart disease*: Cardiomyopathy, or weakened heart muscles.

*Hernia*: A rupture of the wall of an internal organ in the groin area.

*Immune-mediated hemolytic anemia (IMHA)*: Anemia resulting from an immune system mediated destruction of the red blood cells.

*Hereditary kidney hypoplasia*: A condition in which the dog is born with immature kidneys that never develop completely.

*Hip dysplasia*: An abnormal development of the hip joint(s).

*Hydrocephalus*: The accumulation of fluid in the brain.

*Hypothyroidism*: A common disease of thyroid-hormone deficiency. The thyroid regulates your dog's metabolism. A large number of skin problems in dogs are caused by thyroid disease.

*Intervertebral disc disease*: Abnormal development of the discs between the vertebrae.

*Jaw abnormality*: The lower jaw is longer than the upper jaw.

*Osteochondritis dissecans*: Inflammation of the cartilage in the joints. A form of arthritis.

*Osteochondrosis*: An abnormal development of joint cartilage. Most commonly found in the shoulder, elbow, and knee.

*Otitis externa*: An infection of the external structures of the ear.

*Overshot jaw*: A condition in which the upper jaw is too long for the lower jaw.

*Patellar luxation*: The kneecap(s) slips out of place.

*Progressive retinal atrophy (PRA)*: A slow deterioration of the retina, leading to blindness.

*Skin disease*: The American Cocker Spaniel is prone to all types of allergic, autoimmune, hormonal, nutritional, and parasitic skin diseases.

*Skin tumors*: The American Cocker Spaniel is prone to all types of skin tumors.

*Umbilical hernia*: A tear in the muscle wall of the stomach where the umbilical cord was.

*Von Willebrand's disease*: Abnormal blood-clotting defect involving both platelet and coagulation function (factor VIII).

## AMERICAN ESKIMO

*Allergies*: Allergic reactions to flea bites.

*Hip dysplasia*: An abnormal development of the hip joint(s).

*Urolithiasis*: Stones or crystals in the urinary tract.

## AUSTRALIAN CATTLE DOG (BLUE HEELER)

*Blood-clotting disorders*: The Australian Cattle Dog is prone to a blood-clotting disorder due to a deficiency of coagulation factor VIII.

*Cataract*: In older dogs the lens of the eye becomes cloudy, causing a partial or total loss of vision.

*Deafness*: A partial or total loss of hearing.

*Epilepsy*: A brain disorder in which the dog experiences seizures (convulsions).

*Eye abnormalities*: The Australian Cattle Dog is prone to an abnormal development of the retina(s), and a condition where the lens in the eye slips out of place.

*Hernia*: A rupture of the wall of an internal organ in the groin area.

*Hip dysplasia*: An abnormal development of the hip joint(s).

*Hypothyroidism*: A common disease of thyroid-hormone deficiency. The thyroid regulates your dog's metabolism. A large number of skin problems in dogs are caused by thyroid disease.

*Jaw abnormality*: The lower jaw is longer than the upper jaw.

*Liver abnormality*: The Australian Cattle Dog is prone to an abnormal formation of blood vessels in the liver.

*Neuronal ceroid-lipofuscinosis*: An accumulation of fatty pigments in the brain.

*Osteochondritis dissecans*: Inflammation of the cartilage in the joints. A form of arthritis.

*Overshot jaw*: A condition in which the upper jaw is too long for the lower jaw.

*Progressive retinal atrophy (PRA)*: A slow deterioration of the retina, leading to blindness.

*Teeth abnormalities*: The number, placement, or development of the teeth is not normal.

*Umbilical hernia*: A tear in the muscle wall of the stomach where the umbilical cord was.

## AUSTRALIAN KELPIE

*Collie eye anomaly*: An inherited disorder in which the narrow shape of the head causes the eyes to be malformed.

*Progressive retinal atrophy (PRA)*: A slow deterioration of the retina, leading to blindness.

## AUSTRALIAN SHEPHERD

*Cataract*: In older dogs the lens of the eye becomes cloudy, causing a partial or total loss of vision.

*Cleft palate*: A birth defect in which the roof of the mouth doesn't grow properly, leaving a hole from the roof of the mouth into the nose.

*Deafness*: A partial or total loss of hearing.

*Eye abnormalities*: The Australian Shepherd is prone to abnormal development of the retina(s) and collie-eye anomaly, an inherited disorder where the narrow shape of the head causes the eyes to be malformed.

*Hip dysplasia*: An abnormal development of the hip joint(s).

*Hypothyroidism*: A common disease of thyroid-hormone deficiency. The thyroid regulates your dog's metabolism. A large number of skin problems in dogs are caused by thyroid disease.

*Osteochondritis dissecans*: Inflammation of the cartilage in the joints. A form of arthritis.

*Osteochondrosis*: An abnormal development of joint cartilage. Most commonly found in the shoulder, elbow, and knee.

*Pigmentation abnormalities*: A lack of color in the skin.

*Progressive retinal atrophy* (**PRA**): A slow deterioration of the retina, leading to blindness.

*Spina bifida*: A developmental abnormality in which the vertebrae fail to encircle the spinal cord.

*Umbilical hernia*: A tear in the muscle wall of the stomach where the umbilical cord was.

*Von Willebrand's disease*: Abnormal blood-clotting defect involving both platelet and coagulation function (factor VIII).

## BASENJI

*Blood-clotting disorders*: The Basenji is prone to a blood-clotting disorder due to a deficiency of coagulation factor XII.

*Coliform enteritis*: Inflammation of the small intestine caused by bacteria.

*Eye abnormalities*: The Basenji is prone to an abnormal development of the eye(s) or an abnormal development of the retina(s).

*Hernia*: A rupture of the wall of an internal organ in the groin area.

*Hypothyroidism*: A common disease of thyroid-hormone deficiency. The thyroid regulates your dog's metabolism. A large number of skin problems in dogs are caused by thyroid disease.

*Immune-mediated hemolytic anemia (IMHA)*: Anemia resulting from an immune system mediated destruction of the red blood cells.

*Malabsorption*: A condition in which the small intestine does not absorb nutrients properly.

*Progressive retinal atrophy (PRA)*: A slow deterioration of the retina, leading to blindness.

*Pyruvate kinase deficiency*: A symptom of immune-mediated hemolytic anemia in Basenjis. Pyruvate kinase is an essential red-blood-cell enzyme.

*Renal tubular dysfunction*: A condition in which the kidneys don't filter waste properly. In Basenjis, renal tubular dysfunction often leads to glycosuria (excess sugar in the urine).

*Umbilical hernia*: A tear in the muscle wall of the stomach where the umbilical cord was.

## BASSET HOUND

*Addison's disease*: A disease in which the adrenal glands secrete an insufficient amount of cortisone, a steroid hormone.

*Antibody (type IgA) deficiency*: A deficiency in the production of the type IgA antibody, causing a weakened immune system.

*Antibody (type IgG) deficiency*: A deficiency of circulating antibodies, causing a weakened immune system.

*Antibody (type IgM) deficiency*: A deficiency of antibody production during the initial response of the immune system to an antigen.

*Behavioral abnormalities*: A whole range of abnormal behavior patterns, such as aggression and panic disorders.

*Blood-clotting disorders*: The Basset Hound is prone to blood-clotting disorders due to a deficiency of coagulation factors VII or VIII.

*Bone disease*: The Basset Hound is prone to developmental abnormalities of the bones.

*Cryptorchidism*: A developmental condition in which one or both testicles fail to descend into the scrotum.

*Eosinophilic panosteitis:* An inflammatory bone disease found in fast-growing puppies, which is accompanied by increased eosinophils, a type of white blood cell.

*Epilepsy:* A brain disorder in which the dog experiences seizures (convulsions).

*Eye abnormalities:* The Basset Hound is prone to a rolling in or out of the eyelid(s), a protruding third eyelid(s), and a condition where the lens in the eye slips out of place.

**Gastric bloat and torsion:** Gastric bloat is a swelling of the stomach from excess gas and is usually followed by gastric torsion, a twisting of the stomach. Gastric torsion will result in death if not treated immediately.

*Glaucoma:* Pressure on the retina from excess fluid in the eyeball, which causes partial or total loss of vision.

*Globoid cell leukodystrophy:* Degeneration of a type of brain cell.

*Hot spots:* A bacterial skin infection that progresses into severe inflammation from excessive licking and chewing.

*Hernia:* A rupture of the wall of an internal organ in the groin area.

*Hypothyroidism:* A common disease of thyroid-hormone deficiency. The thyroid regulates your dog's metabolism. A large number of skin problems in dogs are caused by thyroid disease.

**Immune-mediated hemolytic anemia (IMHA):** Anemia resulting from an immune system mediated destruction of the red blood cells.

*Intussusception:* A section of the intestinal tract slips into an adjoining section.

*Lung torsion:* A condition where the lung twists upon itself.

**Osteochondritis dissecans:** Inflammation of the cartilage in the joints. A form of arthritis.

**Osteochondrosis:** An abnormal development of joint cartilage. Most commonly found in the shoulder, elbow, and knee.

*Patellar luxation:* The kneecap(s) slips out of place.

*Platelet dysfunction:* Platelets, which are small blood cells needed to control bleeding, do not function properly.

*Progressive retinal atrophy (PRA)*: A slow deterioration of the retina, leading to blindness.

*Sebaceous cyst*: A fluid-filled sac in the sebaceous gland.

*Splenic torsion*: A condition where the spleen twists upon itself.

*T-cell deficiency*: A deficiency of the T-lymphocyte cell, a type of white blood cell, resulting in a weakened immune system.

*Thrombocytopathy*: The small blood cells that are needed to control bleeding are dysfunctional.

*Umbilical hernia*: A tear in the muscle wall of the stomach where the umbilical cord was.

*Vertebra abnormality*: Malformation of third cervical vertebra, which is one of the neck bones in the spinal column.

*Von Willebrand's disease*: Abnormal blood-clotting defect involving both platelet and coagulation function (factor VIII).

*Wobbler's syndrome*: The neck vertebrae are malformed, causing them to slip out of place, and leading to incoordination of the rear legs.

## BEAGLE

*Allergies*: The Beagle is prone to all types of allergies.

*Amyloidosis*: Degeneration of the tissues from a buildup of hard, waxy deposits made of protein and polysaccharides (amyloids).

*Antibody (type IgA) deficiency*: A deficiency in the production of the type IgA antibody, causing a weakened immune system.

*Atopic dermatitis*: A skin disease from inhalant allergies.

*Blood-clotting disorders*: The Beagle is prone to a blood-clotting disorder due to a deficiency of coagulation factors VII or VIII.

*Cancer*: The Beagle is prone to bladder cancer and cancer of the anus.

*Cataract*: In older dogs the lens of the eye becomes cloudy, causing a partial or total loss of vision.

*Cleft palate and/or lip*: Birth defects in which, with cleft palate, the roof of the mouth doesn't grow properly, leaving a hole from the roof of the mouth into the nose or, with cleft lip, the skin below the nose doesn't grow together.

*Corneal dystrophy*: An inherited degenerative condition in which the cornea of the eye becomes cloudy or opaque.

*Demodectic mange*: A skin disease in which canine mites are living in the skin, causing itching, loss of hair, and skin infections. Usually found on the face and front legs.

*Ear infections*: The Beagle is prone to ear infections from dying cells in the ear and surrounding tissue.

*Ehler's-Danlos syndrome*: A connective-tissue disease in which the skin is very fragile and is easily cut or bruised.

*Epilepsy*: A brain disorder in which the dog experiences seizures (convulsions).

*Epiphyseal dysplasia*: Abnormal development of the long bone.

*Eye abnormalities*: The Beagle is prone to abnormally growing eyelashes, protruding third eyelid(s), abnormal development of the retina(s), and malformation of the optic nerve.

*Glaucoma*: Pressure on the retina from excess fluid in the eyeball, which causes partial or total loss of vision.

*Globoid cell leukodystrophy*: Degeneration of a type of brain cell.

*Heart disease*: Malfunctioning valve(s), abnormal development of the heart.

*Immune-mediated hemolytic anemia (IMHA)*: Anemia resulting from an immune system mediated destruction of the red blood cells.

*Intervertebral disc disease*: Abnormal development of the discs between the vertebrae.

*Kidney disease*: The Beagle is prone to abnormal development of the kidney(s) or a condition where there is only one kidney.

*Lipidosis*: An accumulation of lipids (fats) in the nerves.

*Progressive retinal atrophy (PRA)*: A slow deterioration of the retina, leading to blindness.

*Sebaceous cyst*: A fluid-filled sac in the sebaceous gland.

*Thyroid disease*: The Beagle is prone to thyroiditis, lymphocytic thyroiditis, and hypothyroidism. Thyroiditis and lymphocytic thyroiditis are autoimmune diseases that lead to hypothyroidism, a common disease of thyroid-hormone deficiency. The thyroid regulates your dog's metabolism. A large number of skin problems in dogs are caused by thyroid disease.

*Von Willebrand's disease*: Abnormal blood-clotting defect involving both platelet and coagulation function (factor VIII).

## BELGIAN MALINOIS

*Epilepsy*: A brain disorder in which the dog experiences seizures (convulsions).

*Hip dysplasia*: An abnormal development of the hip joint(s).

*Hypothyroidism*: A common disease of thyroid-hormone deficiency. The thyroid regulates your dog's metabolism. A large number of skin problems in dogs are caused by thyroid disease.

*Progressive retinal atrophy (PRA)*: A slow deterioration of the retina, leading to blindness.

## BORDER COLLIE

*Corneal dystrophy*: An inherited degenerative condition in which the cornea of the eye becomes cloudy or opaque.

*Epilepsy*: A brain disorder in which the dog experiences seizures (convulsions).

*Hip dysplasia*: An abnormal development of the hip joint(s).

*Eye abnormalities*: The Border Collie is prone to a condition where the lens in the eye slips out of place.

*Neuronal ceroid-lipofuscinos is*: An accumulation of fatty pigments in the brain.

*Osteochondritis dissecans*: Inflammation of the cartilage in the joints. A form of arthritis.

*Osteochondrosis*: An abnormal development of joint cartilage. Most commonly found in the shoulder, elbow, and knee.

*Progressive retinal atrophy (PRA)*: A slow deterioration of the retina, leading to blindness.

## BRITTANY SPANIEL

*Blood-clotting disorders*: The Brittany Spaniel is prone to a blood-clotting disorder due to a deficiency of coagulation factor VIII.

*Cataract*: In older dogs the lens of the eye becomes cloudy, causing a partial or total loss of vision.

*Cleft palate*: A birth defect in which the roof of the mouth doesn't grow properly, leaving a hole from the roof of the mouth into the nose.

*Eye abnormalities*: The Brittany Spaniel is prone to abnormal development of the retina(s), and abnormally growing eyelashes, a condition where the lens in the eye slips out of place.

*Hereditary glomerulopathy*: A condition in male puppies where the blood vessels of the kidneys become diseased, causing kidney failure. Females can be carriers, remaining healthy until they are older when they also experience kidney failure from diseased blood vessels of the kidney.

*Osteochondritis dissecans*: Inflammation of the cartilage in the joints. A form of arthritis.

*Osteochondrosis*: An abnormal development of joint cartilage. Most commonly found in the shoulder, elbow, and knee.

*Progressive retinal atrophy* (**PRA**): A slow deterioration of the retina, leading to blindness.

## CANAAN DOG

*Hip dysplasia*: An abnormal development of the hip joint(s).

*Thyroid disease*: The Canaan Dog is prone to thyroiditis, lymphocytic thyroiditis, and hypothyroidism. Thyroiditis and lymphocytic thyroiditis are autoimmune diseases that lead to hypothyroidism, a common disease of thyroid-hormone deficiency. The thyroid regulates your dog's metabolism. A large number of skin problems in dogs are caused by thyroid disease.

## CARDIGAN WELSH CORGI

*Antibody (type IgA) deficiency*: A deficiency in the production of the type IgA antibody, causing a weakened immune system.

*Antibody (type IgG) deficiency*: A deficiency of circulating antibodies, causing a weakened immune system.

*Antibody (type IgM) deficiency*: A deficiency of antibody production during the initial response of the immune system to an antigen.

*Dystocia*: Complications giving birth.

*Eye abnormalities*: The Cardigan Welsh Corgi is prone to a rolling in of the eyelid(s), abnormal development of the retina(s), and a condition where the lens in the eye slips out of place.

*Glaucoma*: Pressure on the retina from excess fluid in the eyeball, which causes partial or total loss of vision.

*Intervertebral disc disease*: Abnormal development of the discs between the vertebrae.

*Progressive retinal atrophy (PRA)*: A slow deterioration of the retina, leading to blindness.

*T-cell deficiency*: A deficiency of the T-lymphocyte cell, a type of white blood cell, resulting in a weakened immune system.

## CHINESE SHAR-PEI

*Allergies*: The Chinese Shar-Pei is prone to all types of allergies.

*Antibody (type IgA) deficiency*: A deficiency in the production of the type IgA antibody, causing a weakened immune system.

*Carpal laxity*: Weak carpal (wrist) ligaments.

*Demodectic mange*: A skin disease in which canine mites are living in the skin, causing itching, loss of hair, and skin infections. Usually found on the face and front legs.

*Dermatitis*: An inflammation in the skin folds.

*Eye abnormalities*: The Chinese Shar-Pei is prone to a rolling in or out of the eyelid(s), tight muscles around the eyes causing repetitive blinking, abnormal development of the retina(s), and a condition where the lens in the eye slips out of place.

*Folliculitis*: Inflammation of the hair follicle(s).

*Gastric bloat and torsion*: Gastric bloat is a swelling of the stomach from excess gas and is usually followed by gastric torsion, a twisting of the stomach. Gastric torsion will result in death if not treated immediately.

*Glaucoma*: Pressure on the retina from excess fluid in the eyeball, which causes partial or total loss of vision.

*Hip dysplasia*: An abnormal development of the hip joint(s).

*Hypothyroidism*: A common disease of thyroid-hormone deficiency. The thyroid regulates your dog's metabolism. A large number of skin problems in dogs are caused by thyroid disease.

*Jaw abnormality*: The lower jaw is longer than the upper jaw.

*Malabsorption*: A condition in which the small intestine does not absorb nutrients properly.

*Osteochondritis dissecans*: Inflammation of the cartilage in the joints. A form of arthritis.

*Osteochondrosis*: An abnormal development of joint cartilage. Most commonly found in the shoulder, elbow, and knee.

*Otitis externa*: An infection of the external structures of the ear.

*Patellar luxation*: The kneecap(s) slips out of place.

*Progressive retinal atrophy (PRA)*: A slow deterioration of the retina, leading to blindness.

*Seborrhea*: A skin disease characterized by raw, scaling skin and an excess of sebum (oil-like substance), which causes a rancid body odor.

*Stenotic nares*: A condition where excess flesh causes the openings of the nose (nares) to be too small to breath with ease.

*Tight-lip syndrome*: A condition in which the lower lip is too big and covers the lower teeth.

## ENGLISH COCKER SPANIEL

*Blood-clotting disorders*: The English Cocker Spaniel is prone to a blood-clotting disorder due to a deficiency of coagulation factors II or VIII.

*Cataract*: In older dogs the lens of the eye becomes cloudy, causing a partial or total loss of vision.

*Cryptorchidism*: A developmental condition in which one or both testicles fail to descend into the scrotum.

*Eye abnormalities*: The English Cocker Spaniel is prone to a rolling in or out of the eyelid(s), abnormally growing eyelashes, abnormal development of the retina(s), and a condition where the lens in the eye slips out of place.

*Glaucoma*: Pressure on the retina from excess fluid in the eyeball, which causes partial or total loss of vision.

*Hypothyroidism*: A common disease of thyroid-hormone deficiency. The thyroid regulates your dog's metabolism. A large number of skin problems in dogs are caused by thyroid disease.

*Neuronal ceroid-lipofuscinosis*: An accumulation of fatty pigments in the brain.

*Osteochondritis dissecans*: Inflammation of the cartilage in the joints. A form of arthritis.

*Osteochondrosis*: An abnormal development of joint cartilage. Most commonly found in the shoulder, elbow, and knee.

*Progressive retinal atrophy (PRA)*: A slow deterioration of the retina, leading to blindness.

*Skin disease*: The English Cocker Spaniel is prone to allergic, autoimmune, hormonal, nutritional, and parasitic skin disease.

*Swimmer puppies*: A developmental condition caused by a weakness of the muscles that puppies use to pull their legs together. Newborns are unable to put their feet under them to walk.

*Von Willebrand's disease*: Abnormal blood-clotting defect involving both platelet and coagulation function (factor VIII).

## ENGLISH SPRINGER SPANIEL

*Addison's disease*: A disease in which the adrenal glands secrete an insufficient amount of cortisone, a steroid hormone.

*Allergies*: The English Springer Spaniel is prone to all types of allergies.

*Anasarca*: An accumulation of fluids in various tissues and body cavities in newborn puppies.

*Behavioral abnormalities*: A whole range of abnormal behavioral patterns, such as aggression, panic disorders, and sudden attacks of rage.

*Blood-clotting disorders*: The English Springer Spaniel is prone to a blood-clotting disorder due to a deficiency of coagulation factors VIII, IX, X, or XI.

*Cancer*: The English Springer Spaniel is prone to cancer of the anus, mammary glands, and skin.

*Cataract*: In older dogs the lens of the eye becomes cloudy, causing a partial or total loss of vision.

*Cleft palate and/or lip*: Birth defects in which, with cleft palate, the roof of the mouth doesn't grow properly, leaving a hole from the roof of the mouth into the nose or, with cleft lip, the skin below the nose doesn't grow together.

*Corneal dystrophy*: An inherited degenerative condition in which the cornea of the eye becomes cloudy or opaque.

*Ehler's-Danlos syndrome*: A connective-tissue disease in which the skin is very fragile and is easily cut or bruised.

*Elbow dysplasia*: An abnormal development of the elbow joint(s).

*Epidermoid cyst*: A fluid-filled sac in the outermost layer of the skin.

*Epilepsy*: A brain disorder in which the dog experiences seizures (convulsions).

*Eye abnormalities*: The English Cocker Spaniel is prone to abnormal development of the eye(s), a rolling in or out of the eyelid(s), abnormally growing eyelashes, and abnormal development of the retina(s).

*Glaucoma*: Pressure on the retina from excess fluid in the eyeball, which causes partial or total loss of vision.

*Hereditary kidney hypoplasia*: A condition in which the dog is born with immature kidneys that never develop completely.

*Hernia*: A rupture of the wall of an internal organ in the groin area.

*Hip dysplasia*: An abnormal development of the hip joint(s).

*Hydrocephalus*: The accumulation of fluid in the brain.

*Hypothyroidism*: A common disease of thyroid-hormone deficiency. The thyroid regulates your dog's metabolism. A large number of skin problems in dogs are caused by thyroid disease.

*Immune-mediated hemolytic anemia* (**IMHA**): Anemia resulting from an immune system mediated destruction of the red blood cells.

*Intervertebral disc disease*: Abnormal development of the discs between the vertebrae.

*Jaw abnormality*: The lower jaw is longer than the upper jaw.

*Narcolepsy*: A neurological disorder in which the dog suddenly falls asleep.

*Osteochondritis dissecans*: Inflammation of the cartilage in the joints. A form of arthritis.

*Osteochondrosis*: An abnormal development of joint cartilage. Most commonly found in the shoulder, elbow, and knee.

*Otitis externa*: An infection of the external structures of the ear.

*Overshot jaw*: A condition in which the upper jaw is too long for the lower jaw.

*Patellar luxation*: The kneecap(s) slips out of place.

*Phosphofructokinase deficiency*: A deficiency of a specific red-blood-cell enzyme.

*Progressive retinal atrophy* (**PRA**): A slow deterioration of the retina, leading to blindness.

*Seborrhea*: A skin disease characterized by raw, scaling skin and an excess of sebum (oil-like substance), which causes a rancid body odor.

*Skin tumors*: The English Springer Spaniel is prone to all types of skin tumors.

*Umbilical hernia*: A tear in the muscle wall of the stomach where the umbilical cord was.

*Von Willebrand's disease*: Abnormal blood-clotting defect involving both platelet and coagulation function (factor VIII).

## FIELD SPANIEL

*Anesthetic sensitivity*: A serious condition in which a dog is very sensitive to anesthesia. In many cases the dog is also sensitive to medications and flea-control products that contain pesticides.

*Cataract*: In older dogs the lens of the eye becomes cloudy, causing a partial or total loss of vision.

*Eye abnormalities*: The Field Spaniel is prone to abnormal development of the retina(s).

*Hypothyroidism*: A common disease of thyroid-hormone deficiency. The thyroid regulates your dog's metabolism. A large number of skin problems in dogs are caused by thyroid disease.

*Progressive retinal atrophy* (PRA): A slow deterioration of the retina, leading to blindness.

## FINNISH SPITZ

*Diabetes mellitus*: A disease caused by an insufficient production or use of insulin.

## FRENCH BULLDOG

*Blood-clotting disorders*: The French Bulldog is prone to a blood-clotting disorder due to a deficiency of coagulation factors II, VIII, or IX.

*Cataract*: In older dogs the lens of the eye becomes cloudy, causing a partial or total loss of vision.

*Cleft palate and/or lip*: Birth defects in which, with cleft palate, the roof of the mouth doesn't grow properly, leaving a hole from the roof of the mouth into the nose or, with cleft lip, the skin below the nose doesn't grow together.

*Eye abnormalities*: The French Bulldog is prone to abnormally growing eyelashes and a rolling in of the eyelid(s).

*Vertebra malformation*: A condition in which only half the vertebra is formed.

*Von Willebrand's disease*: Abnormal blood-clotting defect involving both platelet and coagulation function (factor VIII).

## HARRIER

*Epilepsy*: A brain disorder in which the dog experiences seizures (convulsions).

*Hip dysplasia*: An abnormal development of the hip joint(s).

## HUNGARIAN PULI

*Behavioral abnormalities*: A whole range of abnormal behavioral patterns, such as aggression and panic disorders.

*Cataract*: In older dogs the lens of the eye becomes cloudy, causing a partial or total loss of vision.

*Eye abnormalities*: The Hungarian Puli is prone to abnormal development of the retina(s).

*Hip dysplasia*: An abnormal development of the hip joint(s).

*Progressive retinal atrophy (PRA)*: A slow deterioration of the retina, leading to blindness.

## IBIZAN HOUND

*Allergies*: The Ibizan Hound is prone to all types of allergies.

*Anesthetic sensitivity*: A serious condition in which a dog is very sensitive to anesthesia. In many cases the dog is also sensitive to medications and flea-control products that contain pesticides.

*Cataract*: In older dogs the lens of the eye becomes cloudy, causing a partial or total loss of vision.

*Cryptorchidism*: A developmental condition in which one or both testicles fail to descend into the scrotum.

*Eye abnormalities*: The Ibizan Hound is prone to abnormal development of the retina(s).

*Hypothyroidism*: A common disease of thyroid-hormone deficiency. The thyroid regulates your dog's metabolism. A large number of skin problems in dogs are caused by thyroid disease.

*Thrombocytopenia*: An abnormal decrease in the number of blood platelets. Blood platelets play a role in blood clotting. Symptoms are tiny hemorrhages in the skin and mucous membranes.

## IRISH SETTER

*Allergies*: The Irish Setter is prone to all types of allergies.

*Blood-clotting disorders*: The Irish Setter is prone to a blood-clotting disorder due to a deficiency of coagulation factor VIII.

*Bone disease*: Diseases of the bone caused by a metabolic dysfunction.

*Cataract*: In older dogs the lens of the eye becomes cloudy, causing a partial or total loss of vision.

*Corneal dystrophy:* An inherited degenerative condition in which the cornea of the eye becomes cloudy or opaque.

*Elbow dysplasia:* An abnormal development of the elbow joint(s).

*Epilepsy:* A brain disorder in which the dog experiences seizures (convulsions).

*Eye abnormalities:* The Irish Setter is prone to a rolling in of the eyelid(s), abnormal development of the optic nerve, abnormally growing eyelashes, and a condition where the lens in the eye slips out of place.

*Folliculitis:* Inflammation of the hair follicle(s).

*Gastric bloat and torsion:* Gastric bloat is a swelling of the stomach from excess gas and is usually followed by gastric torsion, a twisting of the stomach. Gastric torsion will result in death if not treated immediately.

*Generalized myopathy:* A muscle disorder that affects all muscles.

*Hip dysplasia:* An abnormal development of the hip joint(s).

*Hypothyroidism:* A common disease of thyroid-hormone deficiency. The thyroid regulates your dog's metabolism. A large number of skin problems in dogs are caused by thyroid disease.

*Immune-mediated hemolytic anemia (IMHA):* Anemia resulting from an immune system mediated destruction of the red blood cells.

*Lick granuloma (acral lick dermatitis):* Inflammation or infection of the skin from excessive licking. Usually found on the leg or paw.

*Lymphedema:* An accumulation of fluid in the tissues due to a disorder of the lymphatic system.

*Narcolepsy:* A neurological disorder in which the dog suddenly falls asleep.

*Osteochondritis dissecans:* Inflammation of the cartilage in the joints. A form of arthritis.

*Osteochondrosis:* An abnormal development of joint cartilage. Most commonly found in the shoulder, elbow, and knee.

*Pigmentation abnormalities:* A lack of color in the skin.

*Progressive retinal atrophy (PRA):* A slow deterioration of the retina, leading to blindness.

*Skin disease:* The Irish Setter is prone to deep infections of the skin (boils), infections from allergies, and seborrhea, a skin disease characterized by raw, scaling skin and an excess of sebum (oil-like substance) that causes a rancid body odor.

*Thrombocytopenia:* An abnormal decrease in the number of blood platelets. Blood platelets play a role in blood clotting. Symptoms are tiny hemorrhages in the skin and mucous membranes.

*Wrist subluxation:* The wrist bones are loose and become partially dislocated.

## IRISH TERRIER

*Hyperkeratosis:* An enlargement and thickening of the foot pads causing them to become cracked and infected if not treated.

*Muscular dystrophy:* A progressive muscle disorder that causes a wasting of the muscles. It is an inherited disease with symptoms of slow growth, difficulty eating and swallowing, and weakness.

*Progressive retinal atrophy (PRA):* A slow deterioration of the retina, leading to blindness.

## KERRY BLUE TERRIER

*Blood-clotting disorders:* The Kerry Blue Terrier is prone to a blood-clotting disorder due to a deficiency of coagulation factor XI.

*Cataract:* In older dogs the lens of the eye becomes cloudy, causing a partial or total loss of vision.

*Elbow dysplasia:* An abnormal development of the elbow joint(s).

*Eye abnormalities:* The Kerry Blue Terrier is prone to abnormally growing eyelashes, a rolling in of the eyelid(s), too small an opening between the upper and lower eyelids, and dry eye, a condition in which the eye(s) does not produce enough liquid.

*Hair follicle tumors:* Abnormal growths of the hair follicles.

*Hypothyroidism:* A common disease of thyroid-hormone deficiency. The thyroid regulates your dog's metabolism. A large number of skin problems in dogs are caused by thyroid disease.

*Neuron malfunction*: The neurons in the cerebellum (brain) and spinal cord are malformed.

*Progressive retinal atrophy (PRA)*: A slow deterioration of the retina, leading to blindness.

*Thrombocytopenia*: An abnormal decrease in the number of blood platelets. Blood platelets play a role in blood clotting. Symptoms are tiny hemorrhages in the skin and mucous membranes.

*Von Willebrand's disease*: Abnormal blood-clotting defect involving both platelet and coagulation function (factor VIII).

## MINIATURE BULL TERRIER

*Eye abnormalities*: The Miniature Bull Terrier is prone to a rolling in of the eyelid(s) and a condition where the lens in the eye slips out of place.

*Hypothyroidism*: A common disease of thyroid-hormone deficiency. The thyroid regulates your dog's metabolism. A large number of skin problems in dogs are caused by thyroid disease.

## MINIATURE POODLE

*Allergies*: The Miniature Poodle is prone to all types of allergies.

*Behavioral abnormalities*: A whole range of abnormal behavioral patterns, such as aggression and panic disorders.

*Blood-clotting disorders*: The Miniature Poodle is prone to a blood-clotting disorder due to a deficiency of coagulation factor VIII.

*Bone disease*: The Miniature Poodle is prone to abnormal mineralization of the bones, leading to a weak bone structure.

*Cancer*: The Miniature Poodle is prone to skin cancer and cancer of the toe.

*Cataract*: In older dogs the lens of the eye becomes cloudy, causing a partial or total loss of vision.

*Cushing's disease (hyperadrenocorticism)*: A condition in which the adrenal glands secrete too much cortisol. Cortisol is a steroid hormone which regulates carbohydrate, fat, and protein metabolism.

*Deafness*: A partial or total loss of hearing.

*Epilepsy:* A brain disorder in which the dog experiences seizures (convulsions).

*Epiphyseal dysplasia:* Abnormal development of the long bone.

*Eye abnormalities:* The Miniature Poodle is prone to a rolling in of the eyelid(s) and abnormal development of the eyelashes, tear ducts, optic nerve, and retina(s).

*Glaucoma:* Pressure on the retina from excess fluid in the eyeball, which causes partial or total loss of vision.

*Globoid cell leukodystrophy:* Degeneration of a type of brain cell.

*Heart disease:* Abnormal development of the heart.

*Hemeralopia:* A disorder of the retina causing blindness during the day with partial sight in dim light.

*Hypothyroidism:* A common disease of thyroid-hormone deficiency. The thyroid regulates your dog's metabolism. A large number of skin problems in dogs are caused by thyroid disease.

*Immune-mediated hemolytic anemia (IMHA):* Anemia resulting from an immune system mediated destruction of the red blood cells.

*Intervertebral disc disease:* Abnormal development of the discs between the vertebrae.

*Iris atrophy:* A deterioration of the iris.

*Myasthenia gravis:* An autoimmune disease characterized by progressive muscle fatigue and generalized weakness resulting from the impaired transmission of nerve impulses.

*Osteochondritis dissecans:* Inflammation of the cartilage in the joints. A form of arthritis.

*Osteochondrosis:* An abnormal development of joint cartilage. Most commonly found in the shoulder, elbow, and knee.

*Otitis externa:* An infection of the external structures of the ear.

*Pannus:* Progressive immune-mediated disease in which there is a growth of tissue over the cornea, causing inflammation and possible blindness.

*Patellar luxation:* The kneecap(s) slips out of place.

*Progressive retinal atrophy* (**PRA**): A slow deterioration of the retina, leading to blindness.

*Sebaceous gland tumor*: A skin tumor.

*Skin disease*: The Miniature Poodle is prone to skin disease from allergies and from a deficiency of growth hormones.

*Von Willebrand's disease*: Abnormal blood-clotting defect involving both platelet and coagulation function (factor VIII).

## NORWEGIAN DUNKER HOUND
*Deafness*: A partial or total loss of hearing.

## NORWEGIAN ELKHOUND
*Cataract*: In older dogs the lens of the eye becomes cloudy, causing a partial or total loss of vision.

*Eye abnormalities*: The Norwegian Elkhound is prone to a rolling in of the eyelid(s), abnormally growing eyelashes, and a condition where the lens in the eye slips out of place.

*Glaucoma*: Pressure on the retina from excess fluid in the eyeball, which causes partial or total loss of vision.

*Hip dysplasia*: An abnormal development of the hip joint(s).

*Hereditary kidney hypoplasia*: A condition in which the dog is born with immature kidneys that never develop completely.

*Hypothyroidism*: A common disease of thyroid-hormone deficiency. The thyroid regulates your dog's metabolism. A large number of skin problems in dogs are caused by thyroid disease.

*Keratoacanthoma*: Non-cancerous skin tumor usually found on the face.

*Progressive retinal atrophy* (**PRA**): A slow deterioration of the retina, leading to blindness.

*Sebaceous gland tumor*: A skin tumor.

*Seborrhea*: A skin disease characterized by raw, scaling skin and an excess of sebum (oil-like substance), which causes a rancid body odor.

*Subcutaneous cyst*: A fluid-filled sac located just beneath the skin.

## NOVA SCOTIA DUCK TOLLING RETRIEVER

*Addison's disease*: A disease in which the adrenal glands secrete an insufficient amount of cortisone, a steroid hormone.

*Cataract*: In older dogs the lens of the eye becomes cloudy, causing a partial or total loss of vision.

*Hypothyroidism*: A common disease of thyroid-hormone deficiency. The thyroid regulates your dog's metabolism. A large number of skin problems in dogs are caused by thyroid disease.

*Progressive retinal atrophy (PRA)*: A slow deterioration of the retina, leading to blindness.

## PEMBROKE WELSH CORGI

*Cataract*: In older dogs the lens of the eye becomes cloudy, causing a partial or total loss of vision.

*Cervical spondylosis*: A degenerative disease of the neck vertebrae.

*Corneal dystrophy*: An inherited degenerative condition in which the cornea of the eye becomes cloudy or opaque.

*Ehler's-Danlos syndrome*: A connective-tissue disease in which the skin is very fragile and is easily cut or bruised.

*Dystocia*: Complications giving birth.

*Epilepsy*: A brain disorder in which the dog experiences seizures (convulsions).

*Eye abnormalities*: The Pembroke Welsh Corgi is prone to abnormal development of the retina(s) and a condition where the lens in the eye slips out of place.

*Hypothyroidism*: A common disease of thyroid-hormone deficiency. The thyroid regulates your dog's metabolism. A large number of skin problems in dogs are caused by thyroid disease.

*Progressive retinal atrophy (PRA)*: A slow deterioration of the retina, leading to blindness.

*Von Willebrand's disease*: Abnormal blood-clotting defect involving both platelet and coagulation function (factor VIII).

## PETIT BASSET GRIFFON VENDEEN

*Allergies*: The Petit Basset Griffon Vendeen is prone to all types of allergies.

*Cryptorchidism*: A developmental condition in which one or both testicles fail to descend into the scrotum.

*Eye abnormalities*: The Petit Basset Griffon Vendeen is prone to abnormal development of the retina(s), a condition where the lens slips out of place, and an overproduction of tears.

*Epilepsy*: A brain disorder in which the dog experiences seizures (convulsions).

*Glaucoma*: Pressure on the retina from excess fluid in the eyeball, which causes partial or total loss of vision.

*Hip dysplasia*: An abnormal development of the hip joint(s).

*Patellar luxation*: The kneecap(s) slips out of place.

*Thyroid disease*: The Petit Basset Griffon Vendeen is prone to thyroiditis, lymphocytic thyroiditis, and hypothyroidism. Thyroiditis and lymphocytic thyroiditis are autoimmune diseases that lead to hypothyroidism, a common disease of thyroid-hormone deficiency. The thyroid regulates your dog's metabolism. A large number of skin problems in dogs are caused by thyroid disease.

## PORTUGUESE WATER DOG

*Addison's disease*: A disease in which the adrenal glands secrete an insufficient amount of cortisone, a steroid hormone.

*Cataract*: In older dogs the lens of the eye becomes cloudy, causing a partial or total loss of vision.

*Eye abnormalities*: The Portuguese Water Dog is prone to abnormally growing eyelashes.

*Hypothyroidism*: A common disease of thyroid-hormone deficiency. The thyroid regulates your dog's metabolism. A large number of skin problems in dogs are caused by thyroid disease.

*Lipidosis*: An accumulation of lipids (fats) in the nerves.

*Progressive retinal atrophy (PRA):* A slow deterioration of the retina, leading to blindness.

## SALUKI

*Anesthetic sensitivity:* A serious condition in which a dog is very sensitive to anesthesia. In many cases the dog is also sensitive to medications and flea-control products that contain pesticides.

*Behavioral abnormalities:* A whole range of abnormal behavioral patterns, such as aggression and panic disorders.

*Cataract:* In older dogs the lens of the eye becomes cloudy, causing a partial or total loss of vision.

*Corneal dystrophy:* An inherited degenerative condition in which the cornea of the eye becomes cloudy or opaque.

*Eye abnormalities:* The Saluki is prone to a rolling in of the eyelid and abnormal development of the retina(s).

*Hypothyroidism:* A common disease of thyroid-hormone deficiency. The thyroid regulates your dog's metabolism. A large number of skin problems in dogs are caused by thyroid disease.

*Immune-mediated hemolytic anemia (IMHA):* Anemia resulting from an immune system mediated destruction of the red blood cells.

*Neuronal ceroid-lipofuscinosis:* An accumulation of fatty pigments in the brain.

*Progressive retinal atrophy (PRA):* A slow deterioration of the retina, leading to blindness.

*Thrombocytopenia:* An abnormal decrease in the number of blood platelets. Blood platelets play a role in blood clotting. Symptoms are tiny hemorrhages in the skin and mucous membranes.

*Von Willebrand's disease:* Abnormal blood-clotting defect involving both platelet and coagulation function (factor VIII).

## SKYE TERRIER

*Behavioral abnormalities:* A whole range of abnormal behavioral patterns, such as aggression and panic disorders.

*Epiphyseal dysplasia*: Abnormal development of the long bone.

*Eye abnormalities*: The Skye Terrier is prone to abnormally growing eyelashes and a condition where the lens in the eye slips out of place.

*Hypoplasia of larynx*: Abnormal development of the larynx.

*Myasthenia gravis*: An autoimmune disease characterized by progressive muscle fatigue and generalized weakness resulting from the impaired transmission of nerve impulses.

*Thyroid disease*: The Skye Terrier is prone to thyroiditis, lymphocytic thyroiditis, and hypothyroidism. Thyroiditis and lymphocytic thyroiditis are autoimmune diseases that lead to hypothyroidism, a common disease of thyroid-hormone deficiency. The thyroid regulates your dog's metabolism. A large number of skin problems in dogs are caused by thyroid disease.

*Ulcerative colitis*: A chronic inflammation of the colon that results in the formation of ulcers in the colon.

*Von Willebrand's disease*: Abnormal blood-clotting defect involving both platelet and coagulation function (factor VIII).

## SOFT-COATED WHEATEN TERRIER

*Addison's disease*: A disease in which the adrenal glands secrete an insufficient amount of cortisone, a steroid hormone.

*Allergies*: The Soft-Coated wheaten Terrier is prone to all types of allergies.

*Cataract*: In older dogs the lens of the eye becomes cloudy, causing a partial or total loss of vision.

*Eye abnormalities*: The Soft-Coated wheaten Terrier is prone to abnormal development of the optic nerve and abnormal development of the retina(s).

*Hypothyroidism*: A common disease of thyroid-hormone deficiency. The thyroid regulates your dog's metabolism. A large number of skin problems in dogs are caused by thyroid disease.

*Malabsorption*: A condition in which the small intestine does not absorb nutrients properly.

*Renal dysplasia*: Abnormal development of the kidney(s).

*Von Willebrand's disease:* Abnormal blood-clotting defect involving both platelet and coagulation function (factor VIII).

## STAFFORDSHIRE BULL TERRIER

*Cataract:* In older dogs the lens of the eye becomes cloudy, causing a partial or total loss of vision.

*Cleft palate and/or lip:* Birth defects in which, with the cleft palate, the roof of the mouth doesn't grow properly, leaving a hole from the roof of the mouth into the nose or, with cleft lip, the skin below the nose doesn't grow together.

*Eye abnormalities:* The Staffordshire Bull Terrier is prone to a rolling in of the eyelid(s) and abnormally growing eyelashes.

*Hypothyroidism:* A common disease of thyroid-hormone deficiency. The thyroid regulates your dog's metabolism. A large number of skin problems in dogs are caused by thyroid disease.

*Muscular dystrophy:* A progressive muscle disorder that causes a wasting of the muscles. It is an inherited disease with symptoms of slow growth, difficulty eating and swallowing, and weakness.

*Osteochondritis dissecans:* Inflammation of the cartilage in the joints. A form of arthritis.

*Osteochondrosis:* An abnormal development of joint cartilage. Most commonly found in the shoulder, elbow, and knee.

*Progressive retinal atrophy (PRA):* A slow deterioration of the retina, leading to blindness.

## STANDARD POODLE

*Addison's disease:* A disease in which the adrenal glands secrete an insufficient amount of cortisone, a steroid hormone.

*Allergies:* The Standard Poodle is prone to all types of allergies.

*Behavioral abnormalities:* A whole range of abnormal behavioral patterns, such as aggression and panic disorders.

*Blood-clotting disorders:* The Standard Poodle is prone to a blood-clotting disorder due to a deficiency of coagulation factors VIII or XII.

*Bone disease:* The Standard Poodle is prone to abnormal mineralization of the bones, leading to a weak bone structure.

*Cancer:* The Standard Poodle is prone to cancer of the toe.

*Cataract:* In older dogs the lens of the eye becomes cloudy, causing a partial or total loss of vision.

*Epilepsy:* A brain disorder in which the dog experiences seizures (convulsions).

*Epiphora:* An overproduction of tears.

*Eye abnormalities:* The Standard Poodle is prone to a rolling in of the eyelid(s), a condition where the lens in the eye slips out of place, and abnormal development of the eyelashes, tear ducts, retina, and optic nerve.

*Gastric bloat and torsion:* Gastric bloat is a swelling of the stomach from excess gas and is usually followed by gastric torsion, a twisting of the stomach. Gastric torsion will result in death if not treated immediately.

*Glaucoma:* Pressure on the retina from excess fluid in the eyeball, which causes partial or total loss of vision.

*Hemeralopia:* A disorder of the retina causing blindness during the day with partial sight in dim light.

*Hip dysplasia:* An abnormal development of the hip joint(s).

*Hypothyroidism:* A common disease of thyroid-hormone deficiency. The thyroid regulates your dog's metabolism. A large number of skin problems in dogs are caused by thyroid disease.

*Immune-mediated hemolytic anemia (IMHA):* Anemia resulting from an immune system mediated destruction of the red blood cells.

*Iris atrophy:* A deterioration of the iris.

*Osteochondritis dissecans:* Inflammation of the cartilage in the joints. A form of arthritis.

*Osteochondrosis:* An abnormal development of joint cartilage. Most commonly found in the shoulder, elbow, and knee.

*Pannus:* Progressive immune-mediated disease in which there is a growth of tissue over the cornea, causing inflammation and possible blindness.

*Progressive retinal atrophy (PRA)*: A slow deterioration of the retina, leading to blindness.

*Thrombocytopenia*: An abnormal decrease in the number of blood platelets. Blood platelets play a role in blood clotting. Symptoms are tiny hemorrhages in the skin and mucous membranes.

*Urolithiasis*: Stones or crystals in the urinary tract.

*Von Willebrand's disease*: Abnormal blood-clotting defect involving both platelet and coagulation function (factor VIII).

## STANDARD SCHNAUZER

*Blood-clotting disorders*: The Standard Schnauzer is prone to a blood-clotting disorder due to a deficiency of coagulation factor VIII.

*Cancer*: The Standard Schnauzer is prone to cancer of the anus.

*Cataract*: In older dogs the lens of the eye becomes cloudy, causing a partial or total loss of vision.

*Conjunctivitis*: Inflammation of the eye.

*Eye abnormalities*: The Standard Schnauzer is prone to abnormal development of the retina(s).

*Heart disease*: Malfunctioning valve(s).

*Hypothyroidism*: A common disease of thyroid-hormone deficiency. The thyroid regulates your dog's metabolism. A large number of skin problems in dogs are caused by thyroid disease.

*Osteochondritis dissecans*: Inflammation of the cartilage in the joints. A form of arthritis.

*Osteochondrosis*: An abnormal development of joint cartilage. Most commonly found in the shoulder, elbow, and knee.

*Von Willebrand's disease*: Abnormal blood-clotting defect involving both platelet and coagulation function (factor VIII).

## SUSSEX SPANIEL

*Cataract*: In older dogs the lens of the eye becomes cloudy, causing a partial or total loss of vision.

*Eye abnormalities:* The Sussex Spaniel is prone to abnormally growing eyelashes, a rolling in of the eyelid(s), and abnormal development of the retina(s).

*Heart disease:* Cardiomyopathy, or weakened heart muscles.

## TIBETAN TERRIER

*Anesthetic sensitivity:* A serious condition in which a dog is very sensitive to anesthesia. In many cases the dog is also sensitive to medications and flea-control products that contain pesticides.

*Cataract:* In older dogs the lens of the eye becomes cloudy, causing a partial or total loss of vision.

*Eye abnormalities:* The Tibetan Terrier is prone to a rolling in of the eyelid(s), abnormal development of the retina(s), and a condition where the lens in the eye slips out of place.

*Neuronal ceroid-lipofuscinosis:* An accumulation of fatty pigments in the brain.

*Progressive retinal atrophy (PRA):* A slow deterioration of the retina, leading to blindness.

## WATER SPANIEL

*Cataract:* In older dogs the lens of the eye becomes cloudy, causing a partial or total loss of vision.

*Eye abnormalities:* The Water Spaniel is prone to abnormal development of the retina(s).

## WELSH SPANIEL

*Cataract:* In older dogs the lens of the eye becomes cloudy, causing a partial or total loss of vision.

*Glaucoma:* Pressure on the retina from excess fluid in the eyeball, which causes partial or total loss of vision.

*Hip dysplasia:* An abnormal development of the hip joint(s).

*Progressive retinal atrophy (PRA):* A slow deterioration of the retina, leading to blindness.

# Purebred Small—Up to 20 Pounds

## AFFENPINSCHER

*Anasarca*: An accumulation of fluids in various tissues and body cavities in newborn puppies.

*Cleft palate*: A birth defect in which the roof of the mouth doesn't grow properly, leaving a hole from the roof of the mouth into the nose.

*Patellar luxation*: The kneecap(s) slips out of place.

*Teeth abnormalities*: The number, placement, or development of the teeth is not normal.

*Von Willebrand's disease*: Abnormal blood-clotting defect involving both platelet and coagulation function (factor VIII).

## AUSTRALIAN TERRIER

*Diabetes mellitus*: A disease caused by an insufficient production or use of insulin.

*Eye abnormalities*: The Australian Terrier is prone to abnormal development of the retina(s).

*Legg-Perthes disease*: The blood vessels feeding the thigh bone deteriorate, leading to a deterioration of the femoral head, a part of the hip.

*Progressive retinal atrophy (PRA)*: A slow deterioration of the retina, leading to blindness.

## BEDLINGTON TERRIER

*Bone disease*: The Bedlington Terrier is prone to abnormal mineralization of the bones, leading to a weak bone structure.

*Cataract*: In older dogs the lens of the eye becomes cloudy, causing a partial or total loss of vision.

*Copper metabolism abnormality*: An inability to utilize and store copper properly. Results in liver disease if not treated.

*Eye abnormalities*: The Bedlington Terrier is prone to a rolling out of the eyelid(s) and abnormal development of the tear duct, eyelashes, and retina.

*Hereditary kidney hypoplasia*: A condition in which the dog is born with immature kidneys that never develop completely.

*Progressive retinal atrophy (PRA)*: A slow deterioration of the retina, leading to blindness.

## BICHON FRISE

*Blood-clotting disorders*: The Bichon Frise is prone to a blood-clotting disorder due to a deficiency of coagulation factor IX.

*Cataract*: In older dogs the lens of the eye becomes cloudy, causing a partial or total loss of vision.

*Ciliary dyskinesia*: A condition where the ciliated cells (hairlike cells lining the respiratory tract) are deformed and rigid. Causes pneumonia and other respiratory difficulties.

*Corneal dystrophy*: An inherited degenerative condition in which the cornea of the eye becomes cloudy or opaque.

*Epilepsy*: A brain disorder in which the dog experiences seizures (convulsions).

*Eye abnormalities*: The Bichon Frise is prone to a rolling in of the eyelid(s).

*Patellar luxation*: The kneecap(s) slips out of place.

*Skin allergies*: Allergic reaction that causes inflammation and itching of the skin.

*White dog shaker syndrome*: A condition brought on by stress or overexcitement where the dog has rapid eye movements, tremors, and incoordination.

## BORDER TERRIER

*Cancer*: The Border Terrier is prone to cancer of the neck, aorta, spine, brain, pituitary gland, and mast cells. The mast cell secretes histamine in response to allergens.

*Cataract*: In older dogs the lens of the eye becomes cloudy, causing a partial or total loss of vision.

*Collie eye anomaly*: An inherited disorder in which the narrow shape of the head causes the eyes to be malformed.

*Craniomandibular osteopathy*: Abnormally dense bones in the face and the jaw.

*Cryptorchidism*: A developmental condition in which one or both testicles fail to descend into the scrotum.

*Eye abnormalities*: The Border Terrier is prone to abnormal development of the retina(s) and a condition where the lens in the eye slips out of place.

*Heart disease*: Abnormal development of the heart.

*Histiocytoma*: A tumor that forms beneath the skin.

*Patellar luxation*: The kneecap(s) slips out of place.

*Progressive retinal atrophy (PRA)*: A slow deterioration of the retina, leading to blindness.

*Vertebra malformation*: A condition in which only half the vertebra is formed.

## BOSTON TERRIER

*Allergies*: The Boston Terrier is prone to all types of allergies.

*Anasarca*: An accumulation of fluids in various tissues and body cavities in newborn puppies.

*Cancer*: The Boston Terrier is prone to cancer of the neck, aorta, pituitary gland, and mast cells. The mast cell secretes histamine in response to allergens.

*Cataract*: In older dogs the lens of the eye becomes cloudy, causing a partial or total loss of vision.

*Cleft palate and/or lip*: Birth defects in which, with the cleft palate, the roof of the mouth doesn't grow properly, leaving a hole from the roof of the mouth into the nose or, with cleft lip, the skin below the nose doesn't grow together.

*Corneal dystrophy*: An inherited degenerative condition in which the cornea of the eye becomes cloudy or opaque.

*Corneal ulcer*: A deterioration of the cornea.

*Craniomandibular osteopathy*: Abnormally dense bones in the face and the jaw.

*Cushing's disease (hyperadrenocorticism)*: A condition in which the adrenal glands secrete too much cortisol. Cortisol is a steroid hormone which regulates carbohydrate, fat, and protein metabolism.

*Deafness*: A partial or total loss of hearing.

*Demodectic mange*: A skin disease in which canine mites are living in the skin, causing itching, loss of hair, and skin infections. Usually found on the face and front legs.

*Dermatitis*: An inflammation in the skin folds of the tail.

*Dystocia*: Complications giving birth.

*Esophageal disorder*: Spasms in the muscles of the esophagus.

*Eye abnormalities*: The Boston Terrier is prone to a rolling in of the eyelid(s), abnormally growing eyelashes, abnormal growth of the gland of the third eyelid, a protruding third eyelid, and dry eye, a condition in which the eye(s) does not produce enough liquid.

*Glaucoma*: Pressure on the retina from excess fluid in the eyeball, which causes partial or total loss of vision.

*Hernia*: A rupture of the wall of an internal organ in the groin area.

*Hydrocephalus*: The accumulation of fluid in the brain.

*Hypothyroidism*: A common disease of thyroid-hormone deficiency. The thyroid regulates your dog's metabolism. A large number of skin problems in dogs are caused by thyroid disease.

*Intussusception*: A section of the intestinal tract slips into an adjoining section.

*Patellar luxation*: The kneecap(s) slips out of place.

*Progressive retinal atrophy (PRA)*: A slow deterioration of the retina, leading to blindness.

*Pyometra*: The uterus fills with pus, usually from a severe bacterial infection.

*Sebaceous gland tumor*: A skin tumor.

*Stenotic nares*: A condition where excess flesh causes the openings of the nose (nares) to be too small to breath with ease.

*Swimmer puppies*: A developmental condition caused by a weakness of the muscles that puppies use to pull their legs together. Newborns are unable to put their feet under them to walk.

*Vertebra malformation*: A condition in which only half the vertebra is formed.

## BRUSSELS GRIFFON

*Cataract:* In older dogs the lens of the eye becomes cloudy, causing a partial or total loss of vision.

*Eye abnormalities:* The Brussels Griffon is prone to abnormally growing eyelashes.

*Progressive retinal atrophy (PRA):* A slow deterioration of the retina, leading to blindness.

*Shoulder abnormalities:* Disorders of the shoulder joint from dislocation or malformation.

## CAIRN TERRIER

*Blood-clotting disorders:* The Cairn Terrier is prone to blood-clotting disorders due to a deficiency of coagulation factors VIII or IX.

*Cataract:* In older dogs the lens of the eye becomes cloudy, causing a partial or total loss of vision.

*Cerebellar hypoplasia:* Underdevelopment of a part of the brain called the cerebellum. The cerebellum gives your dog balance, coordination, and posture.

*Craniomandibular osteopathy:* Abnormally dense bones in the face and the jaw.

*Eye abnormalities:* The Cairn Terrier is prone to abnormally growing eyelashes, abnormal development of the retina(s), and a condition where the lens in the eye slips out of place.

*Glaucoma:* Pressure on the retina from excess fluid in the eyeball, which causes partial or total loss of vision.

*Globoid cell leukodystrophy:* Degeneration of a type of brain cell.

*Hernia:* A rupture of the wall of an internal organ in the groin area.

*Hypothyroidism:* A common disease of thyroid-hormone deficiency. The thyroid regulates your dog's metabolism. A large number of skin problems in dogs are caused by thyroid disease.

*Liver abnormalities:* The Cairn Terrier is prone to an abnormal formation of blood vessels in the liver.

*Progressive retinal atrophy* **(PRA)**: A slow deterioration of the retina, leading to blindness.

*Urolithiasis*: Stones or crystals in the urinary tract.

**Von Willebrand's** *disease*: Abnormal blood-clotting defect involving both platelet and coagulation function (factor VIII).

## CAVALIER KING CHARLES SPANIEL

*Cataract*: In older dogs the lens of the eye becomes cloudy, causing a partial or total loss of vision.

*Corneal dystrophy*: An inherited degenerative condition in which the cornea of the eye becomes cloudy or opaque.

*Diabetes mellitus*: A disease caused by an insufficient production or use of insulin.

*Eye abnormalities*: The Cavalier King Charles Spaniel is prone to abnormally growing eyelashes, abnormal development of the retina(s), a rolling in of the eyelid(s), and dry eye, a condition in which the eye(s) does not produce enough liquid.

*Heart disease*: Deterioration of the heart valves.

*Hypothyroidism*: A common disease of thyroid-hormone deficiency. The thyroid regulates your dog's metabolism. A large number of skin problems in dogs are caused by thyroid disease.

*Patellar luxation*: The kneecap(s) slips out of place.

*Progressive retinal atrophy* **(PRA)**: A slow deterioration of the retina, leading to blindness.

*Thrombocytopenia*: An abnormal decrease in the number of blood platelets. Blood platelets play a role in blood clotting. Symptoms are tiny hemorrhages in the skin and mucous membranes.

## CHIHUAHUA

*Blood-clotting disorders*: The Chihuahua is prone to a blood-clotting disorder due to a deficiency of coagulation factor VIII.

*Cleft palate*: A birth defect in which the roof of the mouth doesn't grow properly, leaving a hole from the roof of the mouth into the nose.

*Collapsed trachea*: Malformation of the trachea causes it to collapse easily.

*Corneal dystrophy*: An inherited degenerative condition in which the cornea of the eye becomes cloudy or opaque.

*Eye abnormalities*: The Chihuahua is prone to a rolling in of the eyelid(s), a condition where the lens in the eye slips out of place, and dry eye, a condition in which the eye(s) does not produce enough liquid.

*Glaucoma*: Pressure on the retina from excess fluid in the eyeball, which causes partial or total loss of vision.

*Heart disease*: Abnormal growth of the mitral valve and malfunctioning valves.

*Hydrocephalus*: The accumulation of fluid in the brain.

*Hypoglycemia*: A low level of glucose (blood sugar) in the blood.

*Hypothyroidism*: A common disease of thyroid-hormone deficiency. The thyroid regulates your dog's metabolism. A large number of skin problems in dogs are caused by thyroid disease.

*Iris atrophy*: A deterioration of the iris.

*Liver abnormality*: The Chihuahua is prone to an abnormal formation of blood vessels in the liver.

*Neuronal ceroid-lipofuscinosis*: An accumulation of fatty pigments in the brain.

*Osteochondritis dissecans*: Inflammation of the cartilage in the joints. A form of arthritis.

*Osteochondrosis*: An abnormal development of joint cartilage. Most commonly found in the shoulder, elbow, and knee.

*Patellar luxation*: The kneecap(s) slips out of place.

*Progressive retinal atrophy (PRA)*: A slow deterioration of the retina, leading to blindness.

*Shoulder dislocation*: The shoulder joint slips out of place.

*Vertebra malformation*: An abnormal development of the second vertebra, causing unsteadiness.

## CHINESE CRESTED

*Acne*: Pimples and blackheads on the hairless dogs.

*Cancer*: The Chinese Crested is prone to skin cancer.

*Patellar luxation*: The kneecap(s) slips out of place.

## DACHSHUND

*Elbow dysplasia*: An abnormal development of the elbow joint(s).

*Epilepsy*: A brain disorder in which the dog experiences seizures (convulsions).

*Keratitis*: Inflammation of the cornea.

*Urolithiasis*: Stones or crystals in the urinary tract.

## DANDIE DINMONT TERRIER

*Cataract*: In older dogs the lens of the eye becomes cloudy, causing a partial or total loss of vision.

*Corneal ulcer*: A deterioration of the cornea.

*Elbow dislocation*: The elbow joint slips out of place.

*Eye abnormalities*: The Dandie Dinmont Terrier is prone to a rolling in of the eyelid(s).

*Glaucoma*: Pressure on the retina from excess fluid in the eyeball, which causes partial or total loss of vision.

*Hip dysplasia*: An abnormal development of the hip joint(s).

*Hypothyroidism*: A common disease of thyroid-hormone deficiency. The thyroid regulates your dog's metabolism. A large number of skin problems in dogs are caused by thyroid disease.

*Intervertebral disc disease*: Abnormal development of the discs between the vertebrae.

*Patellar luxation*: The kneecap(s) slips out of place.

*Shoulder abnormalities*: Disorders of the shoulder joint from dislocation or malformation.

*Teeth abnormalities*: The number, placement, or development of the teeth is not normal.

## ENGLISH TOY SPANIEL

*Cataract*: In older dogs the lens of the eye becomes cloudy, causing a partial or total loss of vision.

*Cleft palate*: A birth defect in which the roof of the mouth doesn't grow properly, leaving a hole from the roof of the mouth into the nose.

*Corneal dystrophy*: An inherited degenerative condition in which the cornea of the eye becomes cloudy or opaque.

*Diabetes mellitus*: A disease caused by an insufficient production or use of insulin.

*Eye abnormalities*: The English Toy Spaniel is prone to a rolling in of the eyelid(s) and abnormal development of the retina(s).

*Patellar luxation*: The kneecap(s) slips out of place.

*Umbilical hernia*: A tear in the muscle wall of the stomach where the umbilical cord was.

## HAVANESE

*Cataract*: In older dogs the lens of the eye becomes cloudy, causing a partial or total loss of vision.

*Eye abnormalities*: The Havanese is prone to abnormal development of the retina(s).

*Progressive retinal atrophy (PRA)*: A slow deterioration of the retina, leading to blindness.

## ITALIAN GREYHOUND

*Anesthetic sensitivity*: A serious condition in which a dog is very sensitive to anesthesia. In many cases the dog is also sensitive to medications and flea-control products that contain pesticides.

*Cataract*: In older dogs the lens of the eye becomes cloudy, causing a partial or total loss of vision.

*Corneal dystrophy*: An inherited degenerative condition in which the cornea of the eye becomes cloudy or opaque.

*Cryptorchidism*: A developmental condition in which one or both testicles fail to descend into the scrotum.

*Epilepsy*: A brain disorder in which the dog experiences seizures (convulsions).

*Eye abnormalities*: The Italian Greyhound is prone to abnormal development of the optic nerve.

*Glaucoma*: Pressure on the retina from excess fluid in the eyeball, which causes partial or total loss of vision.

*Progressive retinal atrophy* (*PRA*): A slow deterioration of the retina, leading to blindness.

*Thrombocytopenia*: An abnormal decrease in the number of blood platelets. Blood platelets play a role in blood clotting. Symptoms are tiny hemorrhages in the skin and mucous membranes.

## JACK RUSSELL TERRIER

*Ataxia*: A progressive loss of coordination.

*Blood-clotting disorders*: The Jack Russell Terrier is prone to a blood-clotting disorder due to a deficiency of coagulation factor X.

*Eye abnormalities*: The Jack Russell Terrier is prone to a condition where the lens in the eye slips out of place.

*Myasthenia gravis*: An autoimmune disease characterized by progressive muscle fatigue and generalized weakness resulting from the impaired transmission of nerve impulses.

*Von Willebrand's disease*: Abnormal blood-clotting defect involving both platelet and coagulation function (factor VIII).

## JAPANESE SPANIEL (JAPANESE CHIN)

*Cataract*: In older dogs the lens of the eye becomes cloudy, causing a partial or total loss of vision.

*Cryptorchidism*: A developmental condition in which one or both testicles fail to descend into the scrotum.

*Eye abnormalities*: The Japanese Spaniel is prone to abnormally growing eyelashes and a rolling in of the eyelid(s).

*Glycogen storage disease*: An inability to store and use the complex carbohydrate glycogen, which is primarily stored in the liver and muscle.

*Progressive retinal atrophy (PRA)*: A slow deterioration of the retina, leading to blindness.

## LAKELAND TERRIER

*Cataract*: In older dogs the lens of the eye becomes cloudy, causing a partial or total loss of vision.

*Cryptorchidism*: A developmental condition in which one or both testicles fail to descend into the scrotum.

*Elbow dysplasia*: An abnormal development of the elbow joint(s).

*Eye abnormalities*: The Lakeland Terrier is prone to abnormally growing eyelashes and a condition where the lens in the eye slips out of place.

*Hypothyroidism*: A common disease of thyroid-hormone deficiency. The thyroid regulates your dog's metabolism. A large number of skin problems in dogs are caused by thyroid disease.

*Jaw abnormality*: The lower jaw is longer than the upper jaw.

*Von Willebrand's disease*: Abnormal blood-clotting defect involving both platelet and coagulation function (factor VIII).

## LHASA APSO

*Allergies*: The Lhasa Apso is prone to all types of allergies.

*Cataract*: In older dogs the lens of the eye becomes cloudy, causing a partial or total loss of vision.

*Corneal dystrophy*: An inherited degenerative condition in which the cornea of the eye becomes cloudy or opaque.

*Eye abnormalities*: The Lhasa Apso is prone to abnormally growing eyelashes, a rolling in or out of the eyelid(s), and dry eye, a condition in which the eye(s) does not produce enough liquid.

*Hereditary kidney hypoplasia*: A condition in which the dog is born with immature kidneys that never develop completely.

*Hernia*: A rupture of the wall of an internal organ in the groin area.

*Hypothyroidism*: A common disease of thyroid-hormone deficiency. The thyroid regulates your dog's metabolism. A large number of skin problems in dogs are caused by thyroid disease.

*Patellar luxation*: The kneecap(s) slips out of place.

*Progressive retinal atrophy* (PRA): A slow deterioration of the retina, leading to blindness.

*Von Willebrand's disease*: Abnormal blood-clotting defect involving both platelet and coagulation function (factor VIII).

## MALTESE

*Blindness*: An inability to see from a wide variety of eye diseases.

*Cryptorchidism*: A developmental condition in which one or both testicles fail to descend into the scrotum.

*Deafness*: A partial or total loss of hearing.

*Epiphora*: An overproduction of tears.

*Eye abnormalities*: The Maltese is prone to abnormally growing eyelashes and abnormal development of the retina(s).

*Glaucoma*: Pressure on the retina from excess fluid in the eyeball, which causes partial or total loss of vision.

*Hip dysplasia*: An abnormal development of the hip joint(s).

*Hypoglycemia*: A low level of glucose (blood sugar) in the blood.

*Liver abnormalities*: The Maltese is prone to an abnormal formation of blood vessels in the liver.

*Patellar luxation*: The kneecap(s) slips out of place.

*Progressive retinal atrophy* (PRA): A slow deterioration of the retina, leading to blindness.

*Thyroid disease*: The Maltese is prone to thyroiditis, lymphocytic thyroiditis, and hypothyroidism. Thyroiditis and lymphocytic thyroiditis are autoimmune diseases that lead to hypothyroidism, a common disease of thyroid-hormone deficiency. The thyroid regulates your dog's metabolism. A large number of skin problems in dogs are caused by thyroid disease.

*Von Willebrand's disease*: Abnormal blood-clotting defect involving both platelet and coagulation function (factor VIII).

*White dog shaker syndrome*: A condition brought on by stress or overexcitement where the dog has rapid eye movements, tremors, and incoordination.

## MEXICAN HAIRLESS

*Acne*: Pimples and blackheads on the hairless dogs.

*Cancer*: The Mexican hairless is prone to skin cancer.

*Patellar luxation*: The kneecap(s) slips out of place.

## MINIATURE DACHSHUND

*Acanthosis nigricans*: A rare skin disease characterized by dark skin, hair loss, and inflammation of the skin. Primarily found in the armpits.

*Baldness*: Loss of hair.

*Cataract*: In older dogs the lens of the eye becomes cloudy, causing a partial or total loss of vision.

*Cleft palate and/or lip*: Birth defects in which, with cleft palate, the roof of the mouth doesn't grow properly, leaving a hole from the roof of the mouth into the nose or, with cleft lip, the skin below the nose doesn't grow together.

*Corneal dystrophy*: An inherited degenerative condition in which the cornea of the eye becomes cloudy or opaque.

*Cushing's disease (hyperadrenocorticism)*: A condition in which the adrenal glands secrete too much cortisol. Cortisol is a steroid hormone which regulates carbohydrate, fat, and protein metabolism.

*Deafness*: A partial or total loss of hearing.

*Demodectic mange*: A skin disease in which canine mites are living in the skin, causing itching, loss of hair, and skin infections. Usually found on the face and front legs.

*Diabetes mellitus*: A disease caused by an insufficient production or use of insulin.

**Ehler's-Danlos syndrome:** A connective-tissue disease in which the skin is very fragile and is easily cut or bruised.

**Folliculitis:** Inflammation of the hair follicle(s).

**Hypothyroidism:** A common disease of thyroid-hormone deficiency. The thyroid regulates your dog's metabolism. A large number of skin problems in dogs are caused by thyroid disease.

**Immune-mediated hemolytic anemia (IMHA):** Anemia resulting from an immune system mediated destruction of the red blood cells.

**Intervertebral disc disease:** Abnormal development of the discs between the vertebrae.

**Narcolepsy:** A neurological disorder in which the dog suddenly falls asleep.

**Neuronal ceroid-lipofuscinosis:** An accumulation of fatty pigments in the brain.

**Osteopetrosis:** The bones are abnormally thick and hard.

**Overshot jaw:** A condition in which the upper jaw is too long for the lower jaw.

**Pannus:** Progressive immune-mediated disease in which there is a growth of tissue over the cornea, causing inflammation and possible blindness.

**Pemphigus foliaceous:** An autoimmune skin disease.

**Pigmentation abnormalities:** A lack of color in the skin.

**Progressive retinal atrophy (PRA):** A slow deterioration of the retina, leading to blindness.

**Renal hypoplasia:** A condition in which the kidney(s) do not develop completely.

**Sebaceous gland tumor:** A skin tumor.

**Sterile pyogranuloma syndrome:** A non-infectious disease of the deep layers of the skin characterized by inflammation and sores.

**T-cell deficiency:** A deficiency of the T-lymphocyte cell, a type of white blood cell, resulting in a weakened immune system.

**Von Willebrand's disease:** Abnormal blood-clotting defect involving both platelet and coagulation function (factor VIII).

## MINIATURE PINSCHER

*Cataract:* In older dogs the lens of the eye becomes cloudy, causing a partial or total loss of vision.

*Corneal dystrophy:* An inherited degenerative condition in which the cornea of the eye becomes cloudy or opaque.

*Eye abnormalities:* The Miniature Pinscher is prone to a rolling in of the eyelid(s), and dry eye, a condition in which the eye(s) does not produce enough liquid.

*Hernia:* A rupture of the wall of an internal organ in the groin area.

*Legg-Perthes disease:* The blood vessels feeding the thigh bone deteriorate, leading to a deterioration of the femoral head, a part of the hip.

*Pannus:* Progressive immune-mediated disease in which there is a growth of tissue over the cornea, causing inflammation and possible blindness.

*Progressive retinal atrophy (PRA):* A slow deterioration of the retina, leading to blindness.

*Shoulder dislocation:* The shoulder joint slips out of place.

## MINIATURE SCHNAUZER

*Allergies:* The Miniature Schnauzer is prone to all types of allergies.

*Blood-clotting disorders:* The Miniature Schnauzer is prone to a blood-clotting disorder due to a deficiency of coagulation factor XIII.

*Cataract:* In older dogs the lens of the eye becomes cloudy, causing a partial or total loss of vision.

*Cryptorchidism:* A developmental condition in which one or both testicles fail to descend into the scrotum.

*Cystitis:* Infection of the bladder.

*Dermatitis:* Inflammation between the layers of the skin.

*Esophageal disorder:* Spasms in the muscles of the esophagus.

*Eye abnormalities:* The Miniature Schnauzer is prone to abnormally growing eyelashes and a rolling in of the eyelid(s)

*Fainting:* A sudden, brief state of unconsciousness.

*Heart disease*: Malfunction of the valve(s).

*Hepatic lipidosis*: A degenerative disease in which the liver is unable to excrete fat.

*Hypothyroidism*: A common disease of thyroid-hormone deficiency. The thyroid regulates your dog's metabolism. A large number of skin problems in dogs are caused by thyroid disease.

*Immune-mediated hemolytic anemia* (**IMHA**): Anemia resulting from an immune system mediated destruction of the red blood cells.

*Legg-Perthes disease*: The blood vessels feeding the thigh bone deteriorate, leading to a deterioration of the femoral head, a part of the hip.

*Liver abnormalities*: The Miniature Schnauzer is prone to an abnormal formation of blood vessels in the liver.

*Osteochondritis dissecans*: Inflammation of the cartilage in the joints. A form of arthritis.

*Osteochondrosis*: An abnormal development of joint cartilage. Most commonly found in the shoulder, elbow, and knee.

*Renal dysplasia*: Abnormal development of the kidney(s).

*Schnauzer comedo syndrome*: Blackheads from abnormal development of the hair follicles.

*Stomach hemorrhage*: A serious disorder of the stomach and intestine that comes on suddenly and is characterized by bloody diarrhea.

*Thrombocytopenia*: An abnormal decrease in the number of blood platelets. Blood platelets play a role in blood clotting. Symptoms are tiny hemorrhages in the skin and mucous membranes.

*Urolithiasis*: Stones or crystals in the urinary tract.

*Von Willebrand's disease*: Abnormal blood-clotting defect involving both platelet and coagulation function (factor VIII).

## NORFOLK TERRIER

*Epilepsy*: A brain disorder in which the dog experiences seizures (convulsions).

*Patellar luxation*: The kneecap(s) slips out of place.

*Skin allergies*: Allergic reaction that causes inflammation and itching of the skin.

## NORWICH TERRIER

*Corneal dystrophy*: An inherited degenerative condition in which the cornea of the eye becomes cloudy or opaque.

*Epilepsy*: A brain disorder in which the dog experiences seizures (convulsions).

*Eye abnormalities*: The Norwich Terrier is prone to a condition where the lens in the eye slips out of place.

*Hypothyroidism*: A common disease of thyroid-hormone deficiency. The thyroid regulates your dog's metabolism. A large number of skin problems in dogs are caused by thyroid disease.

*Patellar luxation*: The kneecap(s) slips out of place.

*Skin allergies*: Allergic reaction that causes inflammation and itching of the skin.

*Von Willebrand's disease*: Abnormal blood-clotting defect involving both platelet and coagulation function (factor VIII).

## PAPILLON

*Anasarca*: An accumulation of fluids in various tissues and body cavities in newborn puppies.

*Cataract*: In older dogs the lens of the eye becomes cloudy, causing a partial or total loss of vision.

*Corneal dystrophy*: An inherited degenerative condition in which the cornea of the eye becomes cloudy or opaque.

*Eye abnormalities*: The papillon is prone to a rolling in of the eyelid(s).

*Hypothyroidism*: A common disease of thyroid-hormone deficiency. The thyroid regulates your dog's metabolism. A large number of skin problems in dogs are caused by thyroid disease.

*Patellar luxation*: The kneecap(s) slips out of place.

*Von Willebrand's disease*: Abnormal blood-clotting defect involving both platelet and coagulation function (factor VIII).

## PEKINGESE

*Cataract:* In older dogs the lens of the eye becomes cloudy, causing a partial or total loss of vision.

*Dermatitis:* An inflammation of skin folds in the face.

*Eye abnormalities:* The Pekingese is prone to abnormally growing eyelashes, a rolling in of the eyelid(s), abnormally developed tear ducts, a condition where the lens in the eye slips out of place, and dry eye, a condition in which the eye(s) does not produce enough liquid.

*Hernia:* A rupture of the wall of an internal organ in the groin area.

*Hypothyroidism:* A common disease of thyroid-hormone deficiency. The thyroid regulates your dog's metabolism. A large number of skin problems in dogs are caused by thyroid disease.

*Immune-mediated hemolytic anemia (IMHA):* Anemia resulting from an immune system mediated destruction of the red blood cells.

*Intervertebral disc disease:* Abnormal development of the discs between the vertebrae.

*Keratitis:* Inflammation of the cornea characterized by abnormal pigmentation or the formation of ulcers.

*Pannus:* A progressive immune-mediated disease in which there is a growth of tissue over the cornea, causing inflammation and possible blindness.

*Progressive retinal atrophy (PRA):* A slow deterioration of the retina, leading to blindness.

*Swimmer puppies:* A developmental condition caused by a weakness of the muscles that puppies use to pull their legs together. Newborns are unable to put their feet under them to walk.

*Thrombocytopenia:* An abnormal decrease in the number of blood platelets. Blood platelets play a role in blood clotting. Symptoms are tiny hemorrhages in the skin and mucous membranes.

*Umbilical hernia:* A tear in the muscle wall of the stomach where the umbilical cord was.

*Vertebra malformation:* An abnormal development of the second vertebra, causing unsteadiness.

## POMERANIAN

*Cataract*: In older dogs the lens of the eye becomes cloudy, causing a partial or total loss of vision.

*Collapsed trachea*: Malformation of the trachea causes it to collapse easily.

*Cryptorchidism*: A developmental condition in which one or both testicles fail to descend into the scrotum.

*Cyclic hematopoiesis*: An inherited condition in which, periodically, a type of white blood cell is not produced.

*Eye abnormalities*: The Pomeranian is prone to a rolling in of the eyelid(s), abnormally growing eyelashes, an overproduction of tears, abnormal development of the tear duct(s), and a condition where the lens in the eye slips out of place.

*Globoid cell leukodystrophy*: Degeneration of a type of brain cell.

*Glycogen storage disease*: An inability to store and use the complex carbohydrate glycogen, which is primarily stored in the liver and muscle.

*Growth-hormone-responsive dermatosis*: Skin disorder caused by a deficiency of growth hormones.

*Hypothyroidism*: A common disease of thyroid-hormone deficiency. The thyroid regulates your dog's metabolism. A large number of skin problems in dogs are caused by thyroid disease.

*Liver abnormalities*: The Pomeranian is prone to an abnormal formation of blood vessels in the liver.

*Patellar luxation*: The kneecap(s) slips out of place.

*Progressive retinal atrophy (PRA)*: A slow deterioration of the retina, leading to blindness.

*Shoulder dislocation*: The shoulder joint slips out of place.

*Vertebra malformation*: An abnormal development of the second vertebra, causing unsteadiness.

## PUG

*Allergies*: The Pug is prone to all types of allergies.

*Cancer*: The Pug is prone to cancer of the mast cells. The mast cell secretes histamine in response to allergens.

*Cervical spondylosis*: A degenerative disease of the neck vertebrae.

*Cleft lip*: A birth defect in which the skin below the nose doesn't grow together.

*Collapsed trachea*: Malformation of the trachea causes it to collapse easily.

*Corneal dystrophy*: An inherited degenerative condition in which the cornea of the eye becomes cloudy or opaque.

*Corneal ulcer*: A deterioration of the cornea.

*Cystitis*: Infection of the bladder.

*Demodectic mange*: A skin disease in which canine mites are living in the skin, causing itching, loss of hair, and skin infections. Usually found on the face and front legs.

*Dermatitis*: An inflammation of the skin folds in the face and the tail.

*Dystocia*: Complications giving birth.

*Encephalitis*: Inflammation of the brain. Sometimes a cause of epilepsy.

*Epilepsy*: A brain disorder in which the dog experiences seizures (convulsions).

*Eye abnormalities*: The Pug is prone to a rolling in of the eyelid(s) and dry eye, a condition in which the eye(s) does not produce enough liquid.

*Fainting*: A sudden, brief state of unconsciousness.

*Hip dysplasia*: An abnormal development of the hip joint(s).

*Hypothyroidism*: A common disease of thyroid-hormone deficiency. The thyroid regulates your dog's metabolism. A large number of skin problems in dogs are caused by thyroid disease.

*Intervertebral disc disease*: Abnormal development of the discs between the vertebrae.

*Keratitis*: Inflammation of the cornea characterized by abnormal pigmentation or the formation of ulcers.

*Legg-Perthes disease*: The blood vessels feeding the thigh bone deteriorate, leading to a deterioration of the femoral head, a part of the hip.

*Liver abnormalities*: The Pug is prone to an abnormal formation of blood vessels in the liver.

*Pannus*: A progressive immune-mediated disease in which there is a growth of tissue over the cornea, causing inflammation and possible blindness.

*Patellar luxation*: The kneecap(s) slips out of place.

*Progressive retinal atrophy* (**PRA**): A slow deterioration of the retina, leading to blindness.

*Spondylosis*: A malformation of the vertebrae.

*Stenotic nares*: A condition where excess flesh causes the openings of the nose (nares) to be too small to breath with ease.

*Teeth abnormalities*: The number, placement, or development of the teeth is not normal.

*Urolithiasis*: Stones or crystals in the urinary tract.

## SCHIPPERKE

*Cataract*: In older dogs the lens of the eye becomes cloudy, causing a partial or total loss of vision.

*Diabetes mellitus*: A disease caused by an insufficient production or use of insulin.

*Eye abnormalities*: The schipperke is prone to abnormally growing eyelashes, a rolling in of the eyelid(s), and an abnormal development of the upper and lower eyelids.

*Hypothyroidism*: A common disease of thyroid-hormone deficiency. The thyroid regulates your dog's metabolism. A large number of skin problems in dogs are caused by thyroid disease.

*Legg-Perthes disease*: The blood vessels feeding the thigh bone deteriorate, leading to a deterioration of the femoral head, a part of the hip.

*Pemphigus foliaceous*: An autoimmune skin disease.

*Progressive retinal atrophy* (**PRA**): A slow deterioration of the retina, leading to blindness.

## SCOTTISH TERRIER

*Allergies:* The Scottish Terrier is prone to all types of allergies.

*Blood-clotting disorders:* The Scottish Terrier is prone to a blood-clotting disorder due to a deficiency of coagulation factor IX.

*Cancer:* The Scottish Terrier is prone to bladder cancer, skin cancer, and cancer of the lymphatic system.

*Cataract:* In older dogs the lens of the eye becomes cloudy, causing a partial or total loss of vision.

*Craniomandibular osteopathy:* Abnormally dense bones in the face and the jaw.

*Deafness:* A partial or total loss of hearing.

*Eye abnormalities:* The Scottish Terrier is prone to a condition where the lens in the eye slips out of place.

*Folliculitis:* Inflammation of the hair follicle(s).

*Hypothyroidism:* A common disease of thyroid-hormone deficiency. The thyroid regulates your dog's metabolism. A large number of skin problems in dogs are caused by thyroid disease.

*Immune-mediated hemolytic anemia (IMHA):* Anemia resulting from an immune system mediated destruction of the red blood cells.

*Progressive retinal atrophy (PRA):* A slow deterioration of the retina, leading to blindness.

*Scotty cramp:* Periodic involuntary muscle contractions.

*Von Willebrand's disease:* Abnormal blood-clotting defect involving both platelet and coagulation function (factor VIII).

## SEALYHAM TERRIER

*Allergies:* The Sealyham Terrier is prone to inhalant allergies.

*Cataract:* In older dogs the lens of the eye becomes cloudy, causing a partial or total loss of vision.

*Eye abnormalities:* The Sealyham Terrier is prone to abnormal development of the retina(s) and a condition where the lens in the eye slips out of place.

*Glaucoma:* Pressure on the retina from excess fluid in the eyeball, which causes partial or total loss of vision.

*Hypothyroidism:* A common disease of thyroid-hormone deficiency. The thyroid regulates your dog's metabolism. A large number of skin problems in dogs are caused by thyroid disease.

*Progressive retinal atrophy (PRA):* A slow deterioration of the retina, leading to blindness.

*Skin allergies:* Allergic reaction that causes inflammation and itching of the skin.

## SHETLAND SHEEPDOG

*Blood-clotting disorders:* The Shetland Sheepdog is prone to blood-clotting disorders due to a deficiency of coagulation factors VIII or IX.

*Cataract:* In older dogs the lens of the eye becomes cloudy, causing a partial or total loss of vision.

*Corneal dystrophy:* An inherited degenerative condition in which the cornea of the eye becomes cloudy or opaque.

*Dermatomyositis:* An inflammation of the skin and muscles.

*Discoid lupus erythematosus:* A form of autoimmune disease affecting the skin.

*Eye abnormalities:* The Shetland Sheepdog is prone to an abnormal development of the eye(s), retina(s), eyelashes, and optic nerve(s).

*Folliculitis:* Inflammation of the hair follicle(s).

*Hepatic lipidosis:* A degenerative disease in which the liver is unable to excrete fat.

*Hip dysplasia:* An abnormal development of the hip joint(s).

*Pigmentation abnormalities:* A lack of color in the skin.

*Progressive retinal atrophy (PRA):* A slow deterioration of the retina, leading to blindness.

*Systemic lupus erythematosus:* An autoimmune disease characterized by blood abnormalities, organ disorders, and skin infections.

*Thyroid disease*: The Shetland Sheepdog is prone to thyroiditis, lymphocytic thyroiditis, and hypothyroidism. Thyroiditis and lymphocytic thyroiditis are autoimmune diseases that lead to hypothyroidism, a common disease of thyroid-hormone deficiency. The thyroid regulates your dog's metabolism. A large number of skin problems in dogs are caused by thyroid disease.

*Von Willebrand's disease*: Abnormal blood-clotting defect involving both platelet and coagulation function (factor VIII).

## SHIBA INU

*Hip dysplasia*: An abnormal development of the hip joint(s).

*Patellar luxation*: The kneecap(s) slips out of place.

*Progressive retinal atrophy* (**PRA**): A slow deterioration of the retina, leading to blindness.

## SHIH TZU

*Cataract*: In older dogs the lens of the eye becomes cloudy, causing a partial or total loss of vision.

*Cleft palate and/or lip*: Birth defects in which, with cleft palate, the roof of the mouth doesn't grow properly, leaving a hole from the roof of the mouth into the nose or, with cleft lip, the skin below the nose doesn't grow together.

*Dermoid cyst*: A skin-like growth usually seen on the back.

*Eye abnormalities*: The Shih Tzu is prone to a rolling in or out of the eyelid(s), abnormally growing eyelashes, and abnormal development of the retina(s).

*Hereditary kidney hypoplasia*: A condition in which the dog is born with immature kidneys that never develop completely.

*Hypothyroidism*: A common disease of thyroid-hormone deficiency. The thyroid regulates your dog's metabolism. A large number of skin problems in dogs are caused by thyroid disease.

*Immune-mediated hemolytic anemia* (**IMHA**): Anemia resulting from an immune system mediated destruction of the red blood cells.

*Keratitis*: Inflammation of the cornea., with the formation of ulcers.

*Kidney disease*: Abnormal development of a kidney.

*Liver abnormalities*: The Shih Tzu is prone to an abnormal formation of blood vessels in the liver.

*Progressive retinal atrophy (PRA)*: A slow deterioration of the retina, leading to blindness.

*Thrombocytopenia*: An abnormal decrease in the number of blood platelets. Blood platelets play a role in blood clotting. Symptoms are tiny hemorrhages in the skin and mucous membranes.

*Von Willebrand's disease*: Abnormal blood-clotting defect involving both platelet and coagulation function (factor VIII).

## SILKY TERRIER

*Cataract*: In older dogs the lens of the eye becomes cloudy, causing a partial or total loss of vision.

*Collapsed trachea*: Malformation of the trachea causes it to collapse easily.

*Cryptorchidism*: A developmental condition in which one or both testicles fail to descend into the scrotum.

*Diabetes mellitus*: A disease caused by an insufficient production or use of insulin.

*Hydrocephalus*: The accumulation of fluid in the brain.

*Legg-Perthes disease*: The blood vessels feeding the thigh bone deteriorate, leading to a deterioration of the femoral head, a part of the hip.

*Lipidosis*: An accumulation of lipids (fats) in the nerves.

*Patellar luxation*: The kneecap(s) slips out of place.

*Progressive retinal atrophy (PRA)*: A slow deterioration of the retina, leading to blindness.

*Thrombocytopenia*: An abnormal decrease in the number of blood platelets. Blood platelets play a role in blood clotting. Symptoms are tiny hemorrhages in the skin and mucous membranes.

## SMOOTH FOX TERRIER

*Allergies*: The Smooth Fox Terrier is prone to all types of allergies.

*Cataract:* In older dogs the lens of the eye becomes cloudy, causing a partial or total loss of vision.

*Deafness:* A partial or total loss of hearing.

*Esophageal disorder:* Spasms in the muscles of the esophagus.

*Eye abnormalities:* The Smooth Fox Terrier is prone to abnormally growing eyelashes and a condition where the lens in the eye slips out of place.

*Glaucoma:* Pressure on the retina from excess fluid in the eyeball, which causes partial or total loss of vision.

*Heart disease:* Malfunctioning valve(s).

*Hypothyroidism:* A common disease of thyroid-hormone deficiency. The thyroid regulates your dog's metabolism. A large number of skin problems in dogs are caused by thyroid disease.

*Legg-Perthes disease:* The blood vessels feeding the thigh bone deteriorate, leading to a deterioration of the femoral head, a part of the hip.

*Osteochondritis dissecans:* Inflammation of the cartilage in the joints. A form of arthritis.

*Osteochondrosis:* An abnormal development of joint cartilage. Most commonly found in the shoulder, elbow, and knee.

*Shoulder dislocation:* The shoulder joint slips out of place.

*Skin allergies:* Allergic reaction that causes inflammation and itching of the skin.

*Teeth abnormalities:* The number, placement, or development of the teeth is not normal.

*Von Willebrand's disease:* Abnormal blood-clotting defect involving both platelet and coagulation function (factor VIII).

## STANDARD DACHSHUND

*Acanthosis nigricans:* A rare skin disease characterized by dark skin, hair loss, and inflammation of the skin. Primarily found in the armpits.

*Baldness:* Loss of hair.

*Cataract:* In older dogs the lens of the eye becomes cloudy, causing a partial or total loss of vision.

*Cleft palate and/or lip*: Birth defects in which, with cleft palate, the roof of the mouth doesn't grow properly, leaving a hole from the roof of the mouth into the nose or, with cleft lip, the skin below the nose doesn't grow together.

*Corneal dystrophy*: An inherited degenerative condition in which the cornea of the eye becomes cloudy or opaque.

*Cushing's disease (hyperadrenocorticism)*: A condition in which the adrenal glands secrete too much cortisol. Cortisol is a steroid hormone which regulates carbohydrate, fat, and protein metabolism.

*Deafness*: A partial or total loss of hearing.

*Demodectic mange*: A skin disease in which canine mites are living in the skin, causing itching, loss of hair, and skin infections. Usually found on the face and front legs.

*Dermoid cyst*: A skin-like growth usually seen on the back.

*Diabetes mellitus*: A disease caused by an insufficient production or use of insulin.

*Ehler's-Danlos syndrome*: A connective-tissue disease in which the skin is very fragile and is easily cut or bruised.

*Eye abnormalities*: The standard dachshund is prone to abnormally growing eyelashes, a rolling in of the eyelid(s), abnormal development of the optic nerve, and dry eye, a condition in which the eye(s) does not produce enough liquid.

*Folliculitis*: Inflammation of the hair follicle(s).

*Glaucoma*: Pressure on the retina from excess fluid in the eyeball, which causes partial or total loss of vision.

*Hypothyroidism*: A common disease of thyroid-hormone deficiency. The thyroid regulates your dog's metabolism. A large number of skin problems in dogs are caused by thyroid disease.

*Intervertebral disc disease*: Abnormal development of the discs between the vertebrae.

*Neuronal ceroid-lipofuscinosis*: An accumulation of fatty pigments in the brain.

*Osteopetrosis:* The bones are abnormally thick and hard.

*Overshot jaw:* A condition in which the upper jaw is too long for the lower jaw.

*Pannus:* Progressive immune-mediated disease in which there is a growth of tissue over the cornea, causing inflammation and possible blindness.

*Pemphigus foliaceous:* An autoimmune skin disease.

*Pigmentation abnormalities:* A lack of color in the skin.

*Progressive retinal atrophy* (**PRA**): A slow deterioration of the retina, leading to blindness.

*Renal dysplasia:* Abnormal development of the kidney(s).

*Sebaceous gland tumor:* A skin tumor.

*Sterile pyogranuloma syndrome:* A non-infectious disease of the deep layers of the skin characterized by inflammation and sores.

*Von Willebrand's disease:* Abnormal blood-clotting defect involving both platelet and coagulation function (factor VIII).

## STANDARD MANCHESTER TERRIER

*Cataract:* In older dogs the lens of the eye becomes cloudy, causing a partial or total loss of vision.

*Ehler's-Danlos syndrome:* A connective-tissue disease in which the skin is very fragile and is easily cut or bruised.

*Epilepsy:* A brain disorder in which the dog experiences seizures (convulsions).

*Eye abnormalities:* The Standard Manchester Terrier is prone to a condition where the lens in the eye slips out of place.

*Glaucoma:* Pressure on the retina from excess fluid in the eyeball, which causes partial or total loss of vision.

*Hypothyroidism:* A common disease of thyroid-hormone deficiency. The thyroid regulates your dog's metabolism. A large number of skin problems in dogs are caused by thyroid disease.

*Legg-Perthes disease:* The blood vessels feeding the thigh bone deteriorate, leading to a deterioration of the femoral head, a part of the hip.

*Progressive retinal atrophy (PRA):* A slow deterioration of the retina, leading to blindness.

*Von Willebrand's disease:* Abnormal blood-clotting defect involving both platelet and coagulation function (factor VIII).

## TIBETAN SPANIEL

*Anesthetic sensitivity:* A serious condition in which a dog is very sensitive to anesthesia. In many cases the dog is also sensitive to medications and flea-control products that contain pesticides.

*Progressive retinal atrophy (PRA):* A slow deterioration of the retina, leading to blindness.

## TOY MANCHESTER TERRIER

*Cataract:* In older dogs the lens of the eye becomes cloudy, causing a partial or total loss of vision.

*Eye abnormalities:* The Toy Manchester Terrier is prone to a condition in which the lens in the eye slips out of place.

*Hypothyroidism:* A common disease of thyroid-hormone deficiency. The thyroid regulates your dog's metabolism. A large number of skin problems in dogs are caused by thyroid disease.

*Progressive retinal atrophy (PRA):* A slow deterioration of the retina, leading to blindness.

*Von Willebrand's disease:* Abnormal blood-clotting defect involving both platelet and coagulation function (factor VIII).

## TOY POODLE

*Allergies:* The Toy Poodle is prone to all types of allergies.

*Behavioral abnormalities:* A whole range of abnormal behavioral patterns, such as aggression and panic disorders.

*Blood-clotting disorders:* The Toy Poodle is prone to a blood-clotting disorder due to a deficiency of coagulation factors VIII or XII.

*Bone disease:* The Toy Poodle is prone to abnormal mineralization of the bone.

*Cancer:* The Toy Poodle is prone to skin cancer and cancer of the toe.

*Cataract:* In older dogs the lens of the eye becomes cloudy, causing a partial or total loss of vision.

*Cushing's disease (hyperadrenocorticism):* A condition in which the adrenal glands secrete too much cortisol. Cortisol is a steroid hormone which regulates carbohydrate, fat, and protein metabolism.

*Deafness:* A partial or total loss of hearing.

*Epilepsy:* A brain disorder in which the dog experiences seizures (convulsions).

*Epiphyseal dysplasia:* Abnormal development of the long bone.

*Eye abnormalities:* The Toy Poodle is prone to a rolling in of the eyelid(s), abnormally growing eyelashes, an overproduction of tears, an abnormal development of the tear duct(s), and an abnormal development of the retina(s).

*Glaucoma:* Pressure on the retina from excess fluid in the eyeball, which causes partial or total loss of vision.

*Globoid cell leukodystrophy:* Degeneration of a type of brain cell.

*Growth-hormone-responsive dermatosis:* Skin disorder caused by a deficiency of growth hormones.

*Heart disease:* Abnormal development of the heart.

*Hemeralopia:* A disorder of the retina causing blindness during the with partial sight in dim light.

*Hypothyroidism:* A common disease of thyroid-hormone deficiency. The thyroid regulates your dog's metabolism. A large number of skin problems in dogs are caused by thyroid disease.

*Immune-mediated hemolytic anemia (IMHA):* Anemia resulting from an immune system mediated destruction of the red blood cells.

*Intervertebral disc disease:* Abnormal development of the discs between the vertebrae.

*Iris atrophy:* A deterioration of the iris.

*Liver abnormalities:* The Toy Poodle is prone to an abnormal formation of blood vessels in the liver.

*Osteochondritis dissecans*: Inflammation of the cartilage in the joints. A form of arthritis.

*Osteochondrosis*: An abnormal development of joint cartilage. Most commonly found in the shoulder, elbow, and knee.

*Otitis externa*: An infection of the external structures of the ear.

*Pannus*: Progressive immune-mediated disease in which there is a growth of tissue over the cornea, causing inflammation and possible blindness.

*Patellar luxation*: The kneecap(s) slips out of place.

*Progressive retinal atrophy* (**PRA**): A slow deterioration of the retina, leading to blindness.

*Sebaceous gland tumor*: A skin tumor.

*Skin allergies*: Allergic reaction that causes inflammation and itching of the skin.

*Urolithiasis*: Stones or crystals in the urinary tract.

*Von Willebrand's disease*: Abnormal blood-clotting defect involving both platelet and coagulation function (factor VIII).

## WELSH TERRIER

*Cataract*: In older dogs the lens of the eye becomes cloudy, causing a partial or total loss of vision.

*Eye abnormalities*: The Welsh Terrier is prone to a condition where the lens in the eye slips out of place.

*Glaucoma*: Pressure on the retina from excess fluid in the eyeball, which causes partial or total loss of vision.

*Hypothyroidism*: A common disease of thyroid-hormone deficiency. The thyroid regulates your dog's metabolism. A large number of skin problems in dogs are caused by thyroid disease.

*Von Willebrand's disease*: Abnormal blood-clotting defect involving both platelet and coagulation function (factor VIII).

## WEST HIGHLAND WHITE TERRIER

*Acanthosis nigricans*: A rare skin disease characterized by dark skin, hair loss, and inflammation of the skin. Primarily found in the armpits.

*Addison's disease:* A disease in which the adrenal glands secrete an insufficient amount of cortisone, a steroid hormone.

*Allergies:* The West Highland White Terrier is highly prone to all types of allergies.

*Cataract:* In older dogs the lens of the eye becomes cloudy, causing a partial or total loss of vision.

*Copper metabolism abnormality:* An inability to utilize and store copper properly. Results in liver disease if not treated.

*Craniomandibular osteopathy:* Abnormally dense bones in the face and the jaw.

*Cushing's disease (hyperadrenocorticism):* A condition in which the adrenal glands secrete too much cortisol. Cortisol is a steroid hormone which regulates carbohydrate, fat, and protein metabolism.

*Epidermal dysplasia:* Abnormal development of the outer layer of the skin.

*Eye abnormalities:* The West Highland White Terrier is prone to a condition in which the lens in the eye slips out of place, abnormal development of the retina(s), and dry eye, a condition in which the eye(s) does not produce enough liquid.

*Globoid cell leukodystrophy:* Degeneration of a type of brain cell.

*Hernia:* A rupture of the wall of an internal organ in the groin area.

*Immune-mediated hemolytic anemia (IMHA):* Anemia resulting from an immune system mediated destruction of the red blood cells.

*Legg-Perthes disease:* The blood vessels feeding the thigh bone deteriorate, leading to a deterioration of the femoral head, a part of the hip.

*Seborrhea:* A skin disease characterized by raw, scaling skin and an excess of sebum (oil-like substance), which causes a rancid body odor.

*Skin allergies:* Allergic reaction that causes inflammation and itching of the skin.

*White dog shaker syndrome:* A condition brought on by stress or overexcitement in which the dog has rapid eye movements, tremors, and incoordination.

## WHIPPET

*Baldness*: Loss of hair.

*Cancer*: The Whippet is prone to hemangiosarcoma, a cancer of blood vessels involving liver, skin, or spleen.

*Cataract*: In older dogs the lens of the eye becomes cloudy, causing a partial or total loss of vision.

*Cryptorchidism*: A developmental condition in which one or both testicles fail to descend into the scrotum.

*Demodectic mange*: A skin disease in which canine mites are living in the skin, causing itching, loss of hair, and skin infections. Usually found on the face and front legs.

*Eye abnormalities*: The Whippet is prone to a rolling in of the eyelid(s) and a condition where the lens in the eye slips out of place.

*Hypothyroidism*: A common disease of thyroid-hormone deficiency. The thyroid regulates your dog's metabolism. A large number of skin problems in dogs are caused by thyroid disease.

*Osteochondritis dissecans*: Inflammation of the cartilage in the joints. A form of arthritis.

*Osteochondrosis*: An abnormal development of joint cartilage. Most commonly found in the shoulder, elbow, and knee.

*Progressive retinal atrophy (PRA)*: A slow deterioration of the retina, leading to blindness.

*Von Willebrand's disease*: Abnormal blood-clotting defect involving both platelet and coagulation function (factor VIII).

## WIREHAIRED FOX TERRIER

*Allergies*: The Wirehaired Fox Terrier is prone to inhalant allergies.

*Ataxia*: A progressive loss of coordination.

*Cataract*: In older dogs the lens of the eye becomes cloudy, causing a partial or total loss of vision.

*Deafness*: A partial or total loss of hearing.

*Eye abnormalities:* The Wirehaired Fox Terrier is prone to a rolling in of the eyelid(s), abnormally growing eyelashes, and a condition where the lens in the eye slips out of place.

*Esophageal disorder:* Spasms in the muscles of the esophagus.

*Glaucoma:* Pressure on the retina from excess fluid in the eyeball, which causes partial or total loss of vision.

*Heart disease:* Malfunction of the valve(s) and abnormal development of the heart.

*Legg-Perthes disease:* The blood vessels feeding the thigh bone deteriorate, leading to a deterioration of the femoral head, a part of the hip.

*Progressive retinal atrophy (PRA):* A slow deterioration of the retina, leading to blindness.

*Shoulder dislocation:* The shoulder joint slips out of place.

*Teeth abnormalities:* The number, placement, or development of the teeth is not normal.

*Thyroid disease:* Inflammation of the thyroid.

*Von Willebrand's disease:* Abnormal blood-clotting defect involving both platelet and coagulation function (factor VIII).

## YORKSHIRE TERRIER

*Cataract:* In older dogs the lens of the eye becomes cloudy, causing a partial or total loss of vision.

*Demodectic mange:* A skin disease in which canine mites are living in the skin, causing itching, loss of hair, and skin infections. Usually found on the face and front legs.

*Eye abnormalities:* The Yorkshire Terrier is prone to abnormally growing eyelashes, abnormal development of the retina(s), a rolling in of the eyelid(s) and dry eye, a condition in which the eye(s) does not produce enough liquid.

*Hydrocephalus:* The accumulation of fluid in the brain.

*Hypothyroidism:* A common disease of thyroid-hormone deficiency. The thyroid regulates your dog's metabolism. A large number of skin problems in dogs are caused by thyroid disease.

*Legg-Perthes disease*: The blood vessels feeding the thigh bone deteriorate, leading to a deterioration of the femoral head, a part of the hip.

*Liver abnormalities*: The Yorkshire Terrier is prone to an abnormal formation of blood vessels in the liver.

*Patellar luxation*: The kneecap(s) slips out of place.

*Progressive retinal atrophy (PRA)*: A slow deterioration of the retina, leading to blindness.

*Seborrhea*: A skin disease characterized by raw, scaling skin and an excess of sebum (oil-like substance), which causes a rancid body odor.

*Vertebra malformation*: An abnormal development of the second vertebra, causing unsteadiness.

*Von Willebrand's disease*: Abnormal blood-clotting defect involving both platelet and coagulation function (factor VIII).

# 11

## CBD: The Miracle Remedy For Your Dog

Cannabidiol (CBD), the most well-known and best-studied non-psychoactive cannabinoid, has been found to be non-toxic and non-habit-forming for your dog. Just as importantly, it does not generally cause side effects, so you can give your dog CBD on a daily basis, not just when they are sick or when drugs fail.

### WHAT EXACTLY IS CBD?

CBD is a cannabis-derived compound that is found in abundance in hemp. Most CBD for dogs is derived from hemp oil; therefore, it contains only a trace of tetrahydrocannabinol (THC), the compound that gives marijuana its psychoactive properties. As long as the THC component is less than 0.3%, CBD is legal in all fifty of the United States.

Industrial hemp-derived CBD has significant lifestyle benefits as a "super nutrient" that does not combine the "high" or buzz of other cannabis plants. Quite the opposite. CBD provides the calming, pain-relieving sensation of the cannabis plant *without* the potential intoxicating effects of regular cannabis.

Hemp-based CBD has its origins in the ancient civilizations in Asia.

Here in the United States, the government officially noted the medicinal qualities of hemp back in 1850. However, it took until the 1960s for the establishment to accept CBD as a separate component in cannabis.

CBD has little binding affinity for either of the two cannabinoid receptors; instead, it has an indirect impact on the endocannabinoid system, which influences physiological processes including appetite, pain sensation, mood, and memory.

Dogs have the same natural endogenous cannabinoid receptors as humans. These specific cannabinoid receptor sites—primarily located in the brain, central nervous system, organs, and immune cells—are what influence the calming and relaxing benefits of cannabinoid-based remedies.

CBD can be manufactured into a variety of treatment options that provide both external and internal relief. It can be given in tinctures, or as edibles or oils.

## IS CBD SAFE?

With myriad studies showing the health benefits of CBD, the most encouraging result is that CBD is safe, even when taken in high doses and over extended periods of time. Keep in mind, however, that CBD can decrease the activity of liver enzymes used to metabolize many prescription drugs; therefore, if your dog is currently taking any medication, check with your holistic veterinarian before using CBD.

The bottom line is that CBD can be a healthy, potentially life-saving remedy for your dog. More and more dog owners and holistic vets are being drawn to its diverse and marked health benefits. They feel good knowing that the side effects of CBD are mild, and that their dogs don't appear to be building up a tolerance to it.

## HOW TO CHOOSE CBD FOR YOUR DOG

Not all CBD is the same. When choosing what CBD to administer to your dog, select a high-quality CBD product that has proven results.

When selecting a CBD for your dog:

- Make sure that it is certified "Organic" on the label. If it isn't organic, it could contain dangerous pesticides, herbicides, fungicides, or solvents.
- Look for high-quality and pure products. Make sure your CBD is free of additives, and clearly lists the amount of CBD per serving on the label.
- Ask for a laboratory analysis from a third party. Many oils contain a very small amount of CBD. A reputable manufacturer will be willing to provide you with a certified analysis of the product.
- A tincture is the best form in which to administer CBD to your dog, because it can be given drop by drop. In other words, you can give your dog exactly how much CBD they need.

## HOW DO CANNABINOIDS WORK?

CBD acts on various pathways in the cells through cannabinoid receptors (CBs), which are present not just in humans, but in all mammals. Since cannabinoids have been shown to have valuable therapeutic use in humans, it's logical to think they could also be therapeutic for our dogs.

CBD works for both humans and dogs because we have the same endogenous cannabinoid system. Which doesn't mean that there aren't some differences. Dogs, for example, have a higher number of CB2 receptors in their brain than humans. There are also structural differences of the CBs themselves between the two species, as well as differences in how cannabinoids metabolize in the body.

As discussed, because CBD has not been found to cause many side effects, it can be used not just when your dog is sick or when pharmaceuticals fail. CBD can be a beneficial component of *daily* nutrition for your dog or other pets.

Clinical research shows the following:

- CBD can help with canine conditions such as pain, nausea, seizures, anxiety/stress, arthritis, gastrointestinal distress, and cancer.

- Many pet owners have experienced positive effects using hemp-based CBD for dogs, especially for inflammatory conditions.
- The Journal of the American Holistic Veterinary Medical Association found that of nearly 650 people surveyed, 72% reported having used a hemp-based cannabis product for their canine friend.
- In total, 64% of those surveyed felt that CBD helped their dog.
- According to research at the University of Milan, CBD has long been proven to have anti-cancer and tumor-reducing effects. Other studies have pointed to the possibility that CBD may affect cancer genes by shutting down cancer cellular growth receptors.

## CBD FOR DOGS—PROS AND CONS

Although CBD products are safe, non-toxic alternatives for people like you who desire more transparent treatment options for their dog, the level of openness to cannabis-based products can depend on the social environment in which you live.

For instance, in Colorado, a cannabis mecca, the general thought is: "Why can't my dog experience the same benefits I do?"

People logically need assurance that cannabis products will not harm their pets. There is much misinformation in the public sphere, so it is important to get people to understand the promising medicinal benefits that CBD can provide to your dog. CBD is not going away, and pet owners should consider all sides of the issue when considering whether or not to give CBD products to the furry friend in their life.

## HOW TO USE CBD FOR YOUR DOG

1. **Start Low and Slow.** CBD from hemp can be given to your dog at 1 mg for every 10 pounds of animal weight. The general rule is to be conservative with your CBD dosage.
2. **Use Quality CBD.** It should state on the label the amount of CBD per serving. Ask for a certified three-party laboratory analysis.

3. **Monitor Your Dog.** This is especially important the first time you give CBD to your dog. Keep a dosage and time log of how much and when you administer to your dog; you can then adjust the amount and frequency as needed.

4. **Buy 100% Organic CBD Products.** You don't want to expose your dog to pesticides, herbicides, or insecticides.

5. **Consult with Your Holistic Veterinarian.**

## TEN REASONS TO CONSIDER CBD FOR YOUR DOG

### 1. CBD is not Psychoactive

As discussed above, because CBD is derived from hemp oil, it contains just trace amounts of THC. Therefore, your dog will not experience a "high" from CBD, only relaxation.

### 2. CBD Can Help Reduce Anxiety

CBD helps your dog's anxiety because when it enters a mammal's endocannabinoid system, it activates specific receptors found throughout the body. These are the only receptors that allow for two-way communication between body systems. Because the receptors can talk to each other, CBD makes it easier for the body to calm down, and consequently relieves tension and anxiety.

Dogs can experience two types of anxiety—behavioral and situational. Certain activities that can cause situational anxiety (the majority of those experienced) are:

- Lightning/thunderstorms
- Travel
- Having company or unfamiliar people over
- Fireworks

The calming effects of CBD work well with high-strung dogs that struggle with separation anxiety, depression, and noise phobias. When left alone, they might show disruptive and destructive behaviors such as drooling, urination, barking, pacing, and chewing on objects.

### 3. CBD Can Help Fight Cancer

CBD has been shown to:

- Stop cancer cells from growing, and to increase tumor cell death.
- Decrease cancer treatment systems such as vomiting, loss of appetite, and chronic pain. (see note #5 below)
- Help the immune system's killer cells to cause cancer cell death.
- Kill cancer cells by blocking their ability to produce energy.
- Exhibit anti-tumor properties that slow and inhibit glioma cell growth.
- Help increase the efficacy of conventional cancer treatment.

### 4. CBD Can Help Treat Seizures

One out of every twenty dogs experiences seizures—these dogs are routinely treated with medicines such as potassium bromide and phenobarbital, which can cause damage to the dogs' livers and other organs.

### 5. CBD Can Help Relieve Chronic Pain

According to Dana Scott, founder of *Dogs Naturally Magazine*, "the cannabinoids in CBD work so well for pain that scientists are considering it as a new class of drug for the treatment of chronic pain."

One area in which CBD is beneficial is in the treatment of achy joints, arthritis, and inflammatory joint disease—or any other disease that slows your pet down. CBD can alleviate these joint pains and get your dog moving around again. CBD doesn't simply mask the pain; it helps soothe chronic inflammation that prevents the body from healing properly.

CBD offers the full spectrum of health benefits without the psychoactive effects. It can provide relief from debilitating illnesses that cause low energy levels and overall discomfort. The restorative powers of CBD work just as well for dogs as they do for humans.

There is nothing more devastating to a dog owner than a cancer diagnosis. Fortunately, CBD helps to decrease the symptoms of cancer treatment such as nausea, loss of appetite, and chronic pain. Although CBD cannot cure cancer, it can make your pet feel more comfortable during difficult times.

### 6. CBD Can Help Fight Inflammatory Bowel Disease (IBD)

Although IBD—which can manifest with chronic vomiting or diarrhea—occurs mostly in middle-aged dogs, it can occur in dogs of all ages. CBD cannot only help to prevent colitis, the leading cause of large bowel diarrhea in dogs, but can help to restore normal gut motility in IBD.

### 7. CBD Can Help Reduce Chronic Inflammation and Autoimmune Disease

According to Dana Scott, "CBD has been shown to decrease the production and release of inflammatory cytokines that can cause allergies, hypersensitivities, and autoimmunity. It can also suppress something called Th17 dominance, which is a major cause of autoimmune diseases."

CBD interacts with receptors throughout your dog's body and can act as an anti-inflammatory and immune-boosting agent. It has also been proven to have strong antioxidant properties rivaling those of vitamins C and E.

### 8. CBD Can Protect the Nervous System and Help with Neurodegenerative Diseases

Dana Scott says that CBD shows promise for dogs suffering from degenerative myelopathy and other spine and nerve issues. In humans, it has been shown to help patients with Alzheimer's, Parkinson's, and Amyotrophic Lateral Sclerosis (ALS); there is a hope that it would be equally effective for your dog.

Scott says that "for senior dogs, CBD has been shown to protect the brain from cell death caused by free radicals and toxins."

### 9. CBD Can Increase Appetite and Lessen the Effects of Nausea

CBD can boost your dog's appetite and reduce nausea. It is sensitive enough to alleviate digestive issues while providing necessary relief for pain and digestive issues.

### 10. CBD Can Help Promote Cardiovascular Health

Australian veterinarian Edward Bassingthwaighte has linked use of CBD to the health of a dog's heart. According to Dana Scott, CBD "can reduce the damage from damaged blood vessels and irregular heart rates, protect blood vessels from damage and dilate the arteries, and reduce heart rate and blood pressure associated with stress and anxiety."

**CBD Can Also Help with:**

11. Intestinal Bowel Syndrome (IBS).
12. Arthritis.
13. Minimizing aggressive behavior disorders by calming down a dog who struggles to control their temper.
14. Slowing aging and mental function.
15. Supporting bone health.
16. Colitis support.
17. Degenerative myelopathy.
18. Diabetes.
19. Free radical neutralization.
20. Glaucoma.
21. Infections.
22. Obesity.
23. Obsessive-Compulsive Disorder (OCD).
24. Skin conditions.
25. Spinal injury.

# Resources

## DOG FOOD, SUPPLEMENTS

**Dick Van Patten's Natural Balance
Pet Foods, Inc.**
12924 Pierce Street
Pacoima, CA 91331
Ph: 1-800-829-4493
E-mail: info@naturalbalanceinc.com
Website: www.naturalbalanceinc.com
Look for the organic formula dry dog food

**Dr. Harvey's Healthy
Formulations, Inc.**
180 Main Street
Keansburg, NJ 07734
Ph: 1-866-362-4123
E-mail: info@drharveys.com
Website: www.drharveys.com
Dog food pre-mix for a raw food diet,
supplements

**Green Foods Corporation**
320 North Graves
Oxnard, CA 93030
Ph: 1-800-777-4430
E-mail: info@greenfoods.com
Website: www.greenfoods.com
Barley dog supplement

**Newman's Own Organics**
Website: http://www.newmansown
organics.com
Organic dry and canned dog food
Profits go to organizations that
support animals' well-being

**Orthomolecular Specialties**
P.O. Box 32232
San Jose, CA 95152
Ph: 1-408-227-9334
E-mail: orders@belfield.com
Website: http://www.belfield.com
Supplements developed by Wendell O.
Belfield, DVM

**Rx Vitamins**
200 Myrtle Blvd
Larchmont, NY 10538
Ph: 1-800-792-2222
E-mail: info@rxvitamins.com
Website: www.rxvitamins.com/pets
Supplements

**Solid Gold Health Products for Pets, Inc.**
900 Vernon Way #101
El Cajon, CA 92020
Ph: 1-800-364-4863
E-mail: dane@solidgoldhealth.com
Website: www.solidgoldhealth.com
Organic dry and canned dog food, supplements

**Springtime Inc.**
10942-J Beaver Dam Rd
P.O. Box 1227
Cockeysville, MD 21030
Ph: 1-800-521-3212
E-mail: feedback@springtimeinc.com
Website: www.springtimeinc.com
Supplements

**Wysong Corp.**
7550 Eastman Avenue
Midland, MI 48642
Ph: 1-800-748-0188
E-mail: wysong@wysong.net
Website: www.wysong.net
Organic dry and canned dog food, supplements

## FLEA CONTROL
**Flea Relief by Dr. Goodpet**
P.O. Box 4547
Inglewood, CA 90309
Ph: 1-800-222-9932
E-mail: info@goodpet.com
Website: www.goodpet.com
Homeopathic

**Fleabusters**
Ph: 1-800-666-3532
E-mail: rxforfleas@fleabusters.com
Website: www.fleabuster.com
Products and services

**Fleas Flee**
The Vet at the Barn
790 Chestnut Ridge Road
Chestnut Ridge, NY 10977
Ph: 1-845-356-3838
E-mail: heather@vetatthebarn.com
Website: www.thevetatthebarn.com
Nutritional supplements

**Natural Animal Health Products, Inc.**
7000 U.S. 1 North St.
Augustine, FL 32095
Ph: 1-800-274-7387
E-mail: sales@naturalanimal.com
Website: www.naturalanimal.com
Products, supplements

## LABS THAT DO ANTIBODY TITER TESTS
**Antech Diagnostics**
Ph: East: 1-800-872-1001
Ph: West: 1-800-745-4725
Website: www.antechdiagnostics.com

**Cornell Diagnostic Lab**
P.O. Box 5786
Ithaca, NY 14853
Ph: 1-607-253-3900
E-mail: diagcenter@cornell.edu
Website: www.diaglab.vet.cornell.edu/

**Hemopet**
11330 Markon Drive
Garden Grove, CA 92841
Ph: 1-714-891-2022
E-mail: hemopet@hotmail.com
Website: www.hemopet.com

## WATER FILTERS
**The Aquasana Store**
P.O. Box 521834
Salt Lake City, UT 84152
Ph: 1-877-270-2677
E-mail: contact@aquasanastore.com
Website: www.aquasanastore.com

**Culligan International**
One Culligan Parkway
Northbrook, IL 60062-6209
Ph: 1-847-205-6000
E-mail: feedback@culligan.com
Website: www.culligan.com

**CWR Environmental Products**
100 Carney Street
Glen Cove, NY 11542
Ph: 1-800-444-3563
E-mail: sales@cwrenviro.com
Website: www.cwrenviro.com

## HOMEOPATHIC
**Dr. Goodpet**
P.O. Box 4547
Inglewood, CA 90309
Ph: 1-800-222-9932
E-mail: info@goodpet.com
Website: www.goodpet.com

**HomeoPet**
P.O. Box 147
Westhampton Beach, NY 11978
Ph: 1-800-555-4461
E-mail: info@homeopet.com
Website: www.homeopet.com

**Newton Laboratories**
2360 Rockaway Industrial Blvd
Conyers, GA 30012
Ph: 1-800-448-7256
E-mail: info@newtonlabs.net
Website: www.newtonlabs.net

## ONLINE RESOURCES
**The Academy of Veterinary
   Homeopathy**
Website: www.theavh.org

**Alt Vet Med**—Complementary and
   Alternative Veterinary Medicine
Website: www.altvetmed.org

**American Holistic Veterinary
   Medical Association**
Website: www.ahvma.org

**Environmental Protection Agency**
Website: www.epa.gov/safewater

**International Association for
   Veterinary Homoeopathy**
Website: www.iavh.at

**Merck Veterinary Manual**
Website: www.merckvetmanual.com

**Open Directory Project**
Website: www.dmoz.org/Health/
  Animal/Alternative_Medicine

**A Pet Owner's Guide to Laboratory
  Testing**
Website: www.itsfortheanimals.com/
  BLOOD-TEST-EXPLAINED.HTM

**Veterinary Institute of Integrative
  Medicine**
Website: www.viim.com

**Your Animal's Health**
Website: www.belfield.com

# References

## CHAPTER 1

Case, L, Carey, D, Hirakawa, D. *Canine and Feline Nutrition*. St. Louis, MO: Mosby Year Book, Inc., 1995.

Coffman, H. *The Dry Dog Food Reference*, Nashua, NH: Pig Dog Press, 1995.

Everett, S. *What Many Dog Food Manufacturers Don't Want You to Know*. Unpalatable Dog Food Facts, http://www.albany.net/~sterling/foodfax.htm.

Franklin, D. "Is My Kitchen Faucet Poisoning Me With Lead?" *Health Magazine*. 21: Mar/Apr 1993.

Hallman, JE, et al. "Cellulose, Beet Pulp, and Pectin/Gum Arabic Effects on Canine Colonic Microstructure and Histopathology." *Veterinary Clinical Nutrition*. 2(4):137-142, 1995.

*Health Effects of Lead in Drinking Water*, Pure Water Solutions, http://www.cris.com/~compaid/lead.htm.

Hickman, S. "Focus on Food." *Canine Health Naturally*. 1(1), 1996.

Keller, K. "Water Works Wonders." *Redbook*. 175 D, May 1990.

Lemonick, M, et al. "Toxins on Tap." *Time Magazine*. 142(20), Nov 15, 1993.

"News From Down Under, Dogs On Pet Food Risk Early Death." *The London Sunday Telegraph*. Oct 1, 1995.

Pitcairn, R, Pitcairn, S. *Dr. Pitcairn's Complete Guide to Natural Health for Dogs and Cats*. Emmaus, PA: Rodale Press, Inc., 1995.

Pittman, D. "Health Trends." *Share-Net News*. 1(1), Nov 15, 1993.

Pollack, W. "The Effects of a Natural vs. Commercial Pet Food Diet on the Wellness of Common Companion Animals—A Holistic Perspective." *Journal of the American Holistic Veterinary Medical Association.* 15(4):21–25, 1996-1997.

Rowe, J. "Canine Clinic." *The American Field.* 1995.

Santillo, H. *Food Enzymes: The Missing Link To Radiant Health.* Prescott, AZ: Hohm Press, 1993.

Schachter, M. "The Dangers of Fluoride and Fluoridation." *Nutritional Medicine.* 1996. http://205.180.229.2/library/articles/schacter/fluoride.n.htm.

Volhard, W, Brown, K. *The Holistic Guide For A Healthy Dog.* New York, NY: Howell Book House, 1995.

Wampler, S. *Prevent Disease and Extend Your Life.* Scottsdale, AZ: Health Watchers System, 1995.

Whitney, G. *The Complete Book of Dog Care.* New York, NY: Main Street Book, Doubleday Books, Inc., div. of Bantam Doubleday Dell Publishing Group, 1985.

Williams, D. "Water Quality Alert, Alternatives for the Health Conscious Individual." *Mountain Home Publishing.* 6(24):185–192, Jun 1997.

## CHAPTER 3

Belfield, W, Zucker, M. *How to Have a Healthier Dog.* San Jose, CA: Orthomolecular Specialties, 1981.

Case, L, Carey, D, Hirakawa, D. *Canine and Feline Nutrition.* St. Louis, MO: Mosby Year Book, Inc., 1995.

Goldy, G. "Effects of Measured Doses of Vitamin A Fed to Healthy Beagle Dogs for 26 Weeks." *Veterinary Clinical Nutrition.* 3(2):45-49, 1996.

Hannigan, B. "Diet and Immune Function." *British Journal of Biomedical Sciences.* 51:252-259, 1994.

Hazewinkel, HAW, et al. "Influence of Protein, Minerals, and Vitamin D on Skeletal Development of Dogs." *Veterinary Clinical Nutrition.* 2(3):93–99, 1995.

Kirk, RW. "Nutrition and the Integument." *Journal of Small Animal Practice.* 32:283-288, 1991.

Lazarus, P. *Keep Your Pet Healthy The Natural Way.* New Canaan, CT: Keats Publishing, Inc., 1986.

Mazzotta, M. "Nutrition and Wound Healing." *Journal of the American Podiatric Medical Association*. 84(9):456-462, 1994.

Miller, W. "Nutritional Considerations in Small Animal Dermatology." *Small Animal Practice*. 19(3):497-511, 1989.

Plechner, A, Zucker, M. *Pet Allergies, Remedies For An Epidemic*. Inglewood, CA: Dr. Goodpet Laboratories Very Healthy Enterprises, Inc., 1986.

Robertson, JM, et al. "A Possible Role for Vitamins C and E in Cataract Prevention." *American Journal of Clinical Nutrition*. 53:346S-351S, 1991.

Sheffy, B, et al. "Nutrition and the Immune Response." *Cornell Veterinarian*. 68:48–61, 1978.

Sheffy, B, et al. "Influence of Vitamin E and Selenium on Immune Response Mechanisms." *Federation Proceedings*. 38(7):2139–2143, 1979.

Veterinary Product News Staff Report. "Antioxidants May Improve Pet Health." *Veterinary Product News*. 6(3), 1994.

Volhard, W, Brown, K. *The Holistic Guide For A Healthy Dog*. New York, NY: Howell Book House, 1995.

## CHAPTER 4

Belfield, W, Zucker, M. *How to Have a Healthier Dog*. San Jose, CA: Orthomolecular Specialties, 1981.

Case, L, Carey, D, Hirakawa, D. *Canine and Feline Nutrition*. St. Louis, MO: Mosby Year Book, Inc., 1995.

Falck, G. "High Magnesium Improves the Post Ischemic Recovery of Cardiac Function." *Cardiovascular Research*. 29:439, 1995.

Hazewinkel, HAW, et al. "Influence of Protein, Minerals, and Vitamin D on Skeletal Development of Dogs." *Veterinary Clinical Nutrition*. 2(3):93–99, 1995.

Kirk, RW. "Nutrition and the Integument." *Journal of Small Animal Practice*. 32:283-288, 1991.

Krook, L. "Overnutrition and Skeletal Disease in the Dog." *Overnutrition and Skeletal Disease in the Dog*, Department of Pathology, New York State Veterinary College. 87-89, 1974.

Miller, W. "Nutritional Considerations in Small Animal Dermatology." *Small Animal Practice.* 19(3):497-511, 1989.

Sheffy, B, et al. "Influence of Vitamin E and Selenium on Immune Response Mechanisms." *Federation Proceedings.* 38(7):2139-2143, 1979.

Volhard, W, Brown, K. *The Holistic Guide For A Healthy Dog.* New York, NY: Howell Book House, 1995.

## CHAPTER 5

Belfield, W, Zucker, M. *How to Have a Healthier Dog.* San Jose, CA: Orthomolecular Specialties, 1981.

Carlson, D, Giffin, J. *Dog Owners Home Veterinary Handbook.* New York, NY: Howell Book House, 1992.

Case, L, Carey, D, Hirakawa, D. *Canine and Feline Nutrition.* St. Louis, MO: Mosby Year Book, Inc., 1995.

Faculty and Staff, School of Veterinary Medicine University of California, Davis. *UCDAVIS School of Veterinary Medicine Book of Dogs.* New York, NY: HarperCollins, 1995.

Mazzotta, M. "Nutrition and Wound Healing." *Journal of the American Podiatric Medical Association.* 84(9):456-462, 1994.

Mizelle, HL, et al. "Abnormal Cardiovascular Responses to Exercise During the Development of Obesity in Dogs." *American Journal of Hypertension.* 7: 374-378, 1994.

Morley, J. "Nutritional Modulation of Behavior and Immunocompetence." *Nutrition Reviews.* 52(8):S6-S8, 1994.

Sheffy, B, et al."Nutrition and Metabolism of the Geriatric Dog." *Cornell Veterinarian.* 75:324-347, 1985.

Teare, JA, et al. "Rapid Growth and Skeletal Disease in Dogs." *Proceedings of the Cornell Nutrition Conference.* Cornell University, Ithaca, NY, 126-130, 1980.

## CHAPTER 6

Bogdon, J. "Micronutrient Nutrition and Immunity." *Nutrition Report.* 13(2):1, Feb 1995.

Brennan, M, Eckroate, N. *The Natural Dog*. New York, NY: Penguin Group, 1994.

"Carpet Chemicals May Pose Serious Health Risk: EPA and Carpet Industry Under Fire." *Public Citizen Health Research Group Health Letter*. 9(3):1–3,11, Mar 1993.

Case, L, Carey, D, Hirakawa, D. *Canine and Feline Nutrition*. St. Louis, MO: Mosby Year Book, Inc., 1995.

"CSPI Proposes Modest Increase in Pesticide Tax." *Nutrition Week*. 25(19):4,5, 1995.

Diegelman, N. *Poison In The Grass: The Hazards And Consequences of Lawn Pesticides*. The S.T.A.T.E. Foundation.

Faculty and Staff, School of Veterinary Medicine University of California, Davis. *UCDAVIS School of Veterinary Medicine Book of Dogs*. New York, NY: HarperCollins, 1995.

Hadden, J. "The Treatment of Zinc Deficiency Is an Immunotherapy." *International Journal of Immunopharmacology*. 17(9):697–701, 1995.

Hickman, S. "Focus on Food." *Canine Health Naturally*. 1(1), 1996.

Lewis, RG, et al. "Evaluations of Methods for Monitoring the Potential Exposure of Small Children to Pesticides in the Residential Environment." *Environment Contamination Toxicology*. 26:37-46, 1994.

Lowengart, RA, et al. "Childhood Leukemia and Parents Occupational and Home Exposures." *Journal of the National Cancer Institute*. 79:37–46, 1987.

McCluggage, D. "Vaccinations in Veterinary Medicine —A New Perspective." *Journal of the American Veterinary Medical Association*. 14(2), 1995.

Mockett, A, et al. "Comparing How Puppies with Passive Immunity Respond to Three Canine Parvovirus Vaccines." *Veterinary Medicine*. 430–438, 1995.

"Pesticide Usage." *Nutrition Week*. 25(20):7, 1995.

"Pet Immunizations." *Townsend Letter for Doctors and Patients*. Jun 1996.

Pike, J, et al. "Effect of Vitamin and Trace Element Supplementation on Immune Indices in Healthy Elderly." *International Journal of Vitamin and Nutrition Research*. 65:117–120, 1995.

Pitcairn, R, Pitcairn, S. *Dr. Pitcairn's Complete Guide to Natural Health for Dogs and Cats*. Emmaus, PA: Rodale Press, Inc., 1995.

Plechner, A, Zucker, M. *Pet Allergies, Remedies For An Epidemic*. Inglewood, CA: Dr. Goodpet Laboratories Very Healthy Enterprises, Inc., 1986.

"Pollution—Our Breath-Taking Air." *U.S. News and World Report*. 15, May 20, 1996.

Schoen, AM, Wynn, SG, editors. *Complimentary and Alternative Veterinary Medicine, Principles and Practice*. St. Louis, MO: Mosby, Inc., 1998.

Schueler, T. "Urban Pesticides: From the Lawn to the Stream." *Watershed Protection Techniques*. 2(1), 1995.

Sheffy, B. "Nutrition, Infection and Immunity." *Compendium on Continuing Education for the Practicing Veterinarian*. 7(12):990–997, 1985.

Sheffy, B, et al. "Influence of Vitamin E and Selenium on Immune Response Mechanisms." *Federation Proceedings*. 38(7):2139–2143, 1979.

Smith, C. "Are We Vaccinating Too Much?" *Journal of the American Veterinary Medical Association*. 207(4):421–425, 1995.

Steinman, D, Wisner, M. *Living Healthy In A Toxic World*, Berkeley, CA: Berkeley Publishing Company, 1996.

Taylor, E. "Selenium and Cellular Immunity; Evidence that Selenoproteins May Be Encoded in the +1 Reading Frame Overlapping the Human CD4, CD8, and HLA-DR Genes." *Biological Trace Element Research*. 49:85-95, 1995.

"Veterinary Alternatives Can Help Your Pet." *Alternative Medicine Digest*. 19:94-99, 1997.

Veterinary Product News Staff Report. "Antioxidants May Improve Pet Health." *Veterinary Product News*. 6(3), 1994.

Volhard, W, Brown, K. *The Holistic Guide For A Healthy Dog*. New York, NY: Howell Book House, 1995.

Williams, B. "Latex Allergen in Respirable Particulate Air Pollution." *Journal of Allergy and Clinical Immunology*. 95(1/Part I):88-95, 1995.

Wynn, S. *Vaccination Decisions*. http://www/altvetmed.com/vaccine.html.

## CHAPTER 7

Attia, AM, et al. "Carbaryl-Induced Changes in Indoleamine Synthesis in the Pineal Gland and its Effects on Nighttime Serum Melatonin Concentration." *Journal of Toxicology.* 65:305-314, 1991.

*Dog Watch*, Cornell University College of Veterinary Medicine, Torstar Publications. 1(2), 1997.

Lazarus, Pat. *Keep Your Pet Healthy The Natural Way.* New Canaan, CT: Keats Publishing, 1986.

Pant, N, et al. "Effects of Carbaryl on the Rat's Male Reproductive System." *Journal of Veterinary and Human Toxicology.* 37:421-425, 1995.

Pant, N, et al. "Spermatotoxic Effects of Carbaryl in Rats." *Journal of Human Experimental Toxicology.* 15:736-738, 1996.

Sherman, JD. "Chlorpyrifos (Dursban)-Associated Birth Defects: a Report of Four Cases." *Archives of Environmental Health.* 51:5-8, 1996.

Stein, D. *The Natural Remedy Book For Dogs and Cats.* Freedom, CA: The Crossing Press, 1994.

Takahashi, RN, et al. "Behavioral and Biochemical Changes Following Repeated Administration of Carbaryl to Aging Rats." *Brazilian Journal of Medical and Biological Research.* 23:879-882, 1990.

Takahashi, RN, et al. "Effects of Age on Behavioral and Physiological Responses to Carbaryl in Rats." *Journal of Neurotoxicology Teratology.* 13:21-26, 1991.

## CHAPTER 8

Day, C. *The Homeopathic Treatment of Small Animals: Principals and Practice.* Essex, England: C.W. Daniel Company Limited, 1990.

MacLeod, G. *Dogs: Homeopathic Remedies*, Essex, England: C.W. Daniel Company Limited, 1995.

Pitcairn, R, Pitcairn, S. *Dr. Pitcairn's Complete Guide to Natural Health for Dogs and Cats.* Emmaus, PA: Rodale Press, Inc., 1995.

Schoen, AM, Wynn, SG, editors. *Complimentary and Alternative Veterinary Medicine, Principles and Practice.* St. Louis, MO: Mosby, Inc., 1998.

"Veterinary Alternatives Can Help Your Pet." *Alternative Medicine Digest.* 19:94-99, 1997.

Volhard, W, Brown, K. *The Holistic Guide For A Healthy Dog.* New York, NY: Howell Book House, 1995.

## CHAPTER 9

Belfield, W, Zucker, M. *How to Have a Healthier Dog.* San Jose, CA: Orthomolecular Specialties, 1981.

Brennan, M, Eckroate, N. *The Natural Dog.* New York, NY: Penguin Group, 1994.

Carlson, D, Giffin, J. *Dog Owners Home Veterinary Handbook.* New York, NY: Howell Book House, 1992.

Faculty and Staff, School of Veterinary Medicine University of California, Davis. *UCDAVIS School of Veterinary Medicine Book of Dogs.* New York, NY: HarperCollins, 1995.

Pelton, R, Overholser, L. *Alternatives in Cancer Therapy.* New York, NY: Simon and Schuster, 1994.

Stein, D. *The Natural Remedy Book For Dogs and Cats.* Freedom, CA: The Crossing Press, 1994.

Veterinary Product News Staff Report. "Antioxidants May Improve Pet Health." *Veterinary Product News.* 6(3), 1994.

## CHAPTER 10

Belfield, W, Zucker, M. *How to Have a Healthier Dog.* San Jose, CA: Orthomolecular Specialties, 1981.

Brennan, M. Eckroate, N. *The Natural Dog.* New York, NY: Penguin Group, 1994.

Carlson, D, Giffin, J. *Dog Owners Home Veterinary Handbook.* New York, NY: Howell Book House, 1992.

Faculty and Staff, School of Veterinary Medicine University of California, Davis. *UCDAVIS School of Veterinary Medicine Book of Dogs.* New York, NY: HarperCollins, 1995.

Schoen, AM, Wynn, SG, editors. *Complimentary and Alternative Veterinary Medicine, Principles and Practice.* St. Louis, MO: Mosby, Inc., 1998.

Stein, D. *The Natural Remedy Book For Dogs and Cats*. Freedom, CA: The Crossing Press, 1994.

Veterinary Product News Staff Report. "Antioxidants May Improve Pet Health." *Veterinary Product News*. 6(3), 1994.

## CHAPTER 11

*Canine Consumer Report, A Guide To Hereditary and Congenital Diseases in Dogs*. Davis, CA: The Association of Veterinarians for Animal Rights, 1994.

Fogle, B. *The Encyclopedia of the Dog*. New York, NY: Dorling Kindersley Publishing, Inc., 1995.

Lowell, M. *Your Purebred Puppy, A Buyer's Guide*. New York, NY: Henry Holt and Company, Inc., 1990.

*The Merck Veterinary Manual, 7th Edition*, Rahway, NJ: Merck and Co., Inc., 1991.

Pugnetti, G. *Simon and Schuster's Guide To Dogs*. New York, NY: Simon and Schuster, Inc., 1980.

Streitferdt, U. *Healthy Dog, Happy Dog*. New York, NY: Barron's Educational Series, Inc., 1994.

# References

Scott, Dana. 10 Things You Didn't Know About CBD Oil for Dogs. https:/www.dogsnaturallymagazine.com/cbd-oil-for-dogs/

White AG, Santoro D, Ahrens K, Marsella R. Single-blinded, randomized, placebo-controlled study on the effects of ciclosporin on cutaneous barrier function and immunological response in atopic Beagles. Vet Immunol Immunolpathol. 2018 March; 197;93-101. [PubMed 29475513]

Whalley BJ, Lin H, Bell L, Hill T, Patel A, Gray RA, Elizabeth Roberts C, Devinsky O, Bazelot M, Williams CM, Stephens GJ. Species-specific susceptibility to cannabis-induced convulsions. Br J Pharmacol. 2018 Feb 19. [PubMed 29457829]

Sato K, Sakai M, Hayakawa S, Sakamoto Y, Kagawa Y, Kutara K, Teshima K, Asano K, Watari T. Gallbladder Agenesis in 17 Dogs: 2006-2016. J Vet Intern Med. 2018 Jan; 32(1): 188-194. [PubMed 29377355]

Rotolo MC, Graziano S, Pellegrini M, Corlazzoli D, Antinori L, Porcarelli L, Pichini S. Simple and Fast Gas-chromatography Mass Spectrometry Assay to Assess Delta 9-Tetrahydrocannabinol and Cannabidiol in Dogs Treated with Medical Cannabis for Canine Epilepsy. Curr Pharm Biotechnol. 2017; 18(10): 821-827. [PubMed 29173160]

Liu M, Lo CY, Wang G, Chow HF, Ngo JC, Wan DC, Poon LL, Shaw PC. Identification of influenza polymerase inhibitors targeting polymerase PB2 cap-binding domain through virtual screening. Antiviral Res. 2017 Aug; 144: 186-195. [PubMed 28629986]

Tian Y, Xia M, Zhang S, Fu Z, Wen Q, Liu F, Xu Z, Li T, Tian H. Initial study of sediment antagonism and characteristics of silver nanoparticle-Coated biliary stents in an experimental animal model. Int J Nanomedicine. 2016 Apr 28; 11: 1807-17. [PubMed 27217749]

Istvan Ujvary, Lumir Hanus. Human Metabolites of Cannabidiol: A Review on Their Formation, Biological Activity, and Relevance in Therapy. Cannabis Cannabindoid Res. 2016; 1(1): 90-101. [PubMed 5576600]

Salahaden R. Sultan, Sophie A. Millar, Timothy J. Englan, Saoirse E. O'Sullivan. A Systematic Review and Meta-Analysis of the Haemodynamic Effects of Cannabidiol. Front Pharmacol. 2017; 8: 81. [PubMed 5323388]

A. Galler, B.C. Rutgen, E. Haas, A. Saalmuller, R.A. Hirt, W. Gerner, I Schwendenwein, B. Richter, J.G. Thalhammer, N. Luckschander-Zeller. Immunophenotype of Peripheral Blood Lymphocytes in Dogs with Inflammatory Bowel Disease. J Vet Intern Med. 2017 Nov-Dec; 31(6); 1730-1739. [PubMed 5697185]

Marlein Miranda Cona, Yewei Liu, Ting Yin, Yuanbo Feng, Feng Chen, Stefaan Mulier, Yue Li, Jian Zhang, Raymond Oyen, Yicheng Ni. Rat model of cholelithiasis with human gallstones implanted in cholestasis-induced virtual gallbladder. World J Methodol. 2016 June 26; 6(2); 154-162. [PubMed 4921946]

Atheer Zgair, Jonathan CM Wong, Jong Bong Lee, Jatin Mistry, Olena Sivak, Kishor M Wasan, Ivo M Hennig, David A Barrett, Cris S Constantinescu, Peter M Fischer, Pavel Gershkovich. Dietary fats and pharmaceutical lipid excipients increase systemic exposure to orally administered cannabis and cannabis-based medicines. Am J Transl Res. 2016; 8(8); 3448-3459 [PubMed 5009397]

Yara Mouhamed, Andrey Vishnyakov, Bessi Qorri, Manpreet Sambi, SM Signy Frank, Catherine Nowierski, Anmol Lamba, Umrao Bhatti, Myron R Szewczuk. Therapeutic potential of medical marijuana: an educational primer for health care professionals. Drug Healthc Patient Saf. 2018; 10: 45-66. [PubMed 6001746]

Linda A Parker, Erin M Rock, Cheryl L Limebeer. Regulation of nausea and vomiting by cannabinoids. Br J Pharmacol. 2011 Aug; 163(7): 1411-1422. [PubMed 3165951]

Marta Vascellari, Silvia Ravagnan, Antonio Carminato, Stefania Cazzin, Erika Carli, Graziana Da Rold, Laura Lucchese, Alda Natale, Domenico Otranto, Gioia Capelli. Exposure to vector-borne pathogens in candidate blood donor and free-roaming dogs of northeast Italy. Parasit Vectors. 2016; 9: 369. [PubMed 4928314]

Julie D. Lemetayer, Elizabeth C. Snead, Greg S. Starrak, Brent A. Wagner. Multiple liver abscesses in a dog secondary to the liver fluke *Metorchis conjunctus* treated by percutaneous transhepatic drainage and alcoholization. Can Vet J. 2016 June; 57(6): 605-609. [PubMed 4866664]

# Index

Acanthosis nigricans, 184, 253, 266, 271
Accidents, 133–136. *See also* Wounds, healing
Acetaminophen, 68, 135
*Acid Rain and Transported Air Pollutants*, 86
Acne, 157, 176, 184, 186, 248, 253
Aconite, 109
Aconitum napellus, 111
Acral mutilation, 191, 203
Acrodermatitis, 178
Addison's disease, 164, 172, 191, 199, 201, 215, 223, 233, 234, 236, 237, 272
Adrenaline, 79
Affenpinscher, 241
Afghan hound, 144, 167–168
Aggression. *See* Behavioral abnormalities
Air pollution, 84–87, 136
Airedale terrier, 45, 144, 168–169
Akita, 39, 45, 72, 144, 169–170
ALA (alpha lipoic acid), 130, 140
Alaskan malamute, 39, 40, 51, 144, 146, 170–171
Albon, 31
Alfalfa, 139
Allergies, 136–138, 154, 176, 183, 189, 194, 199, 203, 206, 210, 212, 217, 221, 223, 227, 230, 234, 236, 237, 243, 251, 255, 259, 262, 265, 269, 272, 273. *See also* Skin problems
  breeds prone to, 136
  fleas and, 95–96, 101, 138
  immune system and, 83–84, 136
  natural remedies for, 91, 109, 137–138
Alopecia, 208
Alpha lipoic acid (ALA), 130, 140
Alpo, 6
American Cocker spaniel, 39, 40, 44, 114, 119, 125, 144, 145, 210–212
American Eskimo, 212
American foxhound, 171
*American Journal of Clinical Nutrition*, 33–34
Amyloidosis, 217
Anasarca, 210, 223, 241, 243, 257
Anatolian, 155
Anemia, 11, 46, 48

Anemia with chondrodysplasia, 170
Anesthetic sensitivity, 155, 167, 196, 225, 227, 235, 240, 249, 269
Animal–origin chew toys, 22–24
Antibiotics, 31, 40, 45, 67, 135, 142
Antibodies, 72, 74
Antibody (type IgA) deficiency, 168, 189, 208, 215, 217, 220, 221
Antibody (type IgG) deficiency, 208, 215, 221
Antibody (type IgM) deficiency, 184, 208, 215, 221
Antibody titer tests, 73–74, 76, 77
Antifreeze, 23, 87
Antigens, 71
Antioxidants, 6, 33, 38, 49, 50, 90, 130
Anxiety, 111, 112, 281. *See also* Stress
Apis mellifica, 109, 137
Appetite, 51, 59, 63, 68, 283
Armour (thyroid supplement), 145, 146
Arnica montana, 66, 108, 109
Arrhythmias, 117
Arthritis, 11, 64, 110, 138–139, 282
Ascorbic acid. *See* Vitamin C
Aspirin, 68, 135
Ataxia, 157, 173, 250, 273
Atopic dermatitis, 217
Australian cattle dog (Blue Heeler), 44, 129, 144, 145, 212–213
Australian kelpie, 213
Australian shepherd, 144, 213–214
Australian terrier, 241
Autoimmune disorders, 79, 283

*Baby Gold Bond* powder, 137
Bach flower remedy, 112
Bacterial infections, 49, 90, 109, 117, 137
Bactrovet, 31
Baldness/bald spots, 37, 83, 146, 253, 266, 273
Barking. *See* Behavioral abnormalities
Baryta carbonica, 111
Basenji, 39, 114, 214–215
Basset hound, 9, 39, 44, 45, 131, 145, 215–217
Bassingthwaighte, Edward, 283

Bath time, tips for, 100
B-cells, 72
Beagle, 39, 40, 44, 114, 119, 125, 136, 145, 154, 217–219
Bearded collie, 119, 144, 172
Bedlington terrier, 48, 56, 129, 241–242
Beef. *See* Meat
Beef fat, 8
Beet pulp, 8–9
Begging, 64–65
Behavioral abnormalities, 181, 184, 189, 199, 210, 215, 224, 226, 230, 235, 237, 269. *See also* Stress
    natural remedies for, 31, 111–112, 281
    older dogs and, 62–63
Belfield, Wendell, 33, 34, 121
Belgian malinois, 44, 144, 145, 219
Belgian sheepdog, 44, 144, 145, 172–173
Belgian tervuren, 44, 145, 173
Bernese mountain dog, 9, 129, 131, 144, 173–174
Beta-carotene, 33, 90, 127
*Betadine*, 137
BHA (butylated hydroxyanisole), 6
BHT (butylated hydroxytoluene), 6
Bichon Frise, 44, 45, 136, 145, 148–149, 242
Biotin, 29, 32, 91, 103
Black and tan coonhound, 174
Black-walnut hulls, 96, 97, 103–104
Blindness, 252
Blood-clotting disorders, 40, 155, 159, 165, 167, 168, 170, 174, 176, 179, 184, 187, 189, 194, 196, 199, 201, 202, 205, 206, 207, 209, 210, 212, 214, 215, 217, 220, 222, 224, 226, 227, 229, 230, 237, 239, 242, 245, 246, 250, 255, 262, 263, 269
Bloodhound, 9, 78, 131, 144, 174–175
Blue eyes, 183
Blue Heeler. *See* Australian cattle dog
Bluetick coonhound, 175
Boenninghausen, Baron von, 105
Boils, 178, 183
Bones
    broken, healing, 110
    disease, 157, 165, 215, 227, 230, 238, 241, 269
    nutrition and, 33, 38, 42–43, 44, 48
    pain, remedies for, 68
    puppies and, 57
Bones, in diet, 10, 24, 62, 147
Borax, 101–102
Border collie, 13, 44, 79, 144, 145, 219
Border terrier, 118, 125, 242–243
Boron, 47
Borzoi (Russian wolfhound), 9, 131, 144, 155–156
Boston terrier, 58, 125, 136, 243–244
Bouvier des Flandres, 58, 131, 144, 175–176

Bowel movements. *See* Constipation; Diarrhea
Boxer, 9, 31, 40, 44, 117, 119, 125, 129, 131, 136, 176–178
Breeding dogs. *See* Pregnant and nursing dogs
Breed-specific health problems, 153–275
Brewer's yeast, 31–32, 102
Briard, 9, 131, 144, 178
*British Journal of Biomedical Sciences*, 33
Brittany spaniel, 114, 220
Broderick, R. Geoffrey, 34
Bruises, 66, 108, 109
Brussels Griffon, 245
Bryonia, 109
Bull terrier, 51, 125, 146, 178–179
Bull terrier, Miniature, 230
Bullmastiff, 9, 131, 144, 156–157
Bullous pemphigoid, 180
Bupleurum, 130–131
Butylated hydroxyanisole (BHA), 6
Butylated hydroxytoluene (BHT), 6
By-products, 7

Cairn terrier, 37, 129, 245–246
Calcinosis, 155, 157, 189, 203
Calcium, 42–43
Calendula officinalis, 109, 135, 137
Canaan dog, 220
Cancer, 124–128, 157, 165, 176, 178–179, 180, 183, 184, 186, 189, 191, 194, 196, 198, 199, 205, 207, 209, 210, 217, 224, 230, 238, 239, 242, 243, 248, 253, 260, 262, 270, 273
    bone, 78
    breeds susceptible to, 125
    common locations and types, 124–125
    dog food ingredients and, 6
    prevention and treatment, 31, 33, 50, 78, 89, 91, 94, 124, 126–128, 282
    symptoms, 125
Canine Eye Registration Foundation (CERF) certification, 140
Cannabidiol. *See* CBD
Cappel-King, Beverly, x, 10, 21–22, 23, 34, 78, 88, 115–116, 119, 124, 129, 136, 142, 145, 146
    herbal cream, 133–134
Carbohydrates, 11, 47, 49, 61, 126. *See also* Grains
Cardigan Welsh corgi, 58, 220–221
Cardiomyopathy, 117–118
Cardiovascular disease. *See* Heart disease
Carpal laxity, 221
Carpet
    getting rid of fleas in, 101–102
    toxins and, 84–85
Carson, Rachel, 80–81
Castration-responsive dermatosis, 206
Cataracts, 155, 157, 159–167, 169, 170, 172, 173, 175, 176, 178–181, 183, 184, 186–189, 192–194, 196–199, 201, 203–207, 210, 212,

213, 217, 220, 222, 224–227, 229, 230, 232–243, 245, 246, 249, 250, 251, 253, 255, 257, 258, 259, 261–266, 268–274
    prevention and treatment, 33–34, 140–141
    types, 33–34
Cavalier King Charles spaniel, 119, 246
CBD (cannabidiol), 277–284
    beginning treatment with, 280–281
    benefits, 281–284
    pros and cons, 280
    safety, 278
    selecting products, tips for, 278–279
    therapeutic uses, 279–280
Cerebellar abiotrophy, 180, 196, 204
Cerebellar degeneration/malformation, 173
Cerebellar hypoplasia, 157, 168, 181, 245
Cervical spondylosis, 157, 233, 260
Chamomilla, 111
Chemicals
    allergies and, 137
    in dog food, 5–6
    in flea-control products, 98–99
    in rawhide, 23, 87
    in water, 15, 17–20
Chemotherapy, 124, 126
Chesapeake Bay retriever, 40, 144, 179
Chew toys, 22–24, 87. *See also* Bones, in diet
Chewing, 22
    puppies and, 56, 87, 111
Chihuahua, 6, 129, 246–247
Chinese crested, 248
Chinese Shar-pei, 9, 72, 132, 136, 144, 221–222
Chlorine, in water, 18–20
Choline, 29
Chow chow, 9, 74, 114, 132, 144, 181–182
Chromium, 47
Ciliary dyskinesia, 184, 242
Cleft palate and/or lip, 156, 173, 175, 181, 186, 189, 210, 213, 217–218, 220, 224, 226, 237, 241, 243, 246, 249, 253, 260, 264, 267
*Clinical Toxicology of Commercial Products*, 17
Clumber spaniel, 144, 182
Coat (fur), 45, 48, 51, 154
    monthly health checks of, 3–4
Cobalamin. *See* Vitamin B$_{12}$
Cobalt, 47
Cocculus, 112
Cockapoo, 153
Cocker spaniel, 37, 111, 112, 117, 153
Coenyzme Q$_{10}$ (CoQ$_{10}$), 119, 123
Coliform enteritis, 214
Collagen, 34, 36, 51
Collapsed trachea, 247, 259, 260, 265
Collie, 44, 125, 144, 145, 179–181
Collie eye anomaly, 180, 213, 242
Colostrum, 54, 72
Congestive heart disease, 117
Conjunctivitis, 239

Constipation, 109, 141
Coonhound, 144
Copper, 46, 48, 92, 129
    metabolism abnormality, 48, 129, 184, 241, 272
CoQ$_{10}$ (coenyzme Q$_{10}$), 119, 123
Corneal dystrophy, 162, 167–170, 172, 180, 189, 192, 194, 197, 203, 205, 206, 209, 210, 218, 219, 224, 228, 233, 235, 242, 243, 246, 247, 249, 251, 253, 255, 257, 260, 263, 267
Corneal ulcer, 170, 176, 243, 248, 260
*Cornell Veterinarian*, 39
Cortisone, 31
Cottage cheese, 12, 56, 59, 142
Craniomandibular osteopathy, 185, 188, 199, 207, 242, 243, 245, 262, 272
Cryptorchidism, 215, 223, 227, 234, 243, 250, 251, 252, 255, 259, 265, 273
Curley-coated retriever, 183
Cushing's disease (hyperadrenocorticism), 169, 176, 198, 230, 243, 253, 267, 270, 272
Cutaneous vasculopathy, 189
Cuts. *See* Wounds, healing
Cyclic hematopoisis, 180, 211, 259
Cystitis, 255, 260

Dachshund, 145, 248
Dachshund, Miniature, 39, 115, 253–254
Dachshund, Standard, 115, 266–268
Dairy products. *See* Cottage cheese; Milk; Yogurt
Dalmatian, 45, 56, 125, 136, 144, 183–184
Dandelion, 131
Dandie Dinmont terrier, 144, 248
Day, Stephen, 111, 112
Deafness, 157, 159, 171, 179, 180, 183, 187, 188, 199, 212, 213, 230, 232, 243, 252, 253, 262, 266, 267, 270, 273
Degenerative myelopathy, 31, 157, 167, 189, 283
Demodectic mange, 157, 159, 177, 180, 181, 183, 185, 201, 203, 208, 218, 221, 244, 253, 260, 267, 273, 274
Dental health, 3, 31, 42–43, 44, 62, 117, 147
Depression, 111, 281
Dermatitis, 45, 221, 244, 255, 258, 260
Dermatomyositis, 263
Dermoid cyst, 157, 162, 163, 165, 177, 189, 204, 264, 267
Desiccated thyroid. *See* Armour
Detoxification, 4
DHLPP vaccination, 76, 79–80
Diabetes mellitus, 47, 64, 164, 171, 198, 199, 205, 226, 241, 246, 249, 253, 261, 265, 267
Diarrhea, 4, 8, 19, 109, 110, 141–142
Diatomaceous earth, 101–102
Diet, ix–x, 3–24. *See also* Dog food; Meat; Treats; *Specific ailment; disease*
    changing gradually, 4

home-cooked meals, 4, 10–13, 56
older dogs, 12, 61–62, 63
overweight dogs, 12, 57, 63–65
pregnant and nursing dogs, 59–60
protein, 89
puppies, 54, 56–57
raw foods, 13–14, 32
Digest (ingredient in dog food), 7–8
Digestive enzyme supplements, 61–62, 143
Digestive enzymes, 13–14, 142
Digestive problems, 31, 109, 110, 142–143, 283.
See also Constipation; Diarrhea; Vomiting
Dimethylglycine (DMG), 119
Dirt, 49
Discoid lupus erythematosus, 263
Diseases, natural prevention and treatment of,
113–132
Distemper, 74, 76, 77
DMG (dimethylglycine), 119
Doberman pinscher, 9, 39, 40, 44, 48, 51, 78,
114, 115, 117–118, 119, 125, 129, 132, 144,
146, 184–186
Dog food, 63–64, 113. See also Diet
canned, 5, 7
choosing, 5–7
commercial, 3, 5–10
dry, 5–10, 12
freshness (expiration date), 6–7
home-cooked meals, 4, 10–13, 56
label reading, 7–10
raw foods, 13–14, 32
semi-moist, 5, 47
Dog sizes, 26
Dog treats. See Treats
Dog-food industry, ix, 3, 5, 8, 13, 96
Dogs
breed-specific health problems, 153–275
common ailments, remedies for, 133–149
crossbred, 153–154
disease prevention and treatment, 113–132
giant, 26, 155–167
homeopathy and, 105–112
immune system and, 71–94
large, 26, 167–210
medium, 26, 210–240
mixed-breed, 153
purebred, 153
recovering from illness or surgery, 65–68
small, 26, 241–275
Dr. Bev's Delectable Dog Cookies, 21
Drooling. See Nausea
Dunker. See Norwegian Dunker hound
Dystocia, 186, 197, 221, 233, 244, 260

Ear infections, 218
Ears, clean, 3
Eclampsia, 188, 207
Eczema, 45

Eggs, 9, 12, 32, 56, 59, 89
Ehler's-Danlos syndrome, 165, 177, 183, 189,
197, 211, 218, 224, 233, 254, 267, 268
Elbow dislocation, 248
Elbow dysplasia, 163, 164, 166, 167, 181, 190,
194, 199, 211, 224, 228, 229, 248, 251
Emotional and behavioral problems, 111–112.
See also Stress
Encephalitis, 260
English bulldog, 31, 40, 58, 118–119, 125, 144,
186–187
English cocker spaniel, 40, 222–223
English foxhound, 187
English setter, 9, 132, 144, 145, 187–188
English Springer spaniel, 39, 44, 125, 144, 145,
223–225
English toy spaniel, 249
Environmental Protection Agency. See U.S.
Environmental Protection Agency
Environmental threats, 25, 49, 80–87. See also
Allergies
air pollution, 84–87, 136
eye irritants, 140–141
flea-control products, 98–99
immune system and, 80–87
nutrition for protection against, 87–94
pesticides, 81–83, 116
poisons, 87
water, contaminants in, 15–20
Enzymes. See Digestive enzymes
Eosinophilic panosteitis, 161, 164, 166, 178,
185, 190, 193, 203, 209, 216
Epidermal dysplasia, 272
Epidermoid cyst, 211, 224
Epilepsy, 165, 172, 173, 180, 190, 194, 197, 198,
199, 203, 208, 211, 212, 216, 218, 219, 224,
226, 228, 231, 233, 234, 238, 242, 248, 250,
256, 257, 260, 268, 270. See also Seizures
Epiphora, 238, 252
Epiphyseal dysplasia, 181, 218, 231, 236, 270
Esophageal disorder, 190, 197, 244, 255, 266,
274
Essiac, 67, 115, 124
Ethoxyquin, 6
Exercise, 62, 64, 65, 86, 119, 141, 144
Eye abnormalities, 155–165, 167–169, 171–175,
177, 179–183, 185, 186, 188, 190, 192–194,
196–199, 201, 203–209, 211–214, 216,
218–221, 223, 224, 226–252, 255, 257–264,
266–274
Eyes, 3

Fainting, 118, 177, 185, 255, 260
Fats, 6, 8, 9, 126
Fat-soluble vitamins, 26, 36–40
Fear, 79, 111, 112. See also Stress
Fever, 109, 110
Fiber, 9, 141

Field spaniel, 225–226
Finnish spitz, 226
Flat-coated retriever, 144, 188–189
Fleas, 95–104
    allergies and, 95–96, 101, 138
    collars, shampoos, sprays, powders, and
        pills, 98–100
    herbal products for, 99–100, 101
    life cycle of, 97–98
    natural control methods for, 100–104
Flouride, 17–18, 48
Folic acid (folate), 29, 32, 33, 91, 103, 120–121
Folliculitis, 183, 185, 201, 221, 228, 254, 262,
    263, 267
Food. *See* Diet
Food allergies, 137
*Food Enzymes, The Missing Link to Radiant
    Health*, 13–14
Free radicals, 6, 90, 92
French bulldog, 226
Fright-or-flight response, 79
Fruits, 12, 13–14, 90, 127, 140

Garlic, 89, 95, 97, 103, 123
Gas. *See* Digestive problems
Gastric bloat and torsion, 155, 156, 158, 162,
    165, 166, 173–175, 177, 178, 181, 185, 188,
    190, 196, 197, 200, 209, 216, 222, 228, 238
    breeds susceptible to, 131–132
    diet and, 9, 131, 132
    symptoms, 132
GDV. *See* Gastric bloat and torsion
Gelsemium, 112
Generalized myopathy, 228
Genetics, x
German shepherd, 9, 14, 31, 40, 44, 45, 51, 115,
    118, 119, 125, 132, 136, 144, 145, 146, 153,
    189–191
German shorthaired pointer, 51, 146, 191–192
German short-haired retriever, 119, 125, 144
German wirehaired pointer, 144, 192–193
Giant schnauzer, 39, 144, 193–194
Ginger tea, 59
Glaucoma, 156, 158, 167, 169, 171, 176,
    181, 183, 193, 198, 205, 206, 211, 216, 218,
    221–224, 231, 232, 234, 238, 240, 244, 245,
    247, 248, 250, 252, 263, 266, 267, 268, 270,
    271, 274
Globoid cell leukodystrophy, 175, 183, 216, 218,
    231, 245, 259, 270, 272
Glucosamine, 139
Glutathione (GSH), 130
Glycogen storage disease, 169, 190, 251, 259
Goji berry, 148–149
Golden retriever, 20, 23, 37, 39, 40, 45, 78, 100,
    118, 119, 124, 125, 129, 136, 144, 145, 153,
    154, 194–195
Goldendoodle, 154

Gordon setter, 9, 132, 196
Grains, 56, 59, 89, 142
    in commercial dog food, 8
    in home-cooked meals, 10, 11, 12
Grapeseed extract, 124
Grasses and plants, 49
Great Dane, 44, 45, 51, 118, 119, 125, 132, 144,
    146, 157–159
Great Pyrenees, 45, 144, 159–160
Greater Swiss Mountain Dog, 160
Greyhound, 9, 44, 58, 125, 132, 145, 196–197
Grief, 111
Growth-hormone-responsive dermatosis, 168,
    182, 209, 259, 270
GSH (glutathione), 130
Guinness Book of Records, 13
Gums, 3, 31, 46
    disease, 117, 147

Hahnemann, Samuel, 105–106
Hair follicle tumors, 229
Hair loss. *See* Baldness/bald spots; Skin
    problems
Harrier, 226
Havanese, 249
Health, overall, 148–149
Health checks, monthly, 3–4
Health problems, breed-specific, 153–275
Heart disease, 64, 158, 160, 163, 164, 165, 177,
    185, 186, 190, 194, 198, 205, 211, 218, 231,
    239, 240, 243, 246, 247, 256, 266, 270, 274
    breeds susceptible to, 117–119
    prevention and treatment, 33, 39, 44, 46–47,
        50, 92, 119, 120–123, 283–284
    types, 116–120
Heart murmur, 117
Heartworm, 103–104
Heavy metals. *See* Metals, heavy
Heinz, 6
Hemeralopia, 158, 171, 231, 238, 270
Hepar sulphuris, 109, 137
Hepatic lipidosis, 256, 263
Hepatitis, 76, 128
Hepatocerebellar degeneration, 174
Herbal cream, 133–134
Herbal flea-control products, 99–100, 101
Hereditary glomerulopathy, 220
Hereditary kidney hypoplasia, 171, 190, 198,
    211, 224, 232, 242, 251, 264
Hernia, 179, 180, 211, 212, 214, 216, 224, 244,
    245, 252, 255, 258, 272
High blood pressure, 31, 64
Hip dysplasia, 143–144, 155, 156, 158–169, 171,
    172, 174, 175, 176, 178, 179, 180, 182, 183,
    185, 187–190, 192, 193, 195–197, 200–205,
    207–212, 214, 219, 220, 222, 224, 226–228,
    232, 234, 238, 240, 248, 252, 260, 263, 264
    breeds prone to, 144

prevention and treatment, 34, 144
    puppies and, 57
Histamines, 83, 91
Histiocytoma, 158, 177, 180, 243
*Homeopathic Treatment of Small Animals,*
    *Principals and Practice*, 111
Homeopaths, working with, 107–108
Homeopathy, 66, 68, 105–112, 135
    origin and development, 105–107
    remedies, use and dosage of, 108
    remedies for common ailments, 108–112
Homocysteine, 120
Honey, 59
Hot spots, 45, 109, 137, 159, 168, 169, 200, 216
*How to Have a Healthier Dog*, 33, 121
Hungarian puli, 144, 226–227
Hydrocephalus, 187, 211, 224, 244, 247, 265,
    274
Hygroma, 156, 158, 160, 197
Hyperactivity. *See* Behavioral abnormalities
Hypericum perforatum, 68, 109
Hyperkeratosis, 229
Hypertrophic osteodystrophy, 57, 158, 160, 161,
    163, 166, 167, 193, 200, 209
Hypoallergenic dogs, 154
Hypoglycemia, 188, 200, 247, 252
Hypoplasia of larynx, 236
Hypothyroidism, 155, 156, 159–163, 165,
    166, 168, 169, 171–176, 178, 180, 183, 187,
    188, 189, 192, 196, 197, 198, 200, 202, 203,
    204, 205, 207, 208, 209, 211–214, 216, 219,
    222–224, 226–239, 244–248, 251, 252, 254,
    256–264, 266–271, 273–275
    natural remedies for, 145, 146
    seizures and, 145
    symptoms, 146
Hypotrichosis, 198

Ibizan hound, 227
Ibuprofen, 68, 135
Ignatia, 111, 112
Illness, dogs recovering from, 65–68
Immune system, 71–94, 96. *See also*
    Vaccinations
    allergies and, 83–84, 136
    cancer and, 125, 126, 127–128
    environmental threats, 80–87
    factors affecting, 73
    nutrition for, 31, 33, 38–39, 48, 50–51,
        87–94
    puppies and, 53–54, 75–77
    stress and, 67, 75, 77–80, 91
    surgery and, 66–67
Immune-mediated hemolytic anemia (IMHA),
    39, 163, 164, 170, 171, 185, 193, 195, 201, 211,
    215, 216, 218, 225, 228, 231, 235, 238, 254,
    256, 258, 262, 264, 270, 272
Incontinence, 177, 185, 190, 201

Infections, 61, 89, 91, 109. *See also* Bacterial
    infections
Inflammation, 57, 109, 139, 282, 283
Inflammatory bowel disease (IBD), 283
Injuries. *See* Wounds, healing
Interferon, 91
*International Journal of Immunopharmacology,*
    94
Intervertebral disc disease, 211, 218, 221, 225,
    231, 248, 254, 258, 260, 267, 270
Intussusception, 216, 244
Iodine, 48–49
Iris atrophy, 231, 238, 247, 270
Irish setter, 9, 39, 44, 45, 119, 132, 136, 144, 145,
    227–229
Irish terrier, 229
Irish water spaniel, 197–198
Irish wolfhound, 44, 118, 119, 129, 144,
    160–161
Iron, 46–47, 92–93
Irritability, 110, 111
Italian greyhound, 44, 119, 145, 249–250
Itching. *See* Allergies; Skin problems

Jack Russell terrier, 250
Japanese spaniel (Japanese Chin), 250–251
Jaw abnormality, 182, 208, 209, 211, 213, 222,
    225, 251
*Journal of Federation Proceedings*, 50
*Journal of the American Holistic Veterinary*
    *Medical Association*, 280
*Journal of the American Podiatric Medical*
    *Association*, 34
*Journal of the National Cancer Institute*, 82

Kaopectate, 148
Kava, 68, 80, 135
Keeshond, 44, 119, 125, 129, 145, 198–199
Kennel cough, 76
Keratitis, 180, 190, 248, 258, 260, 264
Keratoacanthoma, 190, 199, 232
Kerry blue terrier, 229–230
Kidney disease, 114, 115–116, 185, 218, 264
Kidney failure, 114–116
    breeds prone to, 114–115
    prevention and treatment, 115–116
    symptoms, 116
King of Dog Cookies, The, 21–22
Komondor, 144, 161
Kuvasz, 144, 161–162

Labradoodle, 154
Labrador retriever, 9, 37, 44, 45, 51, 125, 129,
    132, 136, 145, 146, 153, 199–201
Lakeland terrier, 251
Lambert, N.H., 127
Lameness, 110
L-carnitine, 119

Lead, in water, 16–17
Leaky valve, 117
Ledum palustre, 110
Legg-Perthes disease, 241, 255, 256, 260, 261, 265, 266, 268, 272, 274, 275
Lemmon, Michael W., 98
Leptospirosis, 20, 76
Leukotrienes, 139
Lhaso apso, 45, 115, 136, 251–252
Lick granuloma (acral lick dermatitis), 158, 169, 185, 200, 228
Lipidosis, 188, 192, 218, 234, 265
Lipoic acid. *See* Alpha lipoic acid
Liver abnormalities, 160, 165, 174, 177, 195, 199, 200, 205, 213, 245, 247, 252, 256, 259, 261, 265, 270, 275
Liver disease, 128–131
    breeds prone to, 129
    copper metabolism abnormality and, 48, 129, 184, 241, 272
    prevention and treatment, 129, 130–131
    symptoms and causes, 128–129
Long, Jack, 34
Lung disease, 64
Lung torsion, 216
Lycium Goji berry, 148–149
Lyme disease, 103–104
Lymphedema, 190, 192, 228

Macrominerals, 42–46
Magnesium, 16, 44, 80, 122, 145
Malabsorption, 14, 164, 170, 182, 190, 201, 215, 222, 236
    causes, 42
    copper metabolism abnormality, 48, 129, 184, 241, 272
    zinc, 42, 51, 146, 178
Maltese, 129, 144, 252–253
Maltipoo, 154
Manchester terrier, 40
Manganese, 49–50, 93
Marrow bones, 62, 147
Mastiff, 132, 162
*Materia Medica*, 105–106
Meals, home-cooked, 4, 10–13, 56
Meat, 89
    in commercial dog food, 5–8
    ground, 10
    in home-cooked meals, 10–11
    human grade and/or USDA inspected, 5–6
    muscle, 10
    older dogs and, 61, 63
    organ, 10, 11
    organic, 5, 11
    pregnant and nursing dogs, 59
    puppies, 56
    raw, 11, 13–14, 56, 147
Meat and bone meal, 6

Meat meal, 6, 7–8
Melatonin, 63
Metals, heavy, 16–17, 50
Methionine, 120
Methylsulfonylmethane (MSM), 45, 138
Mexican hairless, 253
Microminerals (trace minerals), 42, 46–51, 92–94
Milk, 13, 43
Milk thistle, 67, 129, 130
Miller, William H., 51
Minerals, 41–51
    macro-, 42–46
    trace, 42, 46–51, 92–94
Miniature bull terrier, 230
Miniature dachshund, 39, 115, 253–254
Miniature English sheepdog, 39
Miniature pinscher, 255
Miniature Poodle, 119, 125, 230–232
Miniature schnauzer, 40, 115, 119, 129, 136, 255–256
Molybdenum, 49
Mosquitoes, 102, 103–104
Motion sickness, 111, 112
MSM (methylsulfonylmethane), 45, 138
Muscle-fiber deficiency, 200
Muscular dystrophy, 158, 172, 182, 195, 200, 205, 229, 237
Myasthenia gravis, 190, 195, 209, 231, 236, 250

Narcolepsy, 168, 169, 171, 185, 200, 210, 225, 228, 254
National Cancer Institute, 19, 126
Natural killer (NK) cells, 72, 90
Natural prevention and treatment of common diseases, 113–132
Natural remedies for common ailments, 133–149
Natural Resources Defense Council, 19, 81
Nausea, 59, 66, 143, 283
Neapolitan mastiff, 144, 162–163
Neck vertebrae malformation, 156, 158, 185, 204
Nerve damage, 68, 109
Nervousness. *See* Stress
Neurological disorders, 31, 204, 283
Neuron malfunction, 230
Neuronal ceroid-lipofuscinosis, 188, 192, 213, 219, 223, 235, 240, 247, 254, 267
Newfoundland, 39, 44, 119, 144, 163–164
Niacin. *See* Vitamin B$_3$
Nightshade vegetables, 139
Norfolk terrier, 145, 256–257
Norwegian Dunker hound, 232
Norwegian elkhound, 115, 144, 232–233
Norwich terrier, 145, 257
Nova Scotia duck tolling retriever, 233
Nursing dogs. *See* Pregnant and nursing dogs

Nutrition. *See* Diet
Nutritional supplements. *See Individual supplements, minerals, and vitamins*
Nuts, 12
Nux vomica, 110, 143

Obesity. *See* Overweight dogs
Old English sheepdog, 39, 144, 201–202
Older dogs, 12, 60–63, 88–89, 110, 125
Omega-3 fatty acids, 139
Onions, 11
Osteoarthritis, 138–139
Osteochondritis dissecans, 157–163, 166, 167, 168, 170, 171, 173–177, 179, 180, 182, 184, 185, 188, 191–197, 200, 201, 202, 204, 205, 207, 208, 211, 213, 214, 216, 219, 220, 222, 223, 225, 228, 231, 237, 238, 239, 247, 256, 266, 271, 273
Osteochondrosis, 57, 157–163, 166, 168, 170, 171, 173–177, 179, 181, 182, 184, 185, 188, 191–197, 200, 202, 204, 205, 207, 208, 211, 214, 216, 219, 220, 222, 223, 225, 228, 231, 237, 238, 239, 247, 256, 266, 271, 273
Osteochondrosis (spinal), 171, 187
Osteopetrosis, 254, 268
Otitis externa, 210, 212, 222, 225, 231, 271
Otterhound, 144, 202
Overshot jaw, 212, 213, 225, 254, 268
Overweight dogs, 12, 57, 63–65
    older dogs, 60–61, 62
Oxidation, 6

Pain, 62, 67–68, 109, 110, 111, 135, 282
Paints, toxins in, 85, 86
Pancreatic insufficiency, 191
Pannus, 169, 172, 173, 182, 184, 191, 192, 197, 204, 207, 231, 238, 254, 255, 258, 261, 268, 271
Papillon, 257
Parainfluenza, 76
Parasites, 89, 96, 103–104, 123. *See also* Fleas
Parvo virus, 34, 74, 76, 77
Patellar luxation, 212, 216, 222, 225, 231, 234, 241, 242, 243, 244, 246, 247, 248, 249, 252, 253, 256, 257, 259, 261, 264, 265, 271, 275
Pauling, Linus, 126
Pekingese, 31, 39, 258
Pembroke Welsh corgi, 40, 58, 145, 233–234
Pemphigus foliaceous, 168, 170, 182, 204, 254, 261, 268
Pepto Bismol, 148
Pericardial disease, 118
Peroxide, 137
Pesticides, 6
    environmental, 81–83, 116
    in flea-control products, 98–99
*Pet Allergies, Remedies for an Epidemic*, 31
Petit Basset Griffon Vendeen, 234

Phagocyte cells, 90
Pharaoh hound, 203
Phosphofructokinase deficiency, 225
Phosphorus, 43
Pigmentation abnormalities, 48, 51, 164, 166, 186, 195, 202, 206, 207, 208, 214, 228, 254, 263, 268
Pillcuring, 143
Pitric acid, 112
Platelet disorders/dysfunction, 160, 216
Platina metallicum, 112
Plechner, Alfred J., 31
Pointer, 44, 144, 145, 203–204
Poisons, 87
Pollutants. *See* Environmental threats
Pomeranian, 31, 129, 259
Poodle, 34, 39, 44, 45, 136, 145, 153, 154
Poodle, Miniature, 119, 125, 230–232
Poodle, Standard, 9, 115, 132, 144, 237–239
Poodle, Toy, 119, 125, 129, 269–271
Portuguese water dog, 234–235
Post-nasal drip, 83
Potassium, 34, 45–46
Poultry. *See* Meat
Poultry bones, 10
Poultry fat, 8
Poultry meal, 7
Pregnant and nursing dogs, 31, 34, 36–37, 57–60
Preservatives, natural, 6
Primor, 31
Probiotics, 40, 45, 67, 135–136, 142
Progressive retinal atrophy (PRA), 37, 156–159, 162, 163, 164, 168–174, 177, 178, 179, 181–184, 186, 188, 189, 191, 192, 193, 195–200, 202, 204–209, 212–215, 217–223, 225–230, 232, 233, 235, 237, 239–247, 249–252, 254, 255, 258, 259, 261–265, 268, 269, 271, 273, 274, 275
Prolapsed rectum, 200
Prolapsed uterus, 200
Propylene glycol, 23, 87
Prostaglandins, 139
Protein, 9, 56, 89
Psyllium seed husk, 141
Pug, 31, 44, 45, 58, 125, 129, 136, 144, 145, 154, 259–261
Puggle, 154
Puppies, 53–57
    chewing and, 56, 87, 111
    feeding, 54, 56–57
    immune system and, 53–54, 75–77
    stress and, 54, 55–56
    vaccinations for, 75–77
    vitamins and, 34, 35–36, 54–56
Pycnogenal, 124
Pyloric stenosis, 187
Pyometra, 244

Pyridoxine. *See* Vitamin B$_6$
Pyrogenium, 110
Pyruvate kinase deficiency, 215

Quercetin, 137–138

Rabies, 74, 76
Radiation, 31, 124, 126
Ralston Purina, 6
Rancid fats and oils, 6
Raw foods, 11, 20, 56
    adding to diet, 13–14, 32
    for dental health, 147
    diarrhea treatment, 142
Rawhide, 22–23, 87
Recipes, for dog treats, 21–22
Red raspberry leaf, 58
Renal dysplasia, 115–116, 236, 256, 268
Renal hypoplasia, 254
Renal tubular dysfunction, 215
Reproductive disorders, 176
Rescue Remedy, 112, 134
Resources, 285–288
Rhodesian ridgeback, 144, 204–205
Rhus toxicodendron, 108, 110
Riboflavin. *See* Vitamin B$_2$
Rottweiler, 39, 119, 144, 164–165
Russian wolfhound, 9, 132, 144, 155–156
Ruta graveolens, 108, 110

Safe Drinking Water Act 1974, 16
Saint Bernard, 9, 44, 118, 119, 125, 129, 132,
    144, 145, 165–166
Salt, 45–46, 48–49, 101
Saluki, 39, 235
Samoyed, 115, 125, 129, 144, 205–206
Samoyed hereditary glomerulopathy, 206
Santillo, Humbart, 13–14
Schipperke, 261
Schnauzer, Giant, 39, 144, 193–194
Schnauzer, Miniature, 40, 115, 119, 129, 136,
    255–256
Schnauzer, Standard, 119, 125, 145, 239
Schnauzer comedo syndrome, 256
Schnoodle, 154
Schultz, Ronald, 73
Scott, Dana, 283–284
Scottish deerhound, 9, 132, 166
Scottish terrier, 40, 45, 72, 125, 262
Scotty cramp, 262
Scratching. *See* Allergies; Skin problems
Sealyham terrier, 45, 136, 262–263
Sebaceous cyst, 199, 202, 206, 217, 218
Sebaceous gland tumor, 232, 244, 254, 268, 271
Seborrhea, 194, 201, 222, 225, 232, 272, 275
Seizures, 145, 282. *See also* Epilepsy
Selenium, 50, 93, 127–128, 139, 145, 146
Separation anxiety, 31, 112, 281

Sex, obsession with, 112
Shark cartilage, 124
Shed-free dogs, 154
Shetland sheepdog, 129, 144, 263–264
Shiba inu, 264
Shih tzu, 39, 115, 129, 264–265
Shihpoo, 154
Shock, 134
Shoulder abnormalities, 245, 248
Shoulder dislocation, 247, 255, 259, 266, 274
Shoulder dysplasia, 201
Shyness, 62–63, 111
Siberian husky, 51, 144, 146, 206–207
*Silent Spring*, 80–81
Silica uroliths, 191
Silicon, 49
Silky terrier, 265
Silymarin (milk thistle), 67, 129, 130
Skeletal problems, 57
Skin problems, 146–147. *See also* Allergies; Hot
    spots; Wounds, healing
    breeds prone to, 37, 146
    causes, 146–147
    disease, 161, 181, 187, 191, 195, 199, 207,
        212, 223, 229, 232
    natural remedies for, 37, 45, 49, 51, 138, 147
    skin allergies, 138, 242, 257, 263, 266, 271,
        272
    tumors, 212, 225
Skye terrier, 235–236
Sleep problems, 63
Smooth fox terrier, 45, 119, 136, 265–266
Sodium, 45–46
Sodium-polyborate powder, 102
Soft-coated wheaten terrier, 45, 115, 136,
    236–237
Soy, 56–57
Spina bifida, 187, 214
Spinal abnormality, 208, 209
Spinone italiano, 207
Splenic torsion, 217
Spondylosis, 177, 261
Sprains, 108, 110
Springer spaniel, 115–116
St. John's wort, 133–134. *See also* Hypericum
    perforatum
Staffordshire bull terrier, 237
Standard Dachshund, 115, 266–268
Standard Manchester terrier, 44, 145, 268–269
Standard Poodle, 9, 115, 132, 144, 237–239
Standard schnauzer, 119, 125, 145, 239
Stenotic nares, 222, 244, 261
Sterile pyogranuloma syndrome, 208, 209, 254,
    268
Steroids, 101, 137
Stomach hemorrhage, 256
Stool hardeners, in dog food, 8–9
Strains, 108, 110

Stress, 60, 77–80
    gastric bloat and torsion and, 131
    immune system and, 67, 75, 77–80, 91
    natural remedies for, 31, 39, 78, 80, 89, 91,
        111–112, 135, 281
    puppies and, 54, 55–56
    vaccinations and, 75
Subaortic stenosis, 192
Subcutaneous cyst, 193, 233
Sugar, 5, 8, 12, 47, 126
Sulfa drugs, 31
Sulfur, 45
Supplements. See Individual supplements,
    minerals, and vitamins
Surgery, 39, 64, 65–68, 89, 109, 110
Sussex spaniel, 44, 119, 239–240
Swallowing. See Nausea
Swimmer puppies, 159, 223, 244, 258
Symphytum, 68, 110
Systemic lupus erythematosus, 191, 263

Tapeworms, 96
Taurine, 119
T-cell deficiency, 210, 217, 221, 254
T-cells, 72, 90, 92
Tea tree oil, 137
Teeth, 3, 117
    breeds prone to abnormalities, 156, 157,
        160, 175, 177, 182, 186, 187, 198, 201, 213,
        241, 248, 261, 266, 274
    breeds prone to disease, 31
    prevention and treatment of disease, 31,
        42–43, 44, 62, 147
Thiamine. See Vitamin B₁
Thrombocytopathy, 171, 192, 202, 217
Thrombocytopenia, 160, 163, 164, 194, 202,
    203, 206, 227, 229, 230, 235, 239, 246, 250,
    256, 258, 265
Thrombosis, 186
Thuja occidentalis, 110–111
Thymus gland, 72, 79
Thyro Complex, 146
Thyroid disease, 156, 158–159, 163–164, 165,
    167, 170, 177, 182, 186, 191, 194, 195, 202,
    219, 220, 234, 236, 252–253, 264, 274. See also
    Hypothyroidism
    prevention and treatment, 48–49, 50, 145
Tibetan mastiff, 144, 166–167
Tibetan spaniel, 269
Tibetan terrier, 240
Ticks, 102, 103–104
Tight-lip syndrome, 222
Tocopherol. See Vitamin E
Torsion. See Gastric bloat and torsion
Toxins. See Environmental threats
Toy breeds, 6, 16, 31, 79
Toy Manchester terrier, 269
Toy Poodle, 119, 125, 129, 269–271

Toys. See Chew toys
Trace minerals (microminerals), 42, 46–51,
    92–94
Trachea hypoplasia, 187
Traumeel cream, 66
Travel, 31, 111, 112
Treats, 20–24, 126. See also Chew toys
Tribrissen, 31
Trihalomethanes, 18–19
Turkey, 10–11

Ulcerative colitis, 178, 186, 191, 236
Umbilical hernia, 169, 170, 174, 176, 179, 181,
    204, 208, 210, 212, 213, 214, 215, 217, 225,
    249, 258
Uric-acid-excretion abnormality, 184
Urinary stones, 178, 184
Urolithiasis, 212, 239, 246, 248, 256, 261, 271
U.S. Centers for Disease Control, 15
U.S. Congressional Office of Technology
    Assessment, 86
U.S. Department of Agriculture (USDA), 5, 6
U.S. Environmental Protection Agency, 15, 19,
    84, 85
U.S. Food and Drug Administration, 99
U.S. Occupational Safety and Health
    Administration (OSHA), 6
U.S. Surgeon General, 81
USP thyroid. See Armour

Vaccinations, 73–77
    nutritional support and, 39, 50, 92
    schedule for, 76–77
    side effects, remedies for, 110–111
    Weirmaraner and, 210
Vaginal hyperplasia, 157, 160, 162, 166, 178,
    187
Valerian, 80, 135
Valvular heart disease, 117
Vegetables, 90, 127, 139, 140, 142
    in home-cooked meals, 10, 11–12
    puppies and, 56
    raw, 13–14
Vertebra abnormality, 217
Vertebra malformation, 168, 187, 226, 243, 244,
    247, 258, 259, 275
Vitamin A, 26, 27, 33, 36–38, 51, 90, 116, 127
    daily dosages, 37–38
    nutritional sources, 38
Vitamin B₁ (thiamin), 27, 32, 91, 102, 103
Vitamin B₂ (riboflavin), 27, 32, 91, 103
Vitamin B₃ (niacin), 27, 32, 91, 103
Vitamin B₅ (pantothenic acid), 28, 32, 34–35,
    91, 103
Vitamin B₆ (pyridoxine), 28, 32, 33, 91, 103,
    120–121
Vitamin B₁₂ (cobalamin), 28, 32, 46, 47, 91, 103,
    120–121

Vitamin B$_{12}$-responsive malabsorption, 194
Vitamin B-complex, 26, 27–29, 30–32, 60, 67, 80, 90–91, 93, 102–103, 115, 116, 120–121, 129
  daily dosages, 32
  nutritional sources, 31–32
Vitamin C, 6, 26, 29, 33–36, 51, 61, 66, 91–92, 93, 115, 116, 121, 126–127, 135, 137, 139, 140
  daily dosages, 35–36
  nutritional sources, 35
  puppies and, 35–36, 54–55
Vitamin D, 26, 30, 38
Vitamin E, 6, 8, 26, 30, 33, 38–39, 50, 51, 60, 61, 67, 92, 93, 119, 121–122, 127, 135, 139, 140
  daily dosages, 39
  nutritional sources, 39
  puppies and, 55–56
Vitamin K, 26, 30, 39–40
Vitamins, 25–40
  fat-soluble, 26, 36–40
  multi-, with minerals, 25–26, 54, 61, 88–89
  reference table of, 27–30
  water-soluble, 26, 30–36
Vizsla, 44, 125, 144, 145, 207–208
Vomiting, 19, 110, 147–148
Von Willebrand's disease, 40, 156, 159, 161, 162, 164, 165, 166, 167, 168, 169, 170, 171, 176, 178, 179, 181, 186, 187, 188, 191, 192, 193, 195, 197, 198, 199, 201, 202, 204, 206, 207, 212, 214, 217, 219, 223, 225, 226, 230, 232, 234, 235, 236, 237, 239, 241, 246, 250, 251, 252, 253, 254, 256, 257, 262, 264, 265, 266, 268, 269, 271, 273, 274, 275

Water, contaminants in, 15–20
Water bowls, 20
Water spaniel, 240
Water-soluble vitamins, 26, 30–36
Weight issues. *See* Overweight dogs
Weirmaraner, 9, 125, 132, 144, 208–210
Welsh spaniel, 144, 240
Welsh terrier, 271

West Highland white terrier, 39, 45, 48, 56, 72, 129, 136, 271–272
Whippet, 125, 273
White blood cells, 71–72, 79, 90, 91
White dog shaker syndrome, 242, 253, 272
Wirehaired fox terrier, 119, 136, 273–274
Wirehaired pointing griffon, 144, 210
Witch hazel, 137
Wobbler's syndrome, 217
Wood, toxins in, 85, 87
Worms, 96, 103–104, 123
Wounds, healing, 133–136
  herbal cream, 133–134
  natural remedies for, 33, 34–35, 45, 49, 51, 109–110, 133–136
  recovery from illness or surgery, 65–68
Wrist subluxation, 201, 229

Yarrow, 131
Yogurt, 12, 59, 61
  antibiotics and, 67
  diarrhea treatment, 142
  puppies and, 56
Yorkshire terrier, 129, 274–275
Yucca, 139

Zinc, 16, 50–51, 94, 129, 133, 137, 146
Zinc-responsive dermatosis, 171
Zucker, Martin, 31

# About the Authors

**Earl Mindell,** R.Ph., Ph.D., is the acclaimed author of more than sixty books on natural health, including *The Vitamin Bible,* the pioneering reference work that revolutionized people's understanding of vitamins and minerals. A registered pharmacist, a master herbalist, and an internationally recognized expert on nutrition, vitamins, and herbal remedies. He is currently an Associate Professor at Chapman University School of Pharmacy and serves on the Deans's Professional Advisory Group, Chapman University School of Pharmacy.

Dr. Mindell lives in Beverly Hills, California

CPSIA information can be obtained
at www.ICGtesting.com
Printed in the USA
LVHW041725120419
613995LV00001B/1/P